DISCREET POWER

DISCREET POWER

How the World Economic Forum
Shapes Market Agendas

Christina Garsten
and Adrienne Sörbom

Stanford University Press
Stanford, California

Stanford University Press
Stanford, California

Printed in the United States of America on acid-free, archival-quality paper

Library of Congress Cataloging-in-Publication Data

Names: Garsten, Christina, author. | Sörbom, Adrienne, author.
Title: Discreet power : how the World Economic Forum shapes market agendas / Christina Garsten and Adrienne Sörbom.
Other titles: Emerging frontiers in the global economy.
Description: Stanford, California : Stanford University Press, 2018. | Series: Emerging frontiers in the global economy | Includes bibliographical references and index.
Identifiers: LCCN 2017050969 | ISBN 9780804794145 (cloth : alk. paper) | ISBN 9781503606043 (pbk : alk. paper) | ISBN 9781503606050 (epub)
Subjects: LCSH: World Economic Forum. | International economic relations. | International relations.
Classification: LCC HF1359 .G37 2018 | DDC 337—dc23
LC record available at https://lccn.loc.gov/2017050969

Typeset by Bruce Lundquist in 10/14 Minion Pro

For Andreas and Tobias, Klara and Sigrid

Contents

Acknowledgments

Exploring the World Economic Forum (WEF)—studying it, thinking about it, and writing about it—has colored our lives for several years. It is with a double feeling of relief and loss that we now leave it behind.

In writing this book, we have benefited greatly from the support of a large number of people. First, we owe our sincere gratitude to the employees, participants, and hangarounds of the WEF, who have generously shared their time, experiences, thoughts, and perspectives with us. We thank in particular Peter Bond and Cassius Luck—you know who you are. Without the support of all of you, our exploration would have been fruitless. Our special thanks go to Kristina Persson, who greatly facilitated our getting in touch with people at the start of this project.

We also extend our thanks to our colleagues in the Govemark network, in which this book has been a continuous discussion point and in which we have enjoyed both stringent academic discussions and joyful moments. Anette Nyqvist, Renita Thedvall, Melissa Fisher, Mikkel Flyverbom, David Westbrook, Mark Maguire, Jamie Saris, Marie-Laure Salles-Djelic, Dan Kärreman, Janine Wedel, Oana Brindusa Albu, and Matilda Dahl deserve special mention for commenting on chapter drafts and contributing sound advice. Many of our colleagues at Score (Stockholm Centre for Organizational Research) at Stockholm University and Stockholm School of Economics have also contributed productive ideas to this book. In particular, we thank Göran Ahrne, Nils Brunsson, Erica Falkenström, and Kristina Tamm Hallström. We are grateful to Måns Ljungstedt and Júlía Birnudóttir Sigurðardóttir for excellent research assistance.

Support and encouragement, and specific gems of insight, have also been provided by colleagues in our broader network. Douglas Holmes, Ulf Hannerz,

Hervé Laroche, Thomas Hylland Eriksen, Afshin Mehrpouya, Steve Barley, Bo Rothstein, Stefan Svallfors, Jana Costas, Chris Grey, and Frank den Hond have—in different ways—supplied us with valuable knowledge and perspectives. Thank you!

Large parts of this book were written during intense periods of writing at two locations: Scancor (Stanford University) and the Sigtuna Foundation. At these locations we also benefited from spirited conversations, among others with John Meyer, Marc Ventresca, Patricia Bromley, Gunlög Sundberg and Mia Kurkiala. We are grateful to these organizations and their staff for generously opening their space to us and providing inspiring writing environments.

The realization of this project was made possible by a research grant from the Swedish Research Council (Vetenskapsrådet). Finally, we extend our sincere thanks to our editors Margo Beth Fleming and J. P. Singh for believing in this project and to Jessica Ling and Olivia Bartz for following this projext through. Thanks also to Nina Colwill for sharp and sensible editing of our prose.

Any factual errors or analytical inadequacies are our responsibility. We also recognize and respect the possibility that your views may not be congruent with those of our interlocutors.

We express our deepest loving gratitude to Peter and Jonas.

Christina Garsten and Adrienne Sörbom
Stockholm and Palo Alto, April 2017

DISCREET POWER

Introduction

The world around us is changing at unprecedented speed. At this tipping point, our traditional concepts of society, meaningful employment, and the nation-state are challenged, and many understandably feel insecure or even threatened. A new model of responsive and responsible leadership is needed to allow us to address the challenges the world faces, from security to the Fourth Industrial Revolution, with long-term, action-oriented thinking and solidarity on both the national and global levels.[1]

These are the words of Klaus Schwab, founder and executive chairman of the World Economic Forum (WEF or the Forum), calling for participation in the Forty-Seventh Annual Meeting in Davos, which took place January 17–20, 2017, under the theme "Responsive and Responsible Leadership." This meeting attracted, among others, United Nations Secretary General António Guterres; the president of the People's Republic of China, Xi Jinping; the managing director of the International Monetary Fund, Christine Lagarde; then US Secretary of State John Kerry; UK Prime Minister Theresa May; over one thousand CEOs of business corporations (among others, CEO of BP Bob Dudley and Google cofounder Sergey Brin); German violinist Anne-Sophie Mutter; Colombian singer Shakira; and Queen Rania of Jordan. All in all, an estimated three thousand world leaders from politics, finance, business, and science attended the meeting.

The WEF has positioned itself as the prime meeting place for top world leaders and as the advocate of burning global issues. According to its worldview, the world is at stake, facing imminent and grave challenges that can be dealt with only by pragmatic and future-oriented actions and positive narratives. Only responsible leadership, courage, and commitment can counter issues such as financial crises, terrorism, environmental disasters, poverty, and social marginalization. The WEF sees itself as providing a critical response to this call. As expressed by Klaus Schwab, "The problem that we have is not globalization. The problem is a lack of global governance, a lack of means to address global issues." In this narrative, the World Economic Forum is the equivalent of the symbolic figure Marianne in the French Revolution—in this case, on the global scene—leading the world to future victories. This self-perception, sense of responsibility, and view of what's wrong with the world and how to tackle it go back to the early days of the organization. As long ago as the late 1980s, Schwab had said:

> We who take charge should not leave the "taking care" to others. Today, taking care means recognizing the interdependence of all people and nations in the world; recognizing the interdependence of the economy and ecology; recognizing the fact that being successful creates special responsibilities towards the world community. The vision of the future is to integrate these two concepts: taking charge and taking care.[2]

Without a given mandate, the Forum has conferred a specific role on itself: "To create global partnerships among those who exercise the highest responsibilities in business, government and academia" in order to "improve the state of the world" (according to its motto). In the WEF's own words, "The best tool to get this done in our complex world is effective, direct and personalized interaction."[3] Against the backdrop of what is perceived to be malfunctioning global governance institutions and stalled international policymaking, the WEF presents itself as offering an alternative global platform for engaging with global problems. It provides a forum for modernized, globalized, and alternative politics. Moreover, it invites world leaders to be part of forging new forms of influence, based not on the legal mandate of state or international institutions but on the exercise of discreet power.

Turning our attention to the WEF, we ask: What type of governance is the WEF aspiring to create? Looking more closely at the processes through which the WEF wields power and authority and the form of governance that is articulated, we also ask: How is global politics possible?

Toward the Summit

Every year in late January, the Forum holds its renowned Annual Meeting at the Swiss ski resort Davos, where invitees and funders flock to mull over the state of the world. In this snowy mountain town, some one thousand industry and finance leaders and two thousand leaders from some one hundred countries, from international and civil society organizations, including nongovernmental organizations (NGOs), labor and faith-based organizations, politics, and academia, present their views on the economy, their visions for the future and their arguments for the best solutions to tough problems.

During this week, Davos changes from a sleepy alpine town to a hub of influence, power, and prestige, addressing pressing global concerns. A wide array of values and priorities, and various ways of reaching defined goals, are articulated and discussed. Lines of convergence and divergence of community and exclusion are drawn as the WEF makes its presence felt. The Davos meeting, however, is not solely a gathering of the world's business leaders, economists, and politicians; a smattering of celebrities also brings glitz and flocks of media people. It is a meeting with many facets: an exclusive elite summit, a glimmering cocktail party, and a marketplace. And the summit is the prime WEF event for which staff in Geneva plan all year.

For three consecutive years (2011–2013), we were there, in Davos. The meeting in 2011 was our first.

Davos, January 2011: In the Power Nexus
Having just arrived in the village, we venture out to explore the area. We had failed to obtain a formal invitation but have decided to crash the summit, to see the extent to which we can participate. This being 2011, the global economy and capitalism are at the top of the agenda, with the theme "Shared Norms for the New Reality." The sense of urgency is still high after the financial crisis, and the event and the town are sprinkled with a certain frenzied activity and nervousness. But there is also a sense of possibility—the opening of new markets for innovation and profit, for global collaboration and mutual benefit.

The streets of Davos are filled with participants in elegant business suits and overcoats, easily identifiable by their badges and briefcases sporting the WEF logo. BMWs, Mercedes, and other pricey cars are conspicuously abundant, as are Western middle-aged businessmen. Banners with the WEF logo hang from buildings and hotel lobbies and are printed on café menus. Buses and houses also display ads for individual countries—India, Brazil, and Mexico among them. On a busy street corner, Canadian Mounties in their red serge pose in front of a stand serving free BeaverTails, a flaky pastry shaped like, yes, beaver tails.

Journalists are roaming the streets, camera equipment and microphones at hand. CNN, BBC, Reuters, and other conglomerates are well represented here and clearly visible by their logos. Now and then we run into a team of journalists who have managed to halt a celebrity or some more ordinary participant to obtain a brief interview. Not every journalist who volunteers to come is welcome, we later learn. Journalists must apply for permission several months ahead, and access is restricted to WEF trusted members of the press.

And then there are the regular visitors to Davos: skiers in their skiing pants, skis on shoulders, jostling with meeting participants, police, military, and maintenance staffs. Only the more economically solvent skiers can afford Davos during this week, when WEF participants and journalists are occupying all the rental apartments and hotel rooms, and prices soar for the few vacancies. The WEF has booked most hotels and apartments well ahead of time. The upside is that the slopes tend to be relatively empty. Nevertheless, some of the skiers appear to be irritated as they make their way through the crowded streets, the busy restaurants, and the fuss of having to navigate around the cordoned-off areas of the village.

As we make our way through the narrow streets, the sunshine sparkles on the snow, illuminating the slopes of the high mountains. The thermometer shows a brisk 14 degrees Fahrenheit, and the air is crisp and light at this altitude of 5,120 feet. We learn that the conference center occupies a large part of the town, now surrounded by high barbed-wire fences. Armed guards secure the gates, and anyone who approaches must present a meeting badge and registration papers.

As we approach, we spot the entrance gates for the meeting compound, with a small shack erected for the occasion. Posted before the two gates are four guards in gray uniforms, automatic weapons on their shoulders. Five more guards are posted on the inside of the gates. It looks like Checkpoint Charlie. We observe guards from the Swiss special police force standing on the roof of the Hotel Belvedere, dressed in camouflage uniforms, heavily equipped and wearing masks. CCTV cameras are posted around the entrance gates and stare at us from above. Swiss Army helicopters hover, and occasionally F/A 18 Hornets, a type of combat jet, intercept their trajectories, drawing white lines across the blue sky. The soundscape created by the air security embeds the small town with a constant pattering noise. After the meeting, we learn that up to five thousand Swiss soldiers took part in the security operation, Alpa Eco Undici, which was staged for the WEF that year.

The guards ask us for our badges, but we have none. Unaware of the entry restrictions, we had arranged for a first meeting with a Scandinavian participant inside the meeting area. Olafur Gunnlaugson, from one of the larger corporate foundations in Scandinavia, has agreed to meet us at Pizzeria Daiano inside the compound, we explain.[4] It's important that we get inside. After a few minutes of arguing, pleading, and looking desperate, the guard decides to let us in, but only as far as the pizzeria, and he never lets us out of his sight until we enter.

Over lunch, Mr. Gunnlaugson, a gracious-mannered man in his fifties, says: "If you are not here, you do not exist"—in other words, every actor or organization with some ambition in the global business arena is here. "The networking is central, but seminars are also very stimulating," he goes on. "The meeting is a melting pot of finance, politics, research, an institution that works. Participating in the Davos summit, one can, in the long run, contribute to improving the world. It's business with social engagement," he asserts.

After lunch, we continue our tour outside the premises, following the wired fence. This walk takes us a good hour, our high-heeled boots get wet and cold from the exercise, and our mood drops. There are a couple of more gateways but nowhere the general public can enter. Having tried our luck with the guards at every entranceway, we venture with disappointment into the town center.

The following day, we make our way toward Café Schneider, where we have arranged for a lunch meeting with Bill Gladstone, president of a CEO-led global association of some two hundred companies dealing with business and sustainable development. Café Schneider is located on the main street of Davos and has been temporarily turned into an important WEF hub. It is housed in a classical Swiss alpine building, with a steeply pitched roof and wooden decor. Gladstone's assistant has reserved a table for us, and the headwaiter directs us to it. The interior of the café reflects a mixture of rustic mountain cabin and smart business style. The white linen cloths and napkins and a tempting menu contribute to our appetite. The snow melts from customers' coats and boots, the smell mixing with the aromas of food cooking in the kitchen.

Mr. Gladstone, a neatly dressed and good-natured man in his sixties, appears ten minutes later. We engage in a long conversation about why it is that someone like him decides to come to Davos, what his organization aims to get out of the meeting, what goes on here, and what, if any, the implications of meetings held here might be. He freely tells us about his motivation. "Nobody is in charge of global problems," he starts out. "Only business has the resources to deal with the serious ones." In his view, governments now understand that they cannot deal with them alone. Cooperation is necessary, not least when it comes to the issue of sustainable development. He goes on to talk about the urgency of the situation in the world, about attempts at regulating carbon emissions, climate agreements, and the like, exemplifying with concrete issues and events. When he has finished painting the global picture, he asserts:

> The World Economic Forum is a platform. It relies on a multistakeholder model, on the idea of bringing diverse interests together around the same table. The World Economic Forum, however, is not a locus for decision making; it is an idea distributor. The WEF doesn't do any advocacy in its own name. Rather, it provides a venue for strategic partners to pursue issues and make decisions.

A little later in the conversation, he adds, "We [the organization] are here, we participate, provide our points of view. We are the leading voice of the global capital."

During our conversation, several well-known people come to greet Gladstone, among them the executive director of the UN Global Compact.

After Gladstone leaves, we remain seated, and note that we are not being asked to leave. Quite the contrary: the waiters pay us continuous attention and do their best to make us comfortable. It appears that we are believed to be of some importance, and this proves to be the case over the following days; the table is kept for us over lunchtime, without our having made the slightest move toward making a reservation. Gladstone's prestige and that of his network have undeservingly rubbed off on us. And for the first time, we feel what it is to be included in the WEF network and how the allure of it works. It rubs off on people who, for various reasons, aspire to get into the new global nobility.

.   .   .

This book builds on four years of our on-and-off ethnographic fieldwork on the WEF. Since that meeting in 2011, we have followed the activities of the organization by attending, or attempting to attend, meetings, seminars, and workshops in various locations across the world. When we have not been given permission to attend, we have circulated the peripheries of meeting compounds, talking to participants, WEF staff, skiers, drivers, members of the Occupy Movement, bartenders, journalists, and others on the margins of events. Whenever we were granted access, we participated in meetings and other events organized by the WEF, chatted in lobby areas, attended cocktail parties, and hung around hotel bars. We have also had conversations and interviews with staff members at the headquarters in Cologny outside Geneva, with funders and participants in meetings, and with others associated with the organization.

Over time, our inroads and positions in the field have given us a rich and varied understanding of the organization. We aim to bring these insights and experiences to bear on a story about the WEF as an organization, articulating many central dimensions of the contemporary world and the challenges associated with global governance. At the core, we want to convey how the WEF works to push its ideas by way of seduction and what we call discretionary governance at the transnational level—the exercise of a discreet form of power and control according to the judgment of the Forum and its members, in ways that escape established democratic controls. We aim to demonstrate how the Forum, together with its funders and invitees, contribute to shaping a fragile political mandate with a significant global sway. Through the strategic use of seductive communicative actions, the WEF and its leaders endeavor to shape the interests and priorities of others, attracting and enticing them into engaging with political issues defined by the Forum and running with them. In the broad sense, seduction entails drawing people in and holding them in one's thrall. It involves radiating some quality that attracts others and stirs their emotions and influences their thoughts in ways desirable to the seducer. Thus seduction is intimately tied up with discretionary governance—the practice of a discreet and subtle form of soft power that works more effectively than coercion.

Governing the World

The contemporary world is characterized by unprecedented globalization. Various parts of the world are now interconnected by way of increased trade and economic activity, faster and thicker communication networks, and intensified points of engagement and tension among cultural groups. Even if globalization occurred long before the term was coined, we are now living in a world where the infrastructure of nation-states and international connections are giving way to a novel geopolitical structure characterized by global and transnational connectivity. Since the end of the Cold War, the driving forces of societal change, of economic, political, and cultural dynamics, have been transnational rather than international.[5] In some instances, we are even experiencing the implications of supranational driving forces, challenging the nation-state as a template for societal coordination and order.[6]

The global political arena is fraught with challenges and contradictions. It is also ripe with opportunities to make a difference and improve the state of the world. As many scholars have noted, globalization is not a unidirectional process but an open-ended, contested, and ambiguous one. People and societies are affected differently, to different degrees and at different speeds. Moreover, some groups of people and some organizations are in more privileged positions not only to harvest the fruits of globalization but also to shape its process, direction, intensity, and speed.

At this time, corporations are among the foremost drivers, setting the parameters for social development. Likewise, organizations sponsored by corporate money, such as think tanks, foundations, and advocacy groups that are able to coordinate corporate interest around particular topics, are gaining leverage on the global scene.[7] In this context, the Forum is a child of its time, reflecting the standing of the transnational corporation and the leverage that can be gained from attracting corporate funding and organizing corporate interest into a larger whole. As a nonprofit think tank with global reach, the WEF builds on the exclusive funding of large transnational corporations to shape the direction of globalization with one overarching ambition: to "improve the world," as the slogan has it.

Globalization has not only accentuated the weaknesses of the geopolitical infrastructure built on the nation-state template, but brought to the fore significant challenges with regard to governance. Nation-state governments are under heavy pressure to regulate and oversee the operations of transnational corporations. Despite international law and conventions, corporations often find loopholes and resort to *forum non conveniens* (that is, relying on courts not to take jurisdiction due to lack of an appropriate forum) to avoid legal sanctions. Voluntary codes and standards may compensate to some extent for the lack of binding transnational legal structures, but they rely on the goodwill of the parties to have effect. Transnational insurgencies and terrorist attacks are laying bare the fractions and tensions brought about by the disjunctures of globalization, for transnational identity politics are not only uniting but also dividing groups of people along new lines that seldom correspond to nation-state orders and regulatory structures. Recent transnational migration waves, propelled by war and conflict, not only alert us to the fickle nature of the global order but also point to the shadow side of globalization and the incapacity of existing structures to govern key policy areas effectively. The Brexit vote, the right-wing populist movements in Hungary and Poland, and the neoconservative tailwind in the United States are prime examples.

The WEF itself is a response to the governance gaps laid bare by intensified globalization. The challenges of the nation-state to effectively regulate transnational trade, the unprecedented global risks associated with climate change, the political insurgencies of recent decades, and the incapacity of the post–World War II global organizational architecture to move forward in the direction of change have made their imprints on its organizational structure and way of functioning.

Established in 1971 by Klaus Schwab, a professor of business policy at the University of Geneva, as the European Management Forum (EMF), based on a nonprofit foundation based in Geneva, Switzerland, the organization aims to provide an alternative to established international organizations, such as the United Nations (UN) and its many suborganizations. In this context, the UN is perceived as being too inert, too slow to set change into motion, and too exclusive in its membership, which rests on nation-states and fails to include the voices of corporations and other organized communities. In addition, the establishment of WEF has a personal side to it. As Chairman Schwab explained to us, the birth of the WEF is an outgrowth of his childhood war experience and his desire to help make the world a better place in which to live. Born in Ravensburg, Germany, in 1938, Schwab experienced World War II, and the human suffering made a strong imprint on him. Trained as an engineer and an economist, he founded the Forum with the aspiration that it would become a platform for public and private cooperation, a driver for reconciliation, and a catalyst for multistakeholder collaboration and initiatives for achieving long-term growth and prosperity.

As Schwab expressed it, "The World Economic Forum is "a response to a need. We were not mandated by anybody. We created . . . a response to a clear need in the international governance system."[8] The organization was thus created to offer a platform for leaders of government, business, and civil society to join forces in making the world a better place. Each January, the organization draws business, political, and civil society leaders from Europe and beyond to Davos for the Annual Meeting. What is described as the collaborative and collegial "spirit of Davos" has thus grown out of four decades of meetings of carefully selected leaders and aspirants.

Organizing for Global Aspirations

In the beginning, WEF meetings were focused primarily on European matters and how European business could catch up with US management practices. In fact, the WEF was initially established under the patronage of the European Commission (EC), and European industrial associations that had a strong interest in strengthening the competitiveness of European business. Soon after, however, the WEF cut loose from EC and turned its focus increasingly toward global issues.

The stakeholder management approach, which over time became a signature model for the WEF, was developed during these early years. This model bases corporate success on managers, taking account of all interests—not merely shareholders, clients, and customers of the corporation, but also employees of the corporation, trade unions, and the communities within which it operates, including government. Schwab outlined the approach in 1971, the same year as the Forum was established, in his book, *Moderne Unternehmensführung im Maschinenbau* (*Modern Enterprise Management in Mechanical Engineering*).[9] In it, he argued that the management of a modern enterprise must serve all stakeholders (*die Interessenten*), "acting as their trustee charged with achieving the long-term sustained growth and prosperity of the company."[10] In 1973, participants at the Annual Meeting codified the approach into a code of ethics, termed "The Davos Manifesto." The first point in the manifesto states that the purpose of professional management is to serve clients, shareholders, workers, and employees, as well as societies, and to harmonize the different interests of the stakeholders.[11] The enterprise shall thus serve not only the shareholders and clients but also employees and society at large. This is to be ensured by securing long-term profit for the enterprise, stated in the manifesto's last point:

> The management can achieve the above objectives through the economic enterprise for which it is responsible. For this reason, it is important to ensure the long-term existence of the enterprise. The long-term existence cannot be ensured without sufficient profitability. Thus, profitability is the necessary means to enable the management to serve its clients, shareholders, employees and society.[12]

Over time, the move from an emphasis on managers to the contemporary emphasis on multistakeholders led to a refinement of the model. The multistakeholder model builds on visions of aligning key priorities and values from various actors. A basic assumption underlying this model therefore is that the values of economic growth and social and environmental sustainability can and must be aligned and balanced in order to reach the universal goal of survival—or at least the goal of improving the state of the world.[13]

Schwab's vision for what would become the WEF grew steadily. Events in 1973—the collapse of the Bretton Woods fixed exchange rate mechanism and the Arab–Israeli War—saw the Annual Meeting expand its focus from management to economic and social issues. Political leaders were invited to Davos for the first time in January 1974. Two years later, the organization introduced a system of funding by incorporating what it referred to as the one thousand leading companies of the world as members. At roughly the same time, the EMF was claimed to be the first NGO to initiate a partnership with China's economic development commissions, spurring economic reform policies in China. Regional meetings around the globe were added to the year's activities. The publication of the first *Global Competitiveness Report* in 1979 saw the organization expand and aspire to become a knowledge hub.[14]

A significant turning point for the Forum was 1987, which marked the transformation of the EMF into the WEF. Now the organization sought to broaden its vision to include the provision of a platform for dialogue for world leaders, not merely European leaders. In its newly established journal, *World Link,* Schwab described how the WEF identified thirty-five thousand leaders across the world. These leaders went under the label "33333" and were drawn into the "World Link system," a communicative network through which Forum leaders wanted to educate and prepare leaders for global action.[15] World Economic Forum Annual Meeting milestones during this time include the Davos Declaration, signed in 1988 by Greece and Turkey, which saw the two countries turn back from the brink of war. In 1989, North and South Korea held their first ministerial-level meetings in Davos. At the same meeting, East German prime minister Hans Modrow and German chancellor Helmut Kohl met to discuss German reunification. In 1992, South African president F. W. de Klerk met Nelson Mandela and Chief Mangosuthu Buthelezi at the Annual Meeting—their first joint appearance outside South Africa and a milestone in the country's political transition.[16]

The alignment of economic, social, and political interests has thus been part of the WEF since the first meeting in 1971. In the 2000s, the WEF launched the Davos Equation in order to emphasize the bond between the economic and social worlds:

> We live in a world which is uncertain and fragile. At the Annual Meeting in Davos, global leaders from all walks of life will confront one basic fact: We will not have strong sustained economic growth across the world unless we have security, but we will not have security in unstable parts of the world without the prospect of prosperity. To have both security and prosperity, we must have peace. This is the Davos Equation: security plus prosperity equals peace.[17]

The equation aims to capture the idea of a balanced and neutral solution to global problems of all kinds: peace, health, education, and so forth. The very notion of "equation" implies symmetry or balance. It implies that diverging tendencies and interests may be reconciled into balance and harmony with each other. The multistakeholder approach is fundamental to this idea, which ideally serves to articulate the priorities and interests of each party. Although parties cannot entirely agree on responsibilities or priorities, they can reach a partial consensus about global issues and development problems. The idea of economic and social values as intricately related to each other, and as unattainable without each other, is part of all Forum settings. In so doing, it seeks to play a role in the alignment of different and sometimes divergent interests and values by assembling groups and people from various spheres of society.

From Cologny and into the World

The activities of the WEF are funded by one thousand companies, called "members" and "partners," which are some of the largest and most highly ranked companies in their fields of business. The highest governing body of the WEF is the foundation board, comprising a smaller number of highly influential persons some of whom are chosen from the funders. In 2015, the Forum was formally recognized as an international organization ("other international body") by the Swiss government[18] and describes itself as

> the International Organization for Public-Private Cooperation. The Forum engages the foremost political, business and other leaders of society to shape global, regional and industry agendas. . . . Our activities are shaped by a unique institutional culture founded on the stakeholder theory, which asserts that an organization is accountable to all parts of society. The institution carefully blends and balances the best of many kinds of organizations, from both the public and private sectors, international organizations and academic institutions.
>
> We believe that progress happens by bringing together people from all walks of life who have the drive and the influence to make positive change.[19]

The WEF has approximately six hundred employees, and counting, located at the headquarters in Cologny outside Geneva and in regional offices with small staffs in Beijing, New York, San Francisco, and Tokyo.[20] Aspiring to be truly global, people of around sixty different nationalities staff the organization.[21] The localities in Cologny have been expanded to house the constantly growing number of staff and address heightened security demands. As visitors approach the entrance to the building, armed guards check their identity, their WEF contact, and purpose of their meeting. After they pass through the gate, they enter the building via a security-screening portal, which checks their bodies and bags for potentially dangerous objects. Inside the building, a receptionist again records their names and the names of their WEF contacts and asks the visitors to sign in to get a visitor's badge. In the waiting lounge, floor-to-ceiling windows offer a breathtaking view of Lake Geneva, and multiple WEF publications are provided, for visitors to browse.

The WEF describes itself as politically neutral, in the sense that it is not tied to any national, political, or partisan interests. It operates as a think tank, networking among and influencing corporate leaders and top politicians, NGO heads, and academics. Although best known for its Annual Meeting in Davos, it regularly hosts a large number of more informal and private meetings around the world, such as the Annual Meeting of the New Champions (targeting emerging economies), the Young Global Leaders Meeting (focusing on promising young leaders), and meetings on the topics of social entrepreneurship and scenario planning. In addition, its strategic insight teams produce reports—for instance, in the fields of economic competitiveness, global risk, and scenario thinking. Moreover, the WEF strives to be and already functions as a private organizer for diplomatic efforts on a range of topics. Such issues as climate agreements, the Israel–Palestine conflict, the war in Syria, global trade tariffs, corruption, and sustainable management of the Arctic are on its agenda. Reports, ratings, and indexes are some of the specific outcomes from these activities, as are ideas about how to move forward and advocate them.

In order to attract people to work for them, engage in panels and deliberations, craft reports, advocate, and, ultimately, instigate change, the WEF organizes its participants into communities. These are, in essence, loosely organized groups of people joined together around issues. The communities constantly vary in number and composition. The Forum's one thousand funding corporations form one of the core communities. They are key players in the Forum's activities, and their financial and organizational support is essential for the Forum's mission.

The Global Future Councils (previously called the Network of Global Agenda Councils) make up another key community. The councils are a network based on invitation-only individuals that study the most pressing issues facing the world. In each of the councils, we find about fifteen to twenty designated "experts," altogether some fifteen hundred "premier thought leaders," who come together to engage in interdisciplinary dialogue, shape agendas, and drive initiatives.[22] Another highly exclusive community is the Informal Gathering of World Economic Leaders (IGWEL). At the Annual Meeting in Davos, political leaders from the G20 and other relevant countries and the heads of international organizations engage in high-level dialogues facilitated by the IGWEL program.

In contrast to these high-profile communities, the Forum also works to create networks for less established but promising individuals. The Global Shapers Community comprises over six thousand young people, and counting, based in more than 450 cities in 170 countries and territories. Organized into a network of "hubs," dedicated to creating local impact, they are meant to constitute a source of grassroots knowledge and global youth perspectives. Global Shapers, as the name suggests, are expected and encouraged to "take action on issues they care about and positively disrupt global policy discussions." The Forum of Young Global Leaders, in its turn, organizes over eight hundred "enterprising, socially-minded men and women selected under the age of 40, who operate as a force for good to overcome barriers that elsewhere stand in the way of progress." The Forum presents the community as made up of "leaders from all walks of life, from every region of the world, and from every stakeholder group in society."[23]

The Global Leadership Fellows community is another highly prestigious community comprising students admitted to the three-year educational program—the Global Leadership Fellows Programme of the World Economic Forum. The program combines intensive on-the-job experience, a learning curriculum, coaching and mentoring, and access to an extensive network of alumni. The program aims to prepare its chosen fellows for leadership in both public and private sectors and to work across all spheres of a globalized society.

The communities are not open for all to join. Candidates are proposed through a qualified nomination process and assessed according to rigorous selection criteria, as set by the Forum.[24] The exclusivity of participation and meeting attendance is often motivated by a perceived need on the part of the WEF to create "safe places" for the invited people to talk freely, under the observance of the Chatham House Rule.[25] In addition, since individuals do not attend as representatives of their nation-states, corporations, NGOs, or political parties, they are expected to feel the need to be thus protected from a broader audience. In the network-like organization, the WEF thus consciously creates an organized network of safe places where invitees can meet in an open and trusting manner.

A New Site for Global Normativity

Surprisingly, given the massive attention of the Davos meeting, the particular organizing model of the Forum largely slips under the radar of both media and academics. Furthermore, the Davos meeting is often misinterpreted as a top meeting among politicians, similar to the summits of the UN, the Organization for Economic Co-operation and Development, or the G20. In fact, the constellation of participants at the Davos Annual Meeting tends to show a majority of business leaders and only a smaller ratio of politicians. According to our calculations, based on a sample of participants in WEF meetings (not merely in Davos) from 2011 to 2013, 41 percent were businesspeople, 16 percent high-level public officials, 16 percent NGO representatives, and 13 percent academics. Media represented 7 percent of the participants, supranational (European Union) politicians 6 percent, and religious community members 1 percent. Among these participants, the average age was fifty-six years. Most commonly, the participants had a PhD or master's degree, which in part or fully was completed at one of the world's ten highest-ranking universities. In 2011, 17 percent of all participants were women; by 2017, the figure had increased to 28 percent.[26]

The WEF is not alone in its endeavor to provide other ways of dealing with the implications of globalization and global governance challenges. Over the past few decades, we have indeed witnessed a formidable growth in the number of organizations with global governance ambitions and a large number of experiments with other forms of governance. Actors in this domain work by crafting and diffusing norms, standards, and codes of conduct and by establishing political programs for the transformation of minds and actions.[27] To use the terminology of sociologist Saskia Sassen, new "sites of normativity" are appearing on the global scene, with power and resources to influence, shape, and fashion the thoughts and actions of others.[28] The existing system of multilateral governance is thus paralleled and transgressed by a rapidly increasing number of organizations without a legal mandate to influence global governance yet with the ambition to do so. These organizations must carve out, construct, and expand their position and mandate. The Forum may therefore be seen as part of an emerging transnational domain that is still under construction.[29]

In the larger picture, the WEF also bears witness to the emergence of a powerful new actor on the global political arena: the think tank. On such pressing issues as climate change, security, and trade policy, think tanks are becoming prominent voices. The UN Climate Meeting in Doha in December 2012, for example, hosted a number of think tanks, including the World

Resources Institute, a global think tank that works with governments, businesses, and renowned individuals to promote a low-carbon future. Another example of the recognition of the role of think tanks in global governance is their positive mention in the United Nations 2030 Agenda for Sustainable Development. Think tanks are in this text seen as significant organizations for policy impact at the national level and critical for achieving a better understanding of the efforts required to mobilize the means of implementation—financing, technology, and trade.[30]

Think tanks were long considered of little importance to social science researchers. A pronounced increase in their sheer numbers,[31] however, coupled with their more articulate ideological positions and intensified advocacy efforts, has contributed to rising academic interest. They offer an institutional innovation that can seamlessly merge research, publicity, and advocacy; in this context, research may become a weapon of political struggle, championing a vision for society and public policy.[32] Yet there are a number of unaddressed questions concerning the role of think tanks as political actors. One of the most urgent questions addresses the forms of legitimacy, authority, and power being constructed by such organizations as the WEF, the Atlas Network, the Club of Rome, and RAND Corporation.

Criticizing the lack of attention given to the way "organizations mold their environments," organizational scholar Stephen R. Barley has mapped organizational links between think tanks and other corporate-funded political actors in the United States.[33] Barley's findings demonstrate how such organizations nationally have succeeded in exerting growing political influence over the past few decades. In this context, think tanks may be viewed as boundary-spanning organizations, specializing in mediating relationships among larger, more established policy fields.[34] At the global level, the WEF serves as a boundary-spanning think tank involved in the brokerage of transnational knowledge domains, contributing in the long run to developing new, transnational forms of power, authority, and legitimacy.[35]

Part of the influence of an organization such as the WEF has to do with the webs of knowledge created around it. Through its activities, the WEF contributes to the establishment of global policy networks and the circulation of knowledge, information, and expertise within those networks. It therefore contributes to the establishment of "epistemic communities" for policy coordination.[36] International relations scholar Diane Stone has convincingly argued that such "knowledge networks are a form of power."[37] The WEF, with its extensive and engaged networks of organizations and associated individuals, has emerged as a central hub in the churning of policy-relevant ideas and knowledge and as a central arena where knowledge from various sources is brought into contact and used to further policy ideas based on assemblages of knowledge.[38]

A challenge for students of governance as pursued by the WEF is that the conventional notions of policy networks, advocates, lobbyists, interest groups, or other notions used to capture organizations and actors with aspirations to influence global governance are no longer able to do the full job. They fail to capture the flexible use of professional affiliations, roles, and skills that comprise new types of policy networks and brokers.[39] And at the organizational level, the power to influence policy and politics derives increasingly from the capacity to create and strategically deploy networks and alliances between diverse forms of organizations. This power builds on a relational capacity, residing in the modes of connections and relationships that are established to produce and leverage specific constellations of knowledge and ideas.[40]

To analyze contemporary power, we also need to rethink the relationships between the state and market actors and the concepts of politics and nonpolitics.[41] We view the organization of the Forum as constituted in and through relationships of collaboration, negotiation, and strategic communication in a larger field of organizations.[42] In this sense, the WEF is a brokering organization, strategically situated as an intermediary between markets and politics on the global arena. Its influence is based on extending its agentic capacity through its network of individuals and associated organizations. This brokerage generates a "partially organized network,"[43] coordinating other actors by establishing and maintaining communities and creating a variety of forms of membership and providing access to certain kinds of resources.[44] In this field, the WEF obtains authority over other actors only if it is recognized as legitimate.[45] The authority of the WEF is therefore fragile: it does not enjoy an official political mandate but must continually construct and maintain its authority and legitimacy. How it builds this recognition is a question of organizing for effective leverage and diffusion of its ideas to the world's top leaders and next-generation leaders. Most important, the Forum's power and authority are built on seductive forms of communication and decisions about agenda setting, meeting participation, and proposed actions made at its own discretion. For this system to work, the discretion of the participants is also required. These practices constitute the base of the WEF's discreet power.

The Seductive Organization

In spite of its potent and spectacular image, the WEF is a small and lean organization, with no legal mandate in international governance. It is not an elected body; heads of state did not create it; it is not a meta-organization, with representatives from various nations. To extend its base and its authority, the WEF must build on a strategic effort to create networks and communities across organizational boundaries. In practice, this entails propelling its ideas and visions through these networks and communities not by coercion but by seduction—that is, by attracting others to its ideas and visions and motivating individuals to work for them and to want the outcomes the WEF wants. The key concept here is seduction, built on ingredients such as status, exclusion, and discretion.

Seduction, as recognized by political scientist Joseph Nye, implies the exercise of a subtle, soft form of power—the ability to shape the preferences of others through appeal and attraction, not by force.[46] At the personal level, we all know the power of attraction and seduction. In politics, as Nye shows, seduction is a staple and tends to be associated by an "attractive personality, culture, political values and institutions."[47] In his view, "seduction is always more effective than coercion."[48] Many values propelled by globalizing organizations and in international diplomatic efforts, such as democracy and human rights, individual opportunities, and sustainability, are deeply seductive. Soft power means getting others to want the outcomes that you want, to move in your direction. It is thus a form of cooptation and constitutes, in Nye's words, "real power."

By way of seductive communication, the Forum aims to attract attention, interest, and engagement and ultimately persuade and convince other individuals and organizations that certain propositions are more reasonable than others. The exercise of such soft, discreet power entails that resources of varying kinds (for example political, financial, social, ideational, knowledge based) are converted into realized power in the sense of obtaining desired outcomes. This in turn requires well-designed strategies and skillful leadership. Global seduction, as exercised by the Forum, thus involves a set of communicative strategies aimed to persuade and convince others to go with the propositions that emerge out of the meetings.

By seduction, the Forum sets the stage for its specific discretionary governance: a form of governance that extends indirect social and communicative influence to larger organizational matters. It involves the exercise of influence and power in line with one's own judgment but outside the realm of customary democratic monitoring.[49] In its efforts to convince its participants and the world at large of the strengths of the normative foundations of the Forum, it employs strategies of communicative seduction and persuasion that are reminiscent of approaches within public diplomacy. Indeed, the rise of the WEF on the global governance scene is linked to developments in the field of diplomacy, and more specifically to the growth of public diplomacy—targeting relations between a diverse set of actors involving not only state officials but also unofficial groups, organizations, and individuals—as a significant reflection of the changing world system toward a multipolar order.[50] One may also note the increased importance of commercial diplomacy as a growing field of interaction between public and private actors.[51]

The WEF's many forms of socializing, associating, networking, and interacting—the staged ceremonial events, the seminars, the small team deliberations, the backstage meetings, the pleasant business lunches, the smooth cocktails, and the extravagant parties—are characteristic of the seductive organization and provides it with a social dynamic and sense of uniqueness.[52] Although WEF meetings and events may appear as somewhat frenzied and disorganized, with people moving back and forth among panels, seminars, networking events, and parties, they are tightly orchestrated. All Forum employees and participants at the events have a mission and understand their role. Each mission, whether it is about initiating a discussion around youth entrepreneurship in West Africa or about investment opportunities in the Arctic, has a long-term and a short-term goal. Each accomplished event brings in return new network contacts, novel information, increased knowledge, or attractive business opportunities.

The particular form of socializing cultivated in and around the Forum centers around the act of seduction, based on selection and elevation of "the best" leaders, experts, and brains. The organization carefully screens, picks, scrutinizes, and evaluates the suitability of its potential invitees. No one—and there are no exceptions—can enter the meeting grounds or participate in seminars without an invitation. The screening process may take a year and involves checking the potential invitee's background, education, work experience, expertise, credentials, credibility, and integrity. The checkup entails references and a process in which the need for the person is carefully weighed. Paola Pakulsky, manager of one of the in-house departments at the Geneva headquarters, is in charge of this process. She is a robust and well-versed woman in her early fifties, with accommodating and considerate manners. She explains:

> We're basically a marketing function in the sense that we provide support to the teams, whether it's the business teams or those dealing with other constituents, in helping them to engage, then, the right people into the right agenda. So our motto is "right person at the right time, in the right agenda."[53]

The screening and selection process is given priority in event planning because the credibility and legitimacy of the Forum relies largely on the performance of the invitees. The other side of this matter is that they need to feel chosen, desired, and wanted. The careful selection process assists in conferring on the invitees a sense of being elevated above the common person and given status distinction. As sociologist Pierre Bourdieu has noted, such processes function simultaneously as a system of power relations and a symbolic system in which minute distinctions become the basis for social judgment.[54] The badge of entrance provided to those who pass the test is indeed a marker of status. Many invitees have conveyed to us the exhilarating sense of elevation they received from having been invited and being present where the action is, among the selected few. Being on the spot with Chancellor Angela Merkel of Germany, singer-songwriter Bono, or Facebook CEO Mark Zuckerberg is different from watching them on television and social media. The WEF badge and their presence at the Forum work as a sort of aphrodisiac, giving them the hype. After having been at the Davos meeting, Amir Shihadeh, the curator of the Amman hub of the Young Global Shapers, a young people's community organized by the Forum, conveys this feeling:

> Literally, get ready for the best experience in your life! As a Global Shaper, the World Economic Forum's Annual Meeting in Davos, Switzerland is the most amazing, passionate, awe-inspiring, phenomenal, and influential event you'll ever attend in your life. Be "present" in both your mind-set and heart while in Davos. Grasp every moment and "internalize" it. Take many "mental pictures." This meeting will remain with you forever, *Insha'Allah* (God willing).[55]

The craving for attention and the allure of proximity is a never-ending process. The invitation is not a given and is reconsidered every year and for every event. Neither is an invitation to participate in one of the working groups or communities a permanent invitation; it is contingent on performance and the priorities of the Forum. With the invitation comes the never-ending anxiety of being thrown out of the circle of nobility and losing the status and privilege that come with belonging. The community of invitees can thus be described as an aspirational class, continuously striving for inclusion.

Enticement in the Emirates

As ethnographers, we have experienced what it means to be enticed by the relevance and grandeur of the organization and its events, but also—and primarily—what it means to be excluded and dismissed. Beyond being a signature ethnographic experience, this double bind is crucial to understanding the operational strategies of the WEF. The following sequence provides a sense of the double character of the Forum—inviting and alluring yet excluding and withdrawing.

. . .

We are all dressed up, in a taxi on the long Al Mina Road in Dubai. We're wearing somewhat uncomfortable high-heeled shoes, tight-fitting pencil skirts, business blouses, and elegant scarves. We have decided to pay a visit to the WEF "brain trust meeting," and we do not want to be met with suspicion or even hesitation because of how we look. We anticipate that we will fail, though, at least in part. Handbags show that we are researchers of some type; they are overloaded with equipment: computers, smart phones, papers, pens, and other necessities.

The Forum staff refer to the Dubai event as the "brain trust meeting," but the proper name is the Summit on the Global Agenda. To this meeting, about fifteen hundred of "the world's best brains" are invited each November to brainstorm and work toward the agenda for the coming Annual Meeting in Davos in January. As usual in the WEF environment, the summit comprises a mix of politicians, civil society people, researchers, and people from funding corporations. (In Chapter 4, we discuss how they come to be identified as the best brains.) Together they contribute to "a network of invitation-only groups that study the most pressing issues facing the world."[56] "All brilliant," one of the staff from the Geneva headquarters described them. And as later vouched for, in the assessment of the Global Agenda Councils, "These councils . . . are creating powerful ideas that are having a measurable impact."[57] By creating what is termed "thought leadership," the councils are meant to influence global public policy, as the results will spread through all possible channels.

We don't feel particularly brilliant, however. As usual, we had tried to be granted access in advance by contacting the Geneva headquarters, informing them about our research interest and the value of giving the world a research perspective on the nature of these meetings. Having been denied, we decided to go anyway. In the taxi on our way to the meeting space, we are not at ease; in fact, we're rather disillusioned and crestfallen. We have no idea how far our efforts to come closer to the meeting core of discussions would take us this time. Will the travel be worthwhile? Will our stylish but uncomfortable shoes help us gain entrance? Our Istanbul endeavor, attending the WEF Regional Meeting in Istanbul a few months ago, had been successful in the sense that we had been able to socialize with staff and participants in the designated networking area set up for the meeting in the hotel lobby. Our recollections of the Turkish military police and the hotel entrance fortified with sandbags and automatic firearms make us a bit shaky, though. What will it be like this time? Is it really a good idea to gate crash a secluded event like this in Dubai?

Surprisingly enough, things go smoothly. Despite the guarded security check, designed and ornamented in the shape of an Arab arch, equipped with screening belts resembling those at airports, we are not searched for the obligatory badges (Photo I.1). We glance at each other with relief and walk ahead steadfastly. We

PHOTO I.1. Entrance to WEF Summit on the Global Agenda, Dubai 2012. Source: Garsten and Sörbom.

are in again, at least in the networking area. This time the networking area has been established in a plaza-looking room, with a high ceiling, wall-to-wall carpeting, and openings to a garden terrace where lunch is being served. The area is full, mostly of men in costumes or *thawbs*, but also women in high heels with expensive handbags. Most of them are showing hair and ankles, but some heads are covered by hijabs, and a few are completely covered by niqabs (Photo I.2).

We make our way toward the garden terrace, resembling scenery from "A Thousand and One Nights," where an extravagant lunch buffet has been set up. Plates in hand, with a small selection from the buffet, we approach one of the tables, where a group of men and one woman have started their lunch and their lunch conversation. They are all smiling kindly at us. After a while, one of them

PHOTO I.2. Networking lounge at WEF Summit on the Global Agenda, Dubai 2012. Source: Garsten and Sörbom.

turns our way, introduces himself as Mathew Tong, and wonders who we are. As usual, we tell the plain truth: "We're researchers from Stockholm University, Sweden, with an interest in understanding how WEF constructs and contributes to global politics." We know from numerous earlier encounters that our chance of keeping his attention is dependent on our short introduction. We would have a window of fifteen to twenty seconds when he would decide if we are interesting enough to talk to.

Mr. Tong, an academic of British origin, an unflappable-looking, gray-haired, and stylish man in his early fifties, apparently finds us entertaining enough and starts describing himself and his relationship to the WEF. He has been part of the brain trust summits for five years and considers himself something of a veteran. He quickly explains, in an ironically kind, smiling, and playful tone, that he never knows what, if anything, they are achieving. "It's a very intangible thing," Tong says. "Mostly I believe that it's about trend spotting. You get a sense of what's going on." The rewards for him are also quite intangible, with a vague sense of contribution once he returns home. "What happens, happens in the councils," he concludes. So he had skipped the first plenary and gone swimming instead. "I am very shallow," he admits. "In general I believe that people come hoping to be invited to Davos. By participating over and over again, they aspire to qualify as participants at 'the summit of summits.'" Tong says that he is certainly hoping to be invited to Davos, although it has not happened yet. When he received his first invitation to Dubai, he said, he had thought that the whole thing was a setup, some kind of a scam. So he phoned the Forum and asked them to e-mail him again. With a half smile, he claims that he has a vague sense of why he was invited: because "I do have a small impact in Hong Kong. I am kind of big there, but it's nothing, of course."

After the short lunch conversation, Mr. Tong invites us to follow him when he returns to a session in the actual council meeting. Experienced as we are with WEF rules, we follow him to the badge checkpoint, with little hope for making it inside. As we assumed would happen, we are not allowed to enter. The guards are firm. We cannot be let in.

At the council meeting entrance, there is a large signpost with an illustration of a schematic beehive, representing a map of the cells in which each council has its meeting. The map is made to look like the inside of a beehive. All the small groups, normally between ten and fifteen persons, including the WEF moderator, meet in these small areas. The idea is that these cubicles shall be closed enough to enable group processes to begin easily, a member of the WEF staff explains in a later conversation, but open enough to allow people to move between the small cells, so that both ideas and people may flow freely (Photo I.3). Struck by this image, standing at the entrance to this social beehive but not being allowed in, we have nothing to do but grasp our cell phones from inside our handbags and take pictures of what we believe to be a portrait of the desired organizational model: the beehive, a key metaphor for the organizing process of the WEF, simultaneously a model *of* and a model *for* the organization.[58]

Mathew Tong hurries inside the beehive to his group. We strike up a conversation with Ruby Balancona who is overseeing badges and the handing out of black conference briefcases with the WEF logo printed on them. She believes that it would in theory be possible for us to participate and initiates the process, trying to sort something out by talking to Simon Kaminsky, one of our earlier interviewees from Cologny. After a few minutes she comes back and says that it is not in her or Kaminsky's hands; we will have to talk to Jean-Luc Bosser who is managing the GACs. Fortunately, we already have a meeting scheduled with Mr. Bosser set up at 4:00 p.m., ninety minutes later. With the groups now in session, the networking area is quite calm. Coffee and water are served from a bar, and we help ourselves while waiting.

PHOTO I.3. Map of the social beehive at the WEF Summit on the Global Agenda, Dubai 2012. Source: Garsten and Sörbom.

We use the time to take notes with our reflections on the situation. What are the chances of gaining entrance? We should try to see this from their perspective. Why would they not let us in? Is this their way of holding us at a distance, saying neither no—so they may still maintain the image of transparency—nor yes. It's a little Kafkaesque, we think, invoking a senseless, disorienting complexity. Is research by gate crashing really the only solution for a social scientist interested in understanding and presenting the Forum to the outside world?

At 4:00 p.m. Jean-Luc Bosser appears and guides us to one of the meeting rooms. He is a composed and anxious-appearing man in his forties, with distinct facial features that clearly express distress at our presence, with a stern look. He closes the door to the event firmly, saying, "No one gets in, no matter who they are and how interested they are in the meeting." He gives us the example of the president of Mexico, who apparently also wanted to join on his own initiative but was refused. "As I have explained earlier, we cannot open the door to all people who want to join," he states emphatically. He is swallowing hard. Disappointed, we leave the conference premises, walk up to the adjacent Mina A'Salam Hotel, where we have an appointment scheduled for next morning with a GAC member we had met before, to check on where the meeting will take place. The summit is not yet over.

Such was our experience of the Forum: at once an organization with the aspiration to gather people "from all walks of life" to work together "to improve the world," by addressing pressing global challenges, and, on the other hand, an organization that prides itself in inviting only "the best brains" and the most resourceful corporations to its meetings behind closed doors. The selectivity and hype cultivated around the organization, the urgency, and the glitz work to further the voice of the WEF in the global political domain. It is, in essence, a truly seductive organization.

Book Outline

We intend this book to provide a narrative of the Forum that captures central dimensions of its workings as an organization. We have also chosen to weave the more analytical discussion into our ethnographic experiences, so as to render the seemingly abstract an embodied quality.

In Chapter 1, we provide a view of the WEF as an ethnographic field and describe our experimental methodological design. We highlight the varying strategies we used to approach the organization—ranging from gate crashing to taking on the insider's role—and the different types of engagements we experienced in meetings and conversational interviews. Apart from displaying the experimentation with the ethnographic method that this research involved, we emphasize the close intertwining of methodology and theory and suggest that what one may learn from denials, rejections, and failure may be just as informative as what is learned by full access and participation. By attempting to study the WEF, by being denied, rejected, and sometimes also welcomed, we learned about the politics of discretion in practice.

Chapter 2 looks at the liquid mandate on which the WEF bases its activities. Against the background of lacking a formal mandate, we describe how it is possible for WEF to position itself as a legitimate actor at the global level. This brings to the fore the seductive strategies in which the Forum is so proficient. With the "right" people attending, legitimacy rubs off on the organization. The network of contacts that WEF organizes, characterized by opacity and a high degree of global sway, is a consequence of the corporate-based mandate they enjoy. We discuss discretionary governance as the specific form of governance by which the Forum operates. In light of the relative lack of democratic characteristics such as representation and accountability, we argue that this type of governance entails a withdrawal of the elites.

In Chapter 3, we describe the authoritative capabilities of the WEF in terms of communicative power. Based on our ethnographic observations and descriptions, we reveal how the activities of WEF are consequential precisely through its communication. Communication, we suggest, is the means by which organizations are designed, created, and sustained and the base of power and authority. At WEF, communication entails working on setting precedence in issues related to global policy and markets, to frame and articulate issues, problems, and solutions. The agenda setting may appear not to involve conflict on the surface. However, the lack of open conflict does not necessarily mean lack of conflict; in fact, conflict is recurrent around the Forum.

Chapter 4 takes a closer look at how the status machinery of the WEF works. The Forum provides an exclusive and closed arena on which a level of hype, urgency, and topicality is produced. The processes by which individuals are selected to participate in discussing, debating, and advocating solutions to urgent global problems are meticulously prepared. The Forum draws into its orbit carefully chosen individuals who are organized into communities of expertise; they engage in cultivating a brain trust, highlighting and celebrating particular individuals, ideas, and actions. We reflect on these processes and how they work to distance the Forum and its selected crowd from the public. By this process, the Forum creates and enhances status distinction and contributes to the formation of a new transnational elite—what we call an aspiring class.

The activities that are distinctly formatted around the future—mobilizing the young and presenting future scenarios—are discussed in Chapter 5. The future is a signature theme at the Forum, one that serves to articulate and postulate future perspectives, agendas, risk, and generations. The emphasis at the Forum is on preparing for the future as it unfolds. In this chapter, we show how the risk scenarios and the future communities are ingredients in the aspirations of shaping the world in a specific direction. They articulate a particular form of anticipatory knowledge, geared to contribute to the shaping of political priorities and agendas, reflecting WEF's central values and priorities.

Chapter 6 unfolds the sometimes conflicting political underpinnings of the Forum. The Forum advocates a specific form of neoliberal thought combined with third way social democracy. This combinatory approach also promotes a set of ideas regarding the role of business in politics, by which economic and social values are seen to be seamlessly aligned. Together these ideas underpin a type of politics that is characterized by a postpolitical paradox in which conflict is seemingly turned into consensus, at the same time as the all-inclusive multistakeholder model turns out to be a differentiating and conflicting force.

In the Conclusion, we return to the exclusivity of the Forum, its liquid mandate, seductive strategies, and discreet power. We reflect on the workings of discretionary governance and the question of how, and if, global politics is possible. And we address what the role of the Forum is at the level of global politics. The WEF is a response to the fragmented global predicament, calling for more transnational cooperation. As a model for future governance, there are democratic challenges but also opportunities for markets, policymaking, and diplomatic relations. The WEF continues working toward its goal "to improve the world" and to show us *one* alternative organizational order.

As we reach the end of the book, we hope to have conveyed how the Forum, together with its funders and invitees, continuously strives to create a fragile political mandate with a significant global sway. This form of power, however soft and discreet it may be, turns out to be seductively sharp.

1 Disentangling Discretionary Governance

"The main challenge for us as an organization is to balance transparency with security," a WEF manager tells us. We are at WEF headquarters in Cologny, talking about all the work required to orchestrate the Davos event and all the issues that must be considered. "One of our goals is to make the organization strong outside and safe inside," he continues. "If you are in, you are in—you are welcome."

Discreet Spaces

The WEF nurtures an image of itself as a transparent organization, an open platform for dialogue. It has received recognition as a meeting ground for discussions and deliberations and for creating a highly visible, agenda-setting platform by working with business leaders, international organizations, and governments to address such issues as corruption, transparency, and emerging-market risks. Although the WEF has no formal, legal mandate, its mission statement is clear: "We believe that progress happens by bringing together people from all walks of life who have the drive and the influence to make positive change.[1] The notion of an open and welcoming arena on which topical global issues are freely discussed is a key signature of the organization. Its striving for transparency is visible even in the architectural design of the headquarters building in Cologny (Photo 1.1). The inside of the building generously opens up to Lake Geneva through its large windows and open layout. The atmosphere is one of openness, lightness, and free space. The words of the WEF manager echo, "You are welcome."

In many ways, the Forum strikes one as an attractive organization that provides a modern, state-of-the-art and progressive alternative to stalled international institutions and ways of doing international diplomacy. Only the most capable and talented people make it here. They represent what we could think of as the new global nobility. It is a seductive space.

From the outside, however, the headquarters building is more like a fortress. Near-black, no windows facing the village street, and strictly guarded

PHOTO 1.1. WEF headquarters in Cologny, Geneva, Switzerland. Source: Flickr.com.

by road barriers, security guards, and security entrance doors equipped with screening devices and surveillance cameras provide visible evidence of what it means to be "strong outside." The architecture speaks to WEF as an organization that seeks to preserve its integrity as "a safe place" for leaders to meet in person, without the prying eyes of the public or the press. Here is where a significant dimension of its value for global leadership resides. The Forum observes the Chatham House Rule, stipulating that when a meeting, or part of a meeting, is being held under the rule, participants are free to use the information received, but they may not reveal the identity or the affiliation of the speaker(s) or that of any other participant. Thus the content of the meetings is anonymous. In that way, the WEF intends to ensure that information regarding who uttered what in private spheres is not disseminated to the outside. In several conversations with meeting participants, we were told that being part of the WEF community entailed being entrusted, with the implication that they would not want to talk too freely about anything related to their involvement in order to protect their bond with the WEF. It also came with a status distinction that made participants eager to protect their access privilege. The ideal of openness is thus combined with the participants' trained ability to remain silent.

One of the participants, Dr. Peel, a polite and talkative woman with a distinct British public school intonation who held a leadership position in a prominent British policy institute and was highly esteemed by the Forum, advised us in lowered tones, "You have to be careful. There are many who want to hide things, since it's so important for them to come back." This kind of advice was given to us more than once and in various forms, and for a reason. We came to understand that a degree of tact and discretion was necessary to be selected for invitation and to be a continuous member of one the organization's communities. This norm of discretion spilled over on us: we too were expected to abide by the unwritten rules of public diplomacy, respect the mission of the organization and its way of operating, observe tact and discretion, and recognize the invisible boundaries of inside and outside.

The WEF can fruitfully be seen as a discretionary space in the way outlined by anthropologist Lilith Mahmoud.[2] In her monograph on Italian Freemasonry, Mahmoud describes how discretion is a key feature of everyday practice, an embodied disposition that allows its members to assert their belonging in a community of initiates while simultaneously allowing them to shield themselves from the intrusive gaze of the media and law enforcement.[3] Similarly, discretion is a way for the WEF to assert its community to the inside and outside worlds and to deter attempts to intrude and question. Knowing when to be discreet is of utmost importance. Moreover, discretion works not by itself but in combination with seductive communicative strategies. The allure of the Forum lies to a large extent in attracting others to do what it wants them to do. Offering opportunities for small-scale, intimate meetings with top executives, eminent politicians, esteemed academics, or illustrious artists—meetings that are sealed off from the outside world—accentuates the attraction of the Forum. In addition, having been selected as a participant for a Forum community or meeting may confer a seductive sense of belonging to a community of elites. Discretion and seduction thus work hand in hand to create the discreet power on which the organization relies.

The ability of the Forum to maintain discretion and integrity is a central asset in all of its dealings. Its very position in the world of global politics, markets, and diplomacy relies strongly on the trust it is able to create between itself and top leaders as a place where critical topics can be discussed without media attention or leakage. One critical dimension of maintaining significance for top world leaders and in the eyes of the public is therefore the continuous staging of the invisible boundaries of inside and outside. The image of high stakes that characterizes the organization relies on the continuous staging of secrecy and exclusivity around the organization and on the perception of an impenetrable core. As Simmel noted, the foundational sociological principle of secrecy builds relationships and communities and works to organize and stratify communities by way of the relative concealment or revelation of knowledge.[4] The WEF takes great care to protect its partners and participants, funders, and guests from unnecessary exposure, keeping large parts of its activities a secret even among participants. Various types of meetings have varying degrees of protection and secrecy around them, and the proper degree of exclusion is a constant concern. Meeting badges provided to participants are color coded, signifying differing degrees of access to meetings. Meeting spaces are differentially secluded, depending on the topic and on participant, media, and public access. Contact information provided to staff and associates is not publicly displayed. The secrecy around the internal workings of the organization, around informal negotiations and financial assets, often makes it difficult to find essential basic information about the organization and its events and to obtain a clear idea of how it functions. There is layer upon layer of secrecy involved, and at times during our research process, we had the impression of peeling an onion, only to find that the essential core slips away.

The dynamic interplay of secrecy and transparency that the Forum draws on for its mobilization takes the form of what we term *discretionary governance*. By this, we mean a form of governance exercised through discretion that is based on the judgment of WEF itself and its participants. It is characterized by low degrees of formal hierarchy, with little emphasis on procedures, norms of accountability, and protocol. Providing open platforms for dialogue and creating safe spaces for deliberation are mechanisms for networking, information sharing, and advocacy, but they are also instruments of discretionary governance. They serve to extend the mechanisms of indirect and discreet political power into other public spheres and organizations, and may have an unaccountable influence on ideological, political, and financial forms of power. The interplay of transparency and secrecy and the everyday politics of discretion are put into action for purposes of discretionary governance and management, but (in)tend to escape social and democratic oversight and regulation. (We discuss this issue more thoroughly in Chapter 2.) Our point here is that the observation of discretion, the making of discreet power, and the exercise of discretionary governance are to be seen not only as abstract theoretical findings; they transpire in the practices of managers, other employees at the Forum, and members of the Forum communities.

Our attempts to get closer to the organization and engage with its communities were largely affected by the workings of discretion. In this chapter, we provide a perspective on the WEF as an ethnographic field and discuss how we approached it methodologically. In particular, we bring into the limelight the varying strategies we used to approach the organization, ranging from gate crashing to taking on the insider's role, and the different types of engagements we experienced in meetings and conversational interviews. Apart from displaying the experimentation with the ethnographic method that this research involved, we emphasize the close intertwining of methodology and theory and suggest that what one may learn from denials, rejections, and failure may be just as informative as what is learned by full access and participation. By attempting to approach the WEF, by being denied, rejected, and welcomed, we learned a great deal about the politics of discretion.

Approaching the Core

In our initial preparations for the project, colleagues told us that researching the WEF would prove to be impossible. "You will not gain access," a renowned professor told us, suggesting that we take another route. And indeed, most earlier research has been based on Internet findings.

How does one approach ethnographically an organization as secluded as the WEF? What types of engagement are possible with people working in the organization and participating in its activities? How does one gain access to its organizational activities, meetings, and events? We both have extensive experience in studying organizations and organizational processes of various sorts, including transnational corporations, multilateral organizations, and social movement organizations, and we had accumulated a repertoire of ways to access and engage with these organizations ethnographically. But the WEF compelled us to try new avenues and experiment in novel ways.

For one thing, the secluded nature of the WEF reinforced the trope of the bounded organization, understandable only "from within." The emphasis on exclusivity and the culture of privilege that the WEF constructs around itself seemed to confirm the appearance of internal consistency in the organization. We chose a different approach. Rather than locating "the field" to be the formal boundaries of the organization, we imagined our field as comprising a more fluid and extended space of relational connections—links that led us to people with varying affiliations to the WEF, other organizations, and public spaces and meeting grounds. For our purposes, the field was more an assemblage of interconnected people, organizations, and sites than a territorially and formally bounded organizational unit. Our field thus was multilocal and global in character, comprising several fields in one.[5] Furthermore, this "global assemblage" is mobile, dynamic, and continuously reconstituted through the shifting interlinkages and frictions among its components. It also defines new relational, discursive, and material relationships.[6]

In the spirit evoked by anthropologist George Marcus, who is devoted to experimental ethnographic ways of studying elites, ethnography is primarily about exploring social relationships and therefore only derivatively about places.[7] Depth of analysis can be achieved through strategic lateral movement through cultural frameworks rather than simply remaining in one spot. In tracing relationships and thus "following" the field, we established both short-term and longer-term relationships with our interlocutors, to some extent replicating some of their experiences. Our ethnographic journey thus took us to Davos, Geneva, Dubai, Istanbul, Cape Town, Stockholm, and yet other places and to numerous meeting grounds: convention centers, hotel lobbies, restaurants and bars, bus stops and airports.[8] We attended the Davos meetings for three consecutive years; spent several stints at the headquarters in Cologny; participated in the regional meetings in Istanbul and Cape Town, the Global Agenda Council Meeting in Dubai, and the Post Davos Nordic Summit in Stockholm. For each of these sites, we calibrated our methodological approach to varying degrees of participation, formality, and scale and to be open to chance happenings. At times, we could engage in the meeting as full-fledged participants, almost on equal terms with other participants. We could walk freely in the gated headquarters office and approach without restraint. At other times, we had to make do with observing— listening, sensing, and seeing what was going on around us. And on yet other occasions, we explored the meaning of being rejected and denied conversations and participation. These polymorphous engagements, however fragmented and single stranded they might appear, together (at least in retrospect) comprise a relatively rich palette of encounters.[9]

Our diversified engagements also implied that we helped to expand the sociality of the meeting spot and the field through our interactions. In this sense, the field was constructed through a play of social relationships established between us and our interlocutors and extending across physical sites. As Simon Coleman and Peter Collins describe in their discussions on space, place, and context in ethnographic fieldwork, dimensions of the field can be captured by the metaphor of performance that sometimes can replace the purely spatial modes of description. This has the advantage of suggesting dynamic, mutual implications in constructing the field, even considering the fact that actors may have different motives, resources, and perspectives. And unlike conventional notions of fixed places, performances can be repeated and transformed over time and created anew. The field is thus, as Coleman and Collins would have it, "constantly in the process of becoming."[10]

WEF staff make use of the beehive as a metaphor intended to capture the essence of the organization. This metaphor is used in meetings; we encountered it for the first time at the Global Agenda Council Meeting in Dubai. The beehive is meant to symbolize the continuous buzz, the networking, and the cross-pollination that occurs between WEF staff and participants in the working groups. A schematic picture of a beehive is often placed centrally in the meeting venues, along with information on meeting spaces for the working groups. The beehive metaphor may be extended beyond the meeting, we suggest, to the wider activities of the organization. To fulfill its mission, the WEF depends entirely on the interactive capacities of participants—their capacity to articulate, disseminate, and mobilize around ideas and arguments, and to pursue them outside the WEF. The aim is to provide a space for networking and interchange of ideas that can then be pushed further, and eventually influence political agendas.

The beehive is a way for the WEF to understand itself as an organization and, in an extended sense, as an assemblage of people, organizations, and sites. There is adjacency here between our way of viewing the field and the way in which WEF staff narrate their organizational space. Adjacency, as social anthropologist Paul Rabinow uses the term, is a space for surprise, provocation, and experimentation, and it was one that we experienced on and off throughout our fieldwork.[11] This space positioned us somewhere between outside and inside, external and internal. In the words of philosopher Colin Koopman, "This location is one from which thought can be offered up as experimental. The adjacent critic gains distance from their object of criticism—but not too much distance."[12] The adjacent critic lives on the edge of the field. In a manner of speaking, we did our fieldwork on the edge.

Gate Crashing
Ethnographic fieldwork on the WEF involved constant negotiations for access, with repeated dismissals. It was no easy matter to invite ourselves into the activities of an organization that prides itself on inviting only a carefully screened

and selected small group of participants. Researching the WEF also proved to be a trying process of tracking people down, trying to get a portion of their time for a conversation or interview, pushing ourselves onto people who were either reluctant to or disinterested in having us around. It tested all of our ethnographic ingenuity.

Having tried our best to negotiate access to meetings with WEF senior managers beforehand, only to be denied most of the time, we ventured to different venues to try our luck. Our ethnographic approach often involved going to events haphazardly, hoping there would be opportunities for us to participate in a few meetings on the spot. Once there, we tried to find ways of getting in, thinking that most of what is relevant is probably going on inside the meeting compound, in the inner circle of events. We did gate crashing in the sense that we tried different ways to approach and gain access to the activities we wanted to take part in or observe. We talked to guards, trying to argue our way in or hoping to direct their attention elsewhere. More than once, we were chased off the grounds by guards demanding to see our badges. We tried walking straight on as if we had the right to pass the security gates without anyone asking us for our badges, a strategy that usually resulted in aggressive deterrence by the guards. On occasion, we had to leave the premises by running as fast as we could in our high heels. We traced the barbed-wire fence around the meeting compound in Davos in hopes of gauging the size of the bounded space and detecting eventual loopholes. We never found one.

The ceaseless failures were highly frustrating and sometimes made us lose faith and courage. We were losing time and proximity to the action. These were challenges we could handle, however; in fact, they sometimes motivated us and goaded us into action. As Woody Allen once said, "Eighty percent of success is showing up." We learned a great deal merely by continuing to try—and by being there. More discomforting was the feeling of shame evoked by the constant denials and reminders of status distinction and discretion. Not being on the list of those of who were welcome, invited, and selected—indeed not being wanted at all—was something that WEF staff often conveyed, however tactfully. This deferential shame arising from deferential treatment is an effective strategy of dissuasion and deterrence. We nevertheless opted to go on with it, thinking that it was part of the learning process. And we soon gathered that we would understand how the organization treats those who are not welcome— ergo the majority of the world's population—and get an idea of how the organization works.

There were other ways in which our access attempts were deterred. WEF staff often tried to divert attention away from our access request toward something that might appear valuable enough to compensate. One time we were trying our best to gain permission for access to a particular regional meeting. We were denied this request but offered a report written by WEF staff and associated experts. The report was presented as "an unofficial report," given only to board members and "shared in trust." In our mind, the report had nothing to do with the meeting we intended to go to, and it could not compensate for the insights we might have obtained by participating. In fact, it was an instance of a "lightning rod strategy," by which the representatives of an organization aim to divert attention away from issues that are seen to be sensitive or otherwise unwanted and toward something that would instead capture some desired characteristics of the organization.[13] Moreover, we discovered, the report appeared on the website a bit later and was not the hot stuff the staff tried to make us believe. Such diversion tactics, we discovered, were often used to uphold the discretion of the organization and steer our attention away from particular interests. Moreover, they constituted an essential resource in maintaining the image of the WEF as a distinct culture of exclusion and privilege.

But gate crashing would sometimes prove worthwhile. At most of the events we attempted to observe, we could attend the designated networking area that the Forum always has at its events. From that position, it was easy to make contact with both staff and participants. Before one of the Davos meetings, we had had a long e-mail conversation with several members of the WEF management team, only to be denied access. We had tried our luck at the gates several times and attempted to compensate for what we considered a failure by talking to service staff and others on the peripheries of the meeting compound. In the afternoon of one of the final meeting days, we had found our way to Sport Central building, where some of the events were held, to see if we could attend one of the seminars—to no avail. Instead, we had a long and informative conversation with a journalist from a European media company. Suddenly we ran into Cassius Luck, one of the senior members of the WEF leadership team, who recognized us in the crowd as the two women who were always hanging around. Mr. Luck is a tall, slender man with ash-blond hair streaked with gray and a manner of interacting that immediately displayed ease of privilege and conviviality. Dressed in other than his usual business attire, he would have appeared more hardcore rock style than the diplomat he now looked like. He was hosting a grand dinner at the end of the Davos meeting and surprised us by saying,

"You ladies are invited to join the dinner tonight unless you have other more interesting invitations." A couple of days earlier, explaining why he had not been able to assist us in getting permission to participate, he had moaned about being drenched by an avalanche of e-mails and not being able to see his wife for a long time. By the time he approached us, though, he could see the end of the event approaching and looked relieved. We accepted the invitation, knowing that we had to change our plans for the evening. He gave us a quick update on the time and location of the dinner and hurried off to his next engagement.

Circling the Peripheries

Being denied most of the time entrance to the meeting proper, we spent considerable time in the peripheral spaces of meeting grounds, talking with activists, journalists, skiers, private drivers, waiters in bars and restaurants, and people on their way to or from seminars. As we gradually learned, being on the periphery was not such a disadvantageous position after all—sometimes quite the contrary. Here, people were freer to talk, eager to air their views, and curious about our research. One invited participant at the Davos meeting said, "The closer you get to the inner core of the meeting ground, the less interesting the discussion gets, since it gets more official." Thus, gaining access to the inner core of meetings did not automatically place us closer to the core of the organization, in the sense of capturing people's perceptions and experiences. The scripted sociality of the more official meetings would not necessarily entail a fuller understanding of the organizational dynamics involved in constructing the WEF as an organization of significance.

At times, adherence to the norms of secrecy provided more information than actual disclosure would have. During a dinner in one of the restaurants in Davos, we were sitting next to a group of young private car drivers, neatly dressed in gray suits, who were having a meal while waiting to drive their clients to the next meeting in a seemingly endless chain of events. On the pretext of asking for directions, we approached their table, map in hand, and soon found ourselves immersed in a conversation over the content of their assignment. Chatting in this manner, we learned that the Davos event is a magnet for young hotel management students in search of interesting job opportunities. Restricted by the codes of conduct in place, they were unable to talk about their clients— the people they were driving, to what meetings, what the client had said on the telephone, and the like. Nonetheless, they told us about the tough competition involved in getting the assignment, the interviews they had gone through, the dress code they were expected to observe, the good money they earned, and the long waiting hours. They told us that they learned how to kill time in between jobs by socializing with each other, for example. And by telling us what they were *not* allowed to tell us, they provided us with more information about the boundaries of secrecy that surround even the logistical parts of the organization of WEF events and the expectations and demands placed on service staff.

Similarly, bartenders, as another category of service staff, often told us about all the fuss involved in preparing for the Davos event and about the hard work in working the late hours. Now and then, we were informed about so-and-so visiting their premises and the security work around the visit. The bartenders appeared to be used to the presence of celebrities—ministers and heads of state, top business leaders and rock stars—and not overly impressed by their concentration in the tiny village of Davos. Meeting participants were often talkative when they were having drinks after hours. They would tell us about the seminars they had participated in, who had been present, and the possible significance of the seminar. Villagers were sometimes willing to talk to us as well, and they could tell about the inconveniences of having their village crowded by visitors and under siege by security measures. "But," they would say, "it's only for a week, and then things will go back to normal." It was easy to tell that they were also flattered by having people like Angela Merkel, German vice chancellor at the time, or Nicolas Sarkozy, the president of France at the time, appear in the lobby in front of their very eyes.

It was also relatively easy to strike up a conversation with participants waiting in a hotel lobby for someone to turn up, for a meeting to start, or just passing time. Often such conversations were comfortable and easygoing. People were generally eager to talk about their experiences and impressions of the meetings, of their motives for accepting the invitation, and about their plans for the day. They were also curious about us and our reasons for being there. More than once, we were given hints as to what the meeting was really about (to meet business partners and strike deals, to get a chance to ease curiosity about the WEF and its circle of attendees, to go skiing and to party, and even responding to the flattery of having been invited) and how we might best advance (by contacting this or that person, tagging along at the meeting, or appearing at a particular cocktail party).

Another group of people we engaged with at the peripheries of meetings were members of the Occupy Movement.[14] At the 2012 Davos meeting, a group of some twenty or thirty people from the Swiss Occupy Movement had camped just outside the WEF meeting compound in the igloos they had erected on an empty parking lot (Photo 1.2). After having received permission from the police and the Forum, they had made themselves at home with sleeping bags and fireplaces. They were dressed to withstand the cold, in sturdy coats and winter boots, but it still looked as if it was cold to stay there. Martha, a young, energetic woman dressed in a heavy down jacket, thick woolen hat, and robust boots and mittens, informed us that she had been sleeping in one of the igloos for three nights and that some of her friends had been asked by the Forum to participate at the Open Forum.

The Open Forum is a meeting platform created in response to criticism about the Davos meeting being secluded from the public at large. Held in a small high school close to the Davos conference center, it is open to everyone who wants to attend; students are especially welcome. There is a program specifically developed for the Open Forum, with daily seminars and panel debates. The Open Forum, as the name suggests, "aims to encourage dialogue and spread awareness on critical issues to the global economy by providing a platform on which

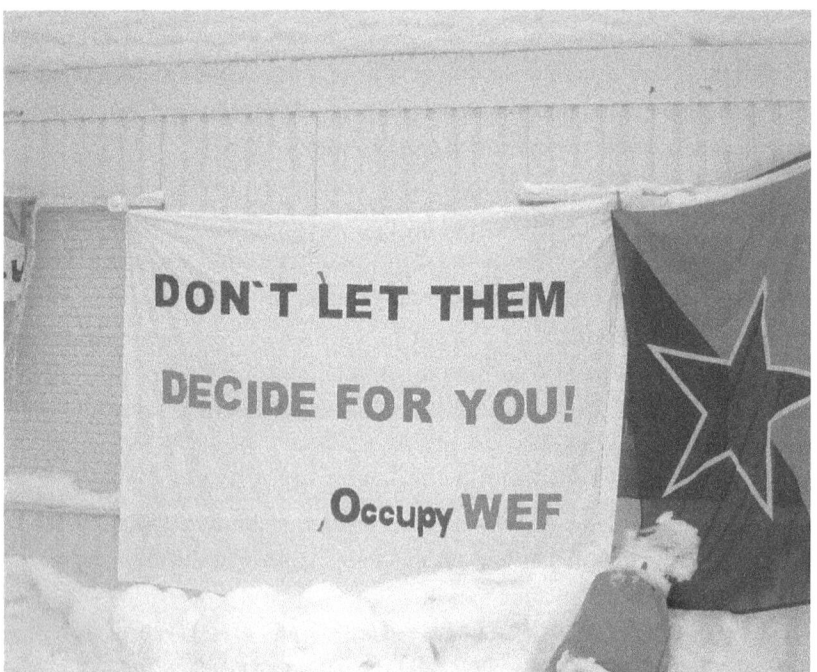

PHOTO 1.2. Occupy WEF in Davos, 2013. Source: Garsten and Sörbom.

ideas, thoughts and questions can be expressed and tackled in an open environment."[15] But to Martha, this was all talk. "Davos is mostly a showcase," she says. We inserted, "The theme this year is 'The Great Transformation: Shaping New Models,' also for the way capitalism should work. Do you think they are open to change?" "They don't want to change anything," she replied. "They are the richest people in the world, and they make money by keeping things the way they are." We hung around with the Occupy Movement people for a while and got to hear some of their opinions about the meeting and what they hoped to accomplish by being there. Such views from the outside were extremely informative and contributed to broadening our field and the context of our focus.

As is evident from these examples, the Forum not only engages in the creation of open spaces for deliberation and in professing transparency as an ideal organizational norm. It also produces silences. Some of these silences are deliberately and intentionally produced, and others are unintentionally produced over time as norms are instilled and sustained. In some cases, the "talk" Martha referred to shields off discussions of the very conditions of deliberation and the basic predicament of democratic engagement. Similarly, the Chatham House Rule makes sure that silence is maintained about the originator of a political opinion, which hampers further action and severs accountability. Circling the peripheries of meetings, we could sense how the production of silences was part and parcel of the way in which the Forum constructs discreet power.[16]

Trojan Horses

Apart from circling the peripheries, we tested ways of getting closer to the inside of the meeting premises. One of these was to jump on the buses that were shuttling participants between hotels and meeting venues. These shuttles are intended for participants with badges, and bus drivers are supposed to check badges of embarking passengers. From a gang of skiers in Davos, we soon learned that they rarely did. We tried and failed a number of times, probably because we did not look the part and displayed too much anxiety, but we eventually learned the ropes.

Hopping onto shuttles became a way of transporting ourselves across social meeting spaces and getting the opportunity to converse with participants. People on the buses were generally traveling alone or in pairs and were open-minded, friendly, and ready to chat. Time on the shuttle buses turned into a kind of speed dating, at which the opening question typically was: "Have you been to any interesting seminars today?" And the subsequent question most often was: "Are you government, NGO, or business?" Our typical response was to talk about the Open Forum seminars that we had access to, and that, yes, we are government, in the sense that we are academics employed by a Swedish public university, doing research on the WEF. Typically, this was followed by, "Oh, how interesting! What have you found?" They would then often tell us how valuable the meeting is for networking and making connections with people from around the world.

During one of those shuttle rides, we chatted with a British participant, a top-level business manager in his sixties, and a younger Chinese participant who was a manager in a high-tech firm. The British manager confessed to us, with a glint in his eye:

> I pretend to be working. But there are lots of parties going on. And Hotel Belvedere is the political center of gravitation for all entertainment. I've been coming here for many years, so it's a great opportunity to meet up with people. I meet a lot of people I haven't seen in a long time. Tonight, I'll be working hard: four parties, but first a business meeting at the Belvedere.

The Chinese meeting participant, we could read from his badge, was a WEF Global Shaper (a young person recognized as having "the passion, dynamism and entrepreneurial spirit to shape the future").[17] He told us that he found the Davos meeting extremely important for connecting with other Shapers and went on to ask us if we know which Swedish politicians were attending the meeting. Luckily, we were able to tell him. Over time, we heard many similar stories, with "confessions" about work being the pretense and partying as the real reason for attending. But we also heard many voices assert the value of face-to-face encounters and unique networking opportunities.

Jumping onto shuttle buses also turned into a way to get past the security barriers of the meeting grounds. The first time, at the Davos summit, we were not even aware that might happen and almost froze with fear as we realized we were inside the premises. As we saw the gates appear ahead of us, we asked the driver to let us off just before. The driver ignored our request and insisted on taking us all the way in, probably thinking he was doing a favor for a couple of busy and tired participants. As we disembarked, guards came to check our badges. Wanting to avoid a conversation about why we were inside the security gates without badges, we started running toward the exit, guards hot on our trail. It was with a sigh of relief that we realized we had been quicker than the guards and could wait inside the small bus shelter where fruit and water were served, until another shuttle bus would take us out of the compound. Later, we became more strategic in using the possibilities of the shuttle buses as Trojan horses, as a way to meet participants.

We learned a great deal not by gaining access, but by circling around the peripheries of the organization, talking to staff, participants, and service people, and trying out Trojan horses. The experimental mode of inquiry required us to try whatever approach appeared sensible and productive at any given moment, thus resembling what media anthropologist Elizabeth Bird calls "opportunistic ethnography" and communication scholar Fay Akindes refers to as "rhizomatic ethnography."[18] The context in which this was done was one of heightened securitization, high wire fences, policy, and military force and arms—in short, a context of latent violence. It was also an assembly of members of a global civil society addressing urgent global problems, trying to shed light on common priorities, and working toward possible solutions. In this tension zone of armed power and dialogical goodwill, issues of opacity and transparency, seclusion and openness become both physically and analytically salient.

We came to choose the Trojan horse approach and the gate crashing mode of fieldwork as a response to the seclusion of WEF activities. The WEF has a right to close its doors to the prying eyes of social scientists, and researchers have the right to ask questions about its doings and analyze its activities. Our openness in relation to the individuals we talked to is key here. We were always open about our roles as researchers; all of our interlocutors knew that we were not ordinary participants. As is the culture at WEF events, we were always ready to exchange business cards instantly when approaching guests, staff, or other groups of people.

Dubai, November 2012: Open, Sesame!

Having done our best to gain access to the Global Agenda Council Meeting in Dubai, to little avail, we decide to pull ourselves together once more. We are tired, sweaty, and frustrated with being rejected and denied permission to join meetings and to meet with WEF staff. We get into a cab that will take us once more from our hotel to the meeting location adjacent to the Mina A'Salam hotel. In the cab, Christina suddenly gets a phone call. The connection is poor, broken by noise and interference. She cannot clearly hear the name of the caller, but we understand that someone from the Forum wants to meet with us at the gates of the meeting. The phone number provides no information. We are somewhat confused by the call. We cannot figure out who the caller is or what the meeting will be about, but we anticipate that something of consequence will happen. The question is, What?

Back at the security gates, the scanning routine from yesterday has changed. Yesterday we could at least get through the security gates by looking the part, relying on the guards not being too meticulous in their screening. Now everybody needs to show a badge. We are stuck in the line at the security gates, guards approaching us. Just as we have put our handbags on the security belt for screening and the guards pulled us aside to check our nonexistent badges, we hear a male voice calling out: "Christina and Adrienne?" As if from nowhere, a WEF director steps forward, and guards immediately let go of us.

This is Cassius Luck, the man on the phone (who invited us to the Davos dinner we already mentioned), saying that he would very much like to help us get into the event. If we would be so kind as to sign in and have our picture taken, he will send off our personal details for security clearance. This last part will take a while to be sorted out, he explains. In the meantime, Mr. Luck walks us up to the lavish Mina A'Salam hotel lobby for a cup of coffee and small talk. On our way, we run into Chairman Schwab and his entourage, coming from the other direction. They are in a hurry, but for a second or two, our eyes meet. In the back of our heads, we both start pondering the fact that that the Chairman now knows that we are here. Has one of our interlocutors perhaps told him that we are to be let in? Mr. Luck takes the opportunity to introduce us, telling Mr. Schwab that we are two researchers from Sweden doing research on the WEF. Schwab looks at us with interest and asks if we would like to sit down and talk for a few minutes. We are asked to contact his assistant to set up a meeting later that afternoon. This in itself is serendipitous. We had tried to contact him several times through his personal assistant and his team of directors, but in vain. Now we are close to a personal meeting with him.

Over coffee, Mr. Luck, who is in charge of communication at the WEF, describes the Forum as "a shy organization." He explains that in contrast to the UN or any state-funded organization, the funding situation of the WEF—the one thousand corporations contributing large funding dues—allows them *not* to show what they are achieving. "We do not need press," he says and continues to explain that what they do is "to provide a brand-free and neutral space." Their slogan, "improving the state of the world," opens up for criticism, Mr. Luck says, "But we do refer to it often." The difficulty with setting up the Dubai event is to get the right people to the right Global Agenda Council (GAC). They usually try to find people with high credibility or from the right institutions, he tells us.

One hour later, our clearance has come through, and we head down to the WEF reception desk in the meeting space—the beehive—for our badges. They are presented, along with conference briefcases containing the meeting program and a thick book listing all meeting participants, other relevant material, and some small gifts. Our white badges say "Media Leader." With badges around our necks and black WEF bags in our hands, all doors are now open. "Do you wish to register for the summit party the same evening?" the assistant asks politely. "Which GAC sessions do you wish to attend?"

In the networking area, we run into Jean-Luc Bosser, in charge of the GAC communities and a key figure in running the meetings. The day before, he had denied us access, telling us, "We cannot open the door to all people who want to join." He now smiles politely when he spots us. Mr. Luck walks up to him to inform him that we are now cleared for access. Would Mr. Bosser now be so kind as to assist us with anything we might need his help with or introduce us to anyone we might want to meet? "I would be much obliged," Mr. Luck says. Mr. Bosser now smiles grudgingly.

A few hours later, having attended a number of sessions, we find ourselves in the temporary office set up for Chairman Schwab. We start by giving the short version of our project, ending with a question for Schwab on what WEF is all about. He enjoys diplomatic status, he says, as if he were from the International Monetary Fund or the World Trade Organization, because the WEF occupies a specific niche in the global governance system. The WEF is a nongovernmental organization (NGO), Schwab says; it serves a mission and is not a private enterprise. Nor is it, in his description, an advocacy group for business. It is 95 percent supported by business, which means to Schwab that business is an asset that must be used in the most efficient way. The Forum is not the voice of business, he underscores by saying:

> That is what the multistakeholder idea is about. Business, research, civil society and politicians must meet, foregrounding the voices of the young, the women, the best expertise, and the good. And in so doing, the Dubai meeting is a way to create dialogue and shape the agenda for the year to come.

Before we leave, we ask if he might be willing to meet us again for a follow-up conversation. We agree that sometime after the next Davos event would be perfect.

· · ·

That moment in Dubai was pivotal: it was the first time we were given full and official access, with badges and all, to an entire meeting. We would later have other opportunities to participate in meetings and to be present at meeting grounds, but never again with the same degree of access. Even so, our research did take us into the inner core of WEF events and allowed us not only to circle the periphery but also to participate in and observe events (Photo 1.3). We realized that our presence had become somewhat conspicuous, however, when one of the top leaders of the WEF remarked, with some irritation: "Are you still around"? We also heard from another researcher who had been in contact with Mr. Luck that he talked of us as "these two researchers from Sweden who are trying to do research on us."

Fieldwork at the WEF also provided openings and occasions to get closer to the core of the organization and its communities. During visits to headquarters in Cologny, we were left to make use of the localities on our own terms, as we met with staff for conversational interviews and absorbed the workplace atmosphere, the interior layout, and decorations. WEF staff often assisted us with requests for meetings with specific people, to obtain documents, and to answer our questions. Moreover, some of the participants and staff we got to know

PHOTO 1.3. Final address at Summit of the Global Agenda, Dubai 2012. HE Sami Dhaen Al Qamzi, Government of Dubai, and Klaus Schwab. Source: Garsten and Sörbom.

were willing to share their views and experiences with us over an extended period. We therefore had the opportunity to try out ideas with some of our interlocutors, for instance, about what the Forum could achieve and its ways of working, something that proved to be highly valuable.

Meetings and Conversational Interviews

Much of our fieldwork was conducted in meetings, which is indicative of the way in which the Forum operates. Formal meetings, ceremonial meetings, big meetings, secluded meetings, open meetings, business meetings, cocktail meetings, lunch meetings, and breakfast meetings—meetings of all sorts were the staple of our fieldwork. As the organized and ritualized social events that they are, meetings provided us with a powerful magnifying glass through which key tenets of the larger organization and the big issues could be carefully observed.[19] Political priorities, economic values, and social priorities were often condensed, played out, and negotiated in formal meetings, turning them into strategic sites from which to observe the organization at large. Meetings, it turned out, are "experiential and experimental sites," to borrow Rabinow's expression, where different versions of interpretations and claims are tested.[20] Even when access was denied or restricted and when people did not want to talk, we realized that that in itself is indicative of what the organization is about and what is at stake in meetings. A small place like the Davos meeting ground is, in our view, one spot in the larger infrastructure of the social world of the WEF and speaks to much bigger stakes concerning participation, voice, and power in global governance matters—issues that may have large-scale implications.

A large part of our fieldwork was made up of conversations with WEF employees, meeting participants, and people circulating on the peripheries of meetings and events. Such conversations were often highly rewarding, since they occurred without planning and on the spot in the middle of action. They would typically evolve around the particular activity in which the person was engaged and thus provide a sense of presence and proximity to our being there. Moreover, such conversations would sometimes lead to a longer relation in which our interlocutors became what Douglas Holmes and George Marcus call "epistemic partners" with whom we could collaborate in the creation of anthropological and sociological knowledge.[21] This was, for instance, the case with our two key informants, Cassius Luck and Peter Bond, with whom we had a number of discussions about the WEF. As we tried to sustain relations over time, we could not only keep track of what was going on in the organization but learn about their ways of learning.

We also conducted a number of regular interviews with WEF staff, funders, meeting participants, and meeting service staff. (See the appendix for details.)[22] Interviews, seen as thematic conversations around particular topics, varied considerably in their format, style, and depth. Many interviews, in particular those with WEF staff, were semistructured, centering around topics the two of us had discussed beforehand and focusing on the staff member's job, position, and experiences in the organization.[23]

Our interviewees were mostly easy to engage with, being used to and trained in meeting the press and choosing their words in interviews. We experienced some of them as being open-minded and reflexive, and others as more polished and formatted. At times, we were frustrated by what appeared to us to be a "Teflon culture" that emerged out of the interviews. It was as if they had been trained in responding to questions without really providing answers. They were skilled in the art of determent, shifting attention away from sensitive issues toward less burning topics or something they would rather talk about. Just as often, however, we were surprised by how much they would reveal of a personal or critical nature, seemingly unaffected by the idea that we might publish what they say. Many of them would give their personalized narrative of the organization, its way of functioning, and what made people join or leave. They would talk freely about organizational challenges and about risks and hazards related to the organization.

Interviews with meeting participants tended to be even more varied in nature. They were often relatively structured and to the point, reflecting the fact that they were squeezed in between a series of meetings and travel arrangements. Other interviews were conducted on the spot—on shuttle buses, in hotel lobbies, at bars, at receptions, or on the premises of other organizations. These interviews were consequently of a more informal and unplanned nature, ranging from five minutes to three hours, and with varying content. A majority of the interviewees expressed themselves relatively freely, airing both their positive and more negative views of what they perceived to be the expectation of the WEF on their participation and their own priorities and perspectives. Their views provided us with a more nuanced and openly reflexive picture of the WEF network as a whole, and both complicated and enriched our understanding of how the organization operates. Moreover, it gave us an idea of the repertoire of rationales involved for the different organizations.

Dyadic Fieldwork

Ethnography has typically been seen as a singular research venture in which a lone researcher engages in the study of a community, group, or organization. The historically engrained notion of the "lone ranger" who develops an interpretation of a cultural setting, based on immersion in it, has (for good and for bad) privileged individual achievement and interpretation. Increasingly, however, ethnographic research takes place in teams, partly reflecting changing notions of how knowledge is constructed and new modalities of engaging with informants.

Team fieldwork can be a productive way to explore what educational scholars Judith Davidson Wassler and Liora Bresler call "the interpretive zone" between the researchers involved.[24] The interpretive zone here refers to an historically and socially situated space of dynamic interaction through which researchers negotiate joint methodological inquiry and group identity. Collaboration has a critically interpretive function that may generate productive possibilities though challenge, conflict, alliances, and overlap.[25]

The WEF, as a dynamically shifting research field and continuously changing organization, appeared to us more easily approachable as a joint venture. Early on, we decided to do what we call dyadic fieldwork—the two of us working together as much as possible. Doing fieldwork together seemed to us to be a way to gain access to an additional perspective, test different approaches and interpretations, and add to the joint stock of memory. And given that our fieldwork would take us to a number of places throughout the world new to us and would involve late nights at cocktail parties and in murky pubs, walking home late on empty streets, we reasoned that we could keep an eye on each other and keep each other safe.

In our case, then, the "fieldworker" turned out to be the two of us, primarily working together and hanging out together. Over time, we learned to make use of our idiosyncrasies to fill in gaps in conversations and interviews, to rely on cues from each other as when to pose a particularly challenging question or when to finish up. We could also motivate each other when one of us was discouraged or dispirited. In this sense, we felt that we expanded our capacities by doing fieldwork together. Our interlocutors quickly noticed this approach, and we were collectively addressed by the expression "ladies" by many of the top—predominantly male—organizational leaders. Somewhat ambivalently, we accepted this title.

Dyadic fieldwork allowed for continuous reflection and discussion of the way to go about things and how to improve. It proved to be a peer review process. We used each other as critical interlocutors, a technique that proved valuable when experimenting with methods.

In the Thick of Paperwork

The use of writing, counting, and documenting, of storing and disseminating information and knowledge, is an elemental feature of organizational life at the Forum, as well as a fundamental feature of striving for influence and authority.[26] Documents permeate the organization, fix contingent conversations onto paper, and transform information and knowledge into fact and opinion. Documents also tie the nodes in the network together by moving in and out of the organization and its units and between members of its communities.

Documents are thus an integral part of the creation and circulation of WEF forms of knowledge, expertise, and governance. As anthropologist Iver Neumann has shown, the generation of knowledge in the format of documents is a key feature of the work of the diplomat, who is caught up in the seemingly endless production of texts: reports, speeches, position papers, and the like.[27] This is also so at the Forum: the creation of texts provides a structuring force and gives rise to a particular rhythm of brainstorming, conceptualizing, framing, researching, editing, and distributing of textual products.

A range of authors publish in various forms under the WEF logo. The Forum annually produces about one hundred in-house reports, often in collaboration with one or several funders and such other partners as renowned universities. These reports reflect the work that is going on in the organization itself and in the various communities, and some of the discussion points and topics that occupy the interest of WEF and its community members. Three of the best-known reports are the *Global Risks Report*, which highlights what the WEF perceives to be the most significant long-term risks worldwide, drawing on the perspectives of experts and global decision makers; the *Global Gender Gap Report*, which attempts to quantify the magnitude of gender disparities and tracks their progress over time; and the *Global Competitiveness Report*, which provides an assessment of the competitiveness of some 140 economies. In addition, Klaus Schwab and staff regularly publish opinion pieces and comments in the predominantly US-based news media and blog on the weforum.org address. These sources provide more articulate views on topical issues and challenges in the contemporary world. The Forum also has Facebook and Instagram accounts, through which it advertises for reports and events. Third, the Forum presents staff, funders, and participants at its own website (even though this type of information has decreased considerably over time). Some participants blog at the Forum web page and earlier wrote in the Forum journal *Global Link* during its period of existence (1988–2001). Altogether, these documents provide access to diverse communicative spaces in and around the WEF organization. We have systematically made use of these presentations, providing an avenue for general information regarding the backgrounds of participants at events and members within the manifold WEF communities.[28]

In brief, then, the WEF is an organization overflowing with paperwork as articulations of bureaucracy and textualization of knowledge. The unceasing flow of documents in an important sense underwrites claims for transparency and accountability. But documents are not the neutral purveyors of discourse they might appear to be, or be invoked to be. They shape the significance of issues they evoke, as well as the relations between the objects they refer to. Climate change, risks, gender gaps, and social entrepreneurship—just to mention of few of the topics regularly treated by the Forum—are brought to life partly by and through documentation. Social anthropologist Matthew Hull succinctly puts it this way: "to restore analytically the visibility of documents, to look at rather than through them, is to treat them as mediators, things that 'transform, translate, distort, and modify the meaning or the elements they are supposed to carry' (Latour 2005, p. 39)."[29] Furthermore, the mediating role of the Forum as an organization risks being made invisible if documents are taken for granted. The generative and performative role of documents should thus not be underestimated. They play important roles in the making of actors, issues, and perspectives that constitute the social world of the organization and its network, and they are thus integral to the exercise of power and influence. We have made use of this plethora of texts along the project. Reading, coding, and analyzing the reports, web presentations, blogs, and so forth, in combination with analysis of field notes and transcribed interviews, constituted the basis for developing our understanding of the WEF and the discreet power it aims for.[30]

Onward

As a discretionary space, the Forum provided a challenging endeavor. The multisited, mobile, and assemblage-like character of the organization encouraged an experimental methodological approach, involving a diverse set of strategies to get access to meetings and events, engage with people in the field, and try alternative interpretations. We have, we believe, tried the full range, from gate crashing to taking on the insider's role; from quick conversational encounters to long and structured interviews; doing dyadic fieldwork and occasionally venturing out alone; and doing number crunching with software as well as engaging in reflexive hermeneutical interpretation. In short, we have experimented with what Akhil Gupta and James Ferguson call "location work," in shifting locations and using a multistranded methodology.[31] Our contention is that by attempting to research the WEF, by being denied, rejected, and welcomed, we have gained knowledge about how the politics of discreet power works and how discretionary governance operates in practice. The engagements we were able to create and sustain, the varying degrees of participation we were granted, the interviews and conversations we were able to obtain, and the rejections we faced were all thematically fused together, along with information about the organizational practices and norms we observed in the Forum.

The methodological implications echo a broader trend within social theory on understanding and following the networks and connections that shape the social. It also resonates with recent attempts to conceptualize the scaling of contemporary fields in inquiry, to understand the epistemological proximity between or among phenomena that may appear to be only partially connected. A recursive conception of scale, along the lines sketched by social anthropologist James Faubion, may better register the local, regional, national, transnational, international, and global scope of the field.[32] In this context, the notion of the bounded field has been disentangled and has become theory rich, multisited, and multiscale rather than an objective place, and ethnography has become intersubjective, co-constructed, and mediated.

For us, the experimental approach also comes with the notion of a grounded ethnography as one that seeks to invent strategies of knowledge production, dissemination, and critique that go beyond the liberal individualism of much of contemporary social science and humanities.[33] Our approach has made us alert to the ways in which the organization makes use of seduction as a strategy to evoke attraction, interest, and commitment among its circles of potential invitees and participants and to create a mandate for itself among other organizations involved in global governance. In a Deleuzian manner, our approach revealed to us the simultaneous and intertwined workings of discreet power and the potentials of desire (both creative and destructive); the ways in which the organization continuously takes shape and ceaselessly leaks; and the in-between, plastic, and always unfinished nature of the organization.[34] It is to these strategies that we now turn.

2 Liquid Mandate

The World Economic Forum is a response to a need. We were not mandated by anybody. We created . . . a response to a clear need in the international governance system.[1]

In March 2013, we sat down in Cologny at the WEF headquarters with Klaus Schwab, WEF founder and Chairman, for a conversation on the role of the WEF in contemporary global governance. The view from the Chairman's meeting room over Lake Geneva was dazzling. The dark brown oval table was shining. Coffee and water were served. The meeting had been rescheduled several times, but now we had the full attention of Chairman Schwab; Mr. Cassius Luck, a senior director; and Ms. Pat Tremblay, one of Schwab's closest associates. The atmosphere in the room was focused and composed. The gravity and firmness of Klaus Schwab, a white man in his mid-seventies with a marked German accent, infused the room. A public figure, he came across as savvy in handling any type of question with great ease and proficiency. The oil portrait outside the meeting room, we noted, failed to capture the restrained buoyancy and curiosity of his facial expression. We knew Cassius Luck from earlier encounters, and now he greeted us as if we were old acquaintances. Pat Tremblay was a newer acquaintance. We had met her only briefly in Dubai, at the Global Agenda Summit a few months before. A North American in her mid-thirties, with a background in engineering and technology at global level, she struck us as Schwab's right hand, carefully keeping an eye on the happenings.

The conversation focused on the evolution of the Forum, its formative moments, and its future challenges. In the midst of the conversation, we asked the Chairman to describe the mandate the organization had built for itself. To our surprise, he denied the existence of a mandate and presented the idea that the Forum is a response to a need in the global government system presented in the quotation at the beginning of this chapter. In a few words, he illustrated a central dilemma related to the constitution of the WEF: its lack of official political mandate means that it is has no authority to act as a representative of other organizations. Rather, it strives to construct legitimacy for itself as an actor in global governance and an arena for political deliberation. Thus, unlike the World Trade Organization (WTO) or the UN, for example, the WEF does not enjoy an ascribed, state-based mandated role to make decisions on matters related to national or transnational affairs. In contrast, it has what we would describe as a liquid mandate, based on corporate money and utterly dependent on the goodwill of its funders and participants, who endow it with a certain, but not completely dependable, trust and agency. Should corporate leaders and politicians stop coming to Davos, even this liquid mandate is at risk. Continuous seduction is therefore essential.

In this chapter, we conceptualize the specific form of external governance of the WEF and analyze the liquid mandate on which it bases its activities. In doing so, we answer the question of how it is possible for WEF to position itself as a legitimate actor in global governance, based on this liquid mandate. Our answer relates to the global seduction and construction of discreet power in which WEF is so proficient. When the "right" people come to attend, their legitimacy rubs off onto the Forum. Like a self-fulfilling prophecy, the Forum is constructed as *the* place to be—as long as it can manage to be seen that way. This image, in turn, requires a nurturing of the attendees' reputation as the world's most committed, brightest, and most excellent.

We begin by presenting what we see as the corporate-based, liquid mandate of WEF, showing its limitations and fragility. Then we analyze its organizational and political consequences. We see the network of contacts that WEF organizes, characterized by opacity and euphemisms as a consequence of this corporate-based mandate. The Forum cannot openly describe itself as an actor in global governance; rather, it refers to itself as an arena that some allegedly important people are invited to attend. It needs to construct its own legitimacy, dressing itself up as an open and democratic international organization. We end the chapter with a discussion of discretionary governance as the specific form of governance that WEF has been able to construct for itself. With the relative lack of democratic characteristics as representation and accountability, this type of governance entails a withdrawal of the elites.

A Postpolitical Vision

In scholarly discussions regarding the nature of politics, there are two general interpretations. One, mainly within political science, follows the lead of political scientist David Easton, focusing on the arenas of politics, such as the parliament, the government, and what is termed the "political system."[2] The other departs from a broader perspective, focusing on the processes of politics, reminiscent of philosophers Gilles Deleuze and Félix Guattari, who claim that "before being there is politics."[3] In their interpretation, *politics* refers to structures predating the individual, shaped and formatted by actors of various sorts—elected politicians, fishermen, pimps, CEOs, midwives, and disc jockeys. Both of these aspects of politics are necessary to keep in mind in order to understand the global politics formed by WEF and the ambivalence related to it as a phenomenon. If politics is seen only from the arena perspective, global politics cannot exist, as the basic governmental characteristics do not occur outside of nation-states. Although voices are raised in favor of a parliament connected to the UN, this has not been realized; nor does a global government exist.[4] Moreover, because organizations such as the WEF do not relate institutionally to any state or to its international counterparts—the UN or the WTO, for instance—and therefore have no right to binding decision making in relation to nation-states, their activities would hardly qualify as politics. It could therefore be tempting to resort to the process perspective and analyze what WEF does in terms of agenda setting or discourse, for example.

To conceptualize the importance of WEF, however, it is vital to develop a double perspective of politics, analyzing the agenda setting and the discursive processes by which it relates to these types of decision-making arenas and other nonpolitical organizations in the established political system. From this double perspective, studying WEF entails an analysis of the forms, distribution, and control of power regarding norms and assets in both state-based organizations pertaining to the political system and such nonstate organizations as corporations, think tanks and nongovernmental organizations (NGOs). In practice, the study of WEF politics regards the study of setting precedence to some options over others and how these options are brought to and used in other organizations.

As becomes clear in the following chapters, WEF is not merely about business, nor is it an exclusive dating agency (which it has been accused of). And clearly none of this is what it aspires to be. The Forum aspires to "improve the state of the world," thereby giving precedence to some projects and norms over others, and it goes about this by establishing an alternative global political framework, placing business at the center, with nation-state representatives and other actors on the flank. Therein lies its discreet power. This is not to say that WEF is merely a political organization. It aims and is used for other purposes as well, and the blending is part of the attraction it has for the many people attending its events and communities. But just as parents have room in their hearts for all their children, the Forum has room for other activities and interests alongside its main engagements.

The particular form of politics staged by and taking place within the Forum relates to contemporary tendencies of governance as a form of doing politics.[5] Thus, the Forum is part of a general trend in contemporary politics in which market actors and other nonstate organizations increasingly participate in activities conventionally perceived as political, as in the case of corporate social responsibility.[6] These changes can be described in terms of the development of a new public domain, in which there is a lack of clarity between the boundaries of what has long been perceived as the spheres of politics, economics, and civil society.[7] In this domain, politics is shaped and pursued in constellations of public and private actors that contain states, international organizations, civil society organizations, and business corporations. Practices within this domain include regulation in various forms, particularly soft regulation, which primarily entails discursive and monitoring activities that embed, frame, stabilize, and reproduce rules and norms.[8]

WEF is both a driver and a consequence of this form of governance, especially in placing corporations at center stage. As we develop in depth in Chapter 6, the Forum plays a vital role in bringing business into what has come to be global politics and reducing conflicts related to this development, while simultaneously helping to construct the postpolitical version of politics.[9] The specific version of governance that the Forum has developed is based on seduction, seclusion, euphemism, and privacy, in which politics is created at the discretion of the organization and based on the discretion of all participants—hence, the term *discretionary governance*.

A New Kid on the Block
Compared to similarly closed meeting spaces, such as the Club of Rome, the Bilderberg Group, and the European Round Table of Industrialists, the WEF stands out because of its impact on media, global outreach, and the number of participants in the network it constructs.[10] It is also much more public than

most other "elite clubs." As such, it has been able to posit itself as a "trusted partner in global politics" (to use the words of the Forum). What is striking about this position and the role it is able to play is the peculiarity of the mandate. It is truly a "new kid on the block," in comparison to other global political organizations. Unlike the Chairman in the quote at the start of this chapter, we maintain that the WEF does have a mandate, but one that differs from those of, for example, intergovernmental organizations (IGOs) and international nongovernmental organizations (INGOs). It is a mandate based on the trust, interests, and financial resources of corporations, as opposed to states or citizens at large. The difference between these mandates is related primarily to the funding and ownership of the WEF, which has several fundamental consequences for how the WEF functions in practice.

The peculiarity of the WEF's liquid mandate and the way the organization functions as an actor in the international system become obvious in comparison with state-based organizations such as IGOs. With few exceptions, the Westphalian international system was built on nation-states, which constituted the international public in that system, manifested in organizations like the UN and the International Monetary Fund (IMF).[11] In the latter part of the 1900s, this domain did expand, however, to include not only INGOs but also transnational corporations (TNC), which together made up the new transnational public domain.

The UN continues to be at the core of this system and constitutes the prime example of IGOs. Born out of World War II, its initial mandate was based on the fifty founding nation-states that wrote the charter, established the organization to secure peace and economic stability in the world, and contributed with substantial funding. In 2011, the UN reached 193 members, when the newly created state of South Sudan joined. The organization has survived over the decades, with varying enthusiasm and increasing difficulties, and still functions as the cornerstone of the international system. The member states are the funders that continuously mandate the UN to act.

· The WEF, in contrast, was established under the patronage of the European Commission (EC) and European Industrial Associations, both of which were concerned that European corporations were falling short in comparison primarily to US corporations. It was Klaus Schwab who personally made contact with the EC president at the time, Jean Rey, explaining the idea of a management forum. Rey liked the idea and suggested two EC commissioners to participate as interlocutors.[12] Shortly after its inception in 1971, the WEF cut loose from the EC, establishing itself as a nonprofit Swiss-based foundation, thereafter leaning for support on business organizations and corporations.

During the first years, the fees charged to attendees of the Davos meetings funded the foundation. But starting in 1976, Schwab reorganized the Forum so that corporations could become "members," paying the foundation's costs by subscription.[13] The reorganization was motivated by the need for stability and predictability. If the corporations that had been recurrent participants at Davos during the first years could be turned into "members," the foundation would have a more secure form of funding. Moreover, the mission of the foundation was soon broadened to include prosperity for European societies on the whole—not merely corporations.

In the late 1980s, the mission was widened even more: the word *European* was replaced by *World* in the name of the organization, and the motto became "improving the state of the world." According to the WEF's internal historiography, the name change was "reflecting the global membership," while acknowledging the "fact that economic policy was at the forefront of its activities."[14] These alterations were, of course, due to changes in the interest of the organization, but the consequence was that funding possibilities were broadened. Instead of merely leaning on European corporations for funding, the WEF now saw the world's largest corporations as potential funders.

Compared to the traditional actor of the international system, the WEF has a background that differs from such organizations and enjoys a new set of funders, providing it with a different base for its mandate. Instead of a nation-state-based mandate, it has a corporate-based mandate. We return to the consequences for the WEF of this mandate. But before that, we need to compare the WEF with INGOs in order to highlight the uniqueness of the WEF, especially in relation to its funders.

Turning the corporate funders into subscribing WEF members, in conjunction with the later formal recognition from the Swiss government of the WEF as an international organization, might have made the WEF appear to be an ordinary INGO, enjoying the same kind of mandate as, for instance, the Red Cross (which also is recognized by the Swiss state as an international organization). A closer look, however, reveals several aspects of the WEF that set it apart from what is usually assumed by the term *association* and certainly many other INGOs. In INGOs and NGOs, funding members commonly have some form of voice in the organizations. They are considered the principals of the association. This is not the case for the WEF. The one thousand corporate funders have restricted accessibility to the core of the organization. Of the twenty-four board of trustee members, only eight come from funding companies; the majority are from international institutions, universities, and NGOs, and from corporations not listed as funders as of January 2018. When we met Klaus Schwab in 2012 in Dubai, he explained that the foundation board was established in such a way as to counter the risk that he would be making all decisions on behalf of the Forum. Yet the limited numbers of funders on the board means that the voices of funders have only partial representation.

Funders of the Forum are also restricted in their ability to influence the organization: the charter for foundation members does not mention how funders may hold the foundation board accountable.[15] The charter dictates how the managing board may terminate a membership, but communication from the funders to the foundation board is not mentioned. Nor does the charter mention how members are part of the election process. Furthermore, the Davos meeting is not used as an annual general meeting at which the foundation members may hold the Forum accountable.

Thus, the membership label applied by the WEF in relation to its funders is partly misleading for those trying to understand the WEF mandate and how the organization functions. Rather, it tells how the WEF would like us to understand it, coming across as an exclusive but otherwise ordinary civil society actor, and it informs us how it communicates with its funders. Yet it is more accurate to describe the relationship between the funders and the WEF as one between a service company and its customers. In this case, however, the service organization is not a company but an actor in global governance. The funders pay for a particular type of service, through which they can be involved in the economic and political fairs and communities that the WEF introduces. But as for customers in general, there are limited ways for a WEF funder to influence what the funding is used for. In this sense, WEF funders are sticking their money into the piggy bank. The primary way for them to be part of directing the actions of the WEF is by paying more, thereby getting somewhat more access to the inner circles. But even this access is restricted, because the Forum decides which members are allowed to boost their membership status by paying more. In short, there is no democratic way of being represented in the organization, making the voice of a funder heard by the board and management of the foundation.

The lack of representative mechanisms is another one of the main differences between WEF and many INGOs and the form of mandate from which they are acting. The WEF does not represent and has no intention of representing the will of its so-called members.[16] In fact, WEF funders are not represented by the WEF as much as the WEF draws on the economic and social capital they provide. Corporations funding the WEF cannot count on the WEF to mirror some form of general corporate interest. This is not to say that funder interests are not taken into account, and throughout the book, we show how this is done. Importantly, though, this lack of representation is vital for the organization, because the WEF needs to be able to show that it is not merely "a global board of commerce seeking to impose its view and order onto the rest of the world," as senior manager Halvard Larsen made clear to us early on.[17] Thus, the WEF needs to show that it is an independent knowledge-based expert organization, although funded by global corporations, in order to be taken seriously by other actors.

Finally, the WEF also differs from many INGOs in determining who may become a member. Taking the example of the International Trade Union Confederation (ITUC) as a typical INGO, all trade unions accepting ITUC's charter are accepted as members. The WEF limits its members to no more than one thousand. Any company that sees itself as important enough, and with the economic resources for paying the substantial fees, is welcome to apply for membership. Being a private organization, however, the Forum will always reserve the right to decide who gets to fund and take part in its activities.

So although the WEF shares some basic configurations with other organizations, mainly other INGOs, it is a new kid on the block in comparison to other global organizations. Fundamentally, it is based on a different type of mandate—a liquid mandate—characterized by discretion, choice, and euphemistic global rhetoric. In order to be treated as a legitimate actor in global policymaking, despite its exceptional composition and curious mandate, it dresses itself up as an ordinary international organization at times. It talks of "members" and "annual meetings" and claims adherence to democratic procedures, even as it draws heavily on privacy, security, and lack of representation and accountability. Political life is rife with misleading implications and euphemisms such as these, and the WEF is no exception in this respect.[18] Moreover, euphemisms and deceptions, intentional or not, are common ingredients and acceptable in many day-to-day settings.[19] Applying makeup or wearing a wig is a common artifice around the world. In the case of the WEF, the use of social euphemism is a way of dealing with the limitations of its organizational constitution and its corporate-based mandate. This is not a straightforward task, however, because this restraint is also a prime asset. Dressing up to look like any other INGO or IGO also runs the risk of losing what makes it unique.

What's in a Corporate-Based Mandate?

As organizational theorist Steven Barley says, "Corporations have played the game of influencing policy since the corporate form first emerged."[20] But nation-states all over the world generally restrict corporate interference in political affairs by demanding that politicians show their holding of shares, for example. Essentially, modern politics and government are built on the idea of one citizen, one vote—not one corporation, one vote. Thus, because corporate engagements in politics are restricted, often by law, they need to organize accordingly should they want to be seen as legitimate political actors.

For an organization such as the WEF, mandated and funded by corporations, this skepticism of corporations in politics means that it needs to show that it has agency and legitimacy on its own, that it has actorhood in itself, in spite of being dependent on corporate funders.[21] The Forum resolves this issue by bringing other actors in, borrowing some of their agency and legitimacy. A core motivation for the Forum to invite prime ministers, ministers, presidents of nation-states, and civil society organizations, and, indeed, the secretary general of the UN and managing director of the IMF, is that these people bring some of their legitimacy and agency to the Forum setting. In practice, this functions as a form of decoupling from the corporations, whereby the corporate-funded mandate is downplayed, even as the agency of the Forum increases and a dissociated political mandate takes form. This agency, and the decoupling of business, is largely built on the capacity of the Forum to relate strategically to individuals, especially leaders, of other organizations. As long as people—that is, "the right people"—keep coming to meetings and events, the Forum will be able to mobilize a sense of agency and a mandate to act beyond the agency of its funders. But it is a mandate dependent on the active participation and support of these right people. It is not a nation-state-based mandate, as Chairman Schwab highlighted in our conversation. In this sense, it is liquid and unstable, remaining only as long as funders and participants continue to attend its meetings.

The functioning of this liquid mandate can be understood in terms of a self-fulfilling prophecy, as described by Robert Merton.[22] Merton's analysis of this social mechanism starts with acknowledging the theorem set forth by sociologist W. I. Thomas, who stated, "If men define the situation as real, it is real in its consequences."[23] Merton then goes on to exemplify how this works in practice by recounting the story of how the US-based Last National Bank went from a flourishing institution into bankruptcy in virtually a single day in 1932. The rumors that the bank was in trouble gave rise to trouble, so "the prophecy of collapse led to its own fulfillment."[24] In the WEF case, the self-fulfilling mechanism has so far worked the other way around. The engagement of presidents and CEOs in Forum activities sends the message that this is *the* place to be. Indeed, as our informants readily told us, "If you are not there, you do not count." The WEF has successfully come to be defined by others as real, and therefore it is real in its consequences. In the 1932 case that Merton recalls, the resources of the bank on its very last Wednesday were "liquid without being watered."[25] The same goes for the Forum: its mandate to do politics may look stable until suddenly it does not.

Switzerland's recognition of the Forum as an international organization has been a leap forward in strengthening the position of the WEF at a global level. Managing director Cassius Luck explained a few months after the recognition was announced:

> I think it's part of Klaus's vision, which is that he sees the organization as on a journey, from being a private foundation to being a public international institution. And part of that journey for him is about creating the structures to give the organization longevity and relevance. And I think that's important.[26]

The Forum still runs the risk of being bypassed in the global domain, however, by other actors that are perceived as more relevant and rewarding. This introduces a degree of vulnerability.

The liquid character of WEF's corporate-based mandate is reinforced by the fact that the organization has an unstable funding base. Its corporate funders can leave whenever they want. Again, comparing the situation of WEF to that of the UN makes this point evident. It is simply much easier for a business corporation to leave the WEF than for a nation-state to leave the UN. Although the UN is constantly described as being in crisis and some countries have threatened to withhold their funding, withdrawal from the UN is not even provided by its charter, and there is no form of praxis for the process of leaving the organization. Once a state is a member of the UN, it remains a member. WEF funders, however, do leave the WEF, and there is a constant buzz of critical voices surrounding the Forum. Erwin Koopman, director general of a state agency in the Netherlands and a recurrent participant at WEF events, described the situation to us:

> It is critical what will happen these coming years. As things stand now, the WEF loses members—there are several that chose to withdraw as members. And I

know, therefore, that the WEF is thinking of broadening its membership base by letting other foundations be members, for example: the Bill and Melinda Gates Foundation, NGOs, and internationals. They're doing this to develop their funding. But it also entails a broadening of their mandate. I mean, they have to choose. There are other platforms for us to use.[27]

Other informants talk about the importance of the Chairman as the base of the organization. Schwab is the charismatic leader on whom the organization is built. Although many see his unquestioned leadership as a core asset, others are more critical about this role. Mr. Koopman says he is not impressed by how leadership is run within the Forum. He goes on to argue that "the organization needs to be developed; it is a bit outdated," leading to greater risks that the WEF could lose its attraction. Peter Bond, a high-level director at one of the Strategic Partners of WEF, a global corporation that has been a WEF member for many years, depicts an organization that has let no one but Chairman Schwab take a leading role: "When he resigns there is great uncertainty concerning the future of the organization." Schwab's strong position is underscored in the foundation statutes, where it stated, that "Mr Klaus Schwab who created the Foundation, or at least one member by his immediate family designated by it, is a member of the Foundation board."[28] Schwab's wife, Hilde Schwab, is also a strong voice in the organization; she is chairperson and cofounder of the Schwab Foundation for Social Entrepreneurship, as well as adviser and project manager for numerous Forum activities. Leadership in the organization thus resides to a great extent in the hands of the Schwab family. The succession of leadership is an issue surrounded by much insecurity and opacity, according to our informants.

Thus, although the funders of the Forum may dispose of substantial economic assets and may exercise political power in both the broader and wider sense of the term, the Forum has but a limited and fragile mandate, characterized by discretion and choice.[29] There is a constant risk that funding corporations may choose to leave the WEF, in which case the Merkels, the Clintons, and the Gateses may well prefer going elsewhere.

Building Networks, Borrowing Agency
Because of its liquid mandate, the Forum has to build its legitimacy on the support and engagement of others who are seen as legitimate. Crudely put, if the chancellor of Germany and the secretary general of the UN participate, some of their legitimacy rubs off on the Forum, rendering it some agency as a politi-

cal actor. This is essentially why the WEF must stage itself as an international organization that "is committed to improving the state of the world through public–private *cooperation*."[30] It must rely on other organizations to pursue its agendas in other organizational contexts. This agency, however, is not yet an institutionalized agency. It is there only as long the Forum enjoys the trust and loyalty of these individuals and the status accorded to them. It may well be that the next chancellor of Germany or the next International Monetary Fund director will not find the Forum alluring enough to accept a potential invitation. Or, given the role that the WEF is able to play in the context of global governance gaps, it may endure and even expand.

The option that the Forum chose in order to achieve agency is to build an organized network of communities through which it can influence issues of priority in global governance. Internally this network is often talked about as "a community of communities." This is how managing director Martin Lesoto describes the WEF network:

> So for me, that's been the secret of the Forum—being able to create that community feeling. Not to get too philosophical, but even Davos is like a community for every single person that goes, you know. I always use this analogy that, again, don't get too hung up on our content. I mean the content is important, but nobody ever goes or doesn't go to Davos because of the theme: "Oh I don't like the theme this year, I'm not gonna come." What we do is like the church, like people go to church on a Sunday—I don't know about you in Sweden . . . but people go to church because they, first and foremost, wanna reconnect with their community, and they don't care what the sermon is, they don't know who the guest minister is. They go because that's actually how they reconnect. The first thing they say to each other is, "How are the kids doing?" "What's happening?" "Is your daughter feeling better?" And in a way that community also governs the minister, so the congregation gives . . . in a way they supervise the minister. Obviously there's rituals and symbols involved . . . so for me the analogy of the Forum is like replicating this. That's actually one of Professor Schwab's, in my view, geniuses—understanding this approach.[31]

As Martin Lesoto describes, the secret to WEF—and, according to him, the genius of Klaus Schwab—is the creation of "that community feeling." Participants experience a sense of belonging to something that rewards them socially, emotionally, and perhaps even financially. It is like being part of a church community, as Lesoto describes it—not being there primarily to listen to what the minister says but to meet others. Sociologist Emile Durkheim argued that every society needs to reaffirm and uphold its collective sentiments and collective ideals in order to function as a society—a need that requires reunions, assemblies, and meetings.[32] From Durkheim's perspective, it is easy to understand Davos, Dubai, and the many other WEF events as meetings aimed at constructing and reaffirming community. What the WEF succeeds in doing is to create and shape community relations analogous to those termed *communal* by Durkheim's contemporary, sociologist Max Weber. The relationship, he would have argued, rests on "a subjective feeling of the parties, whether affectual or traditional, that they belong together."[33] The WEF events generate an imagined, transnational space that offers a sense of belonging—a space that also has the merit of rendering high status to those who are chosen and choose to participate.[34] It may well be that the Forum and its participants choose to opt out of the relationship. This space is indeed only one of many that funders and invitees nurture, and they may vary in intensity, reciprocity, and dependence. But as long as both parts—the Forum and the individual participant—orient toward each other, a sense of collective identity is sustained and translates into a sense of belonging.[35] The strength of the WEF, and a main reason for its funders and invitees to return and lend the organization some agency, is that it offers a feeling of belonging, a sense of being included in an emerging global nobility—a new transnational elite community.

Discretionary Governance

The liquid and circumscribed corporate mandate of the Forum has several critical consequences. One is that it makes the Forum vulnerable. Furthermore, another consequence of its liquid mandate is that it lays the foundation for networking activities. The networking priority is essential due to the lack of external decision-making capacity. Consequently, the Forum needs to disseminate its ideas through the network and rely on the members of its networks and communities to spread the gospel.[36]

In addition, there is a third consequence, one of great significance: the emphasis on transparency and accountability. This is where the intimate relation to corporations appears as a true asset. Playing the role of an accepted partner in the field of global governance means, in practice, that the Forum must answer to the same needs for transparency and accountability as do intergovernmental and multilateral organizations.[37] Therefore, the Forum disseminates a virtually innumerable number of reports, press statements, Tweets, and podcasts; arranges the Open Forum in Davos; and allows the press to attend parts of the Davos Annual Meeting. Given its organizational status, however, the WEF can largely decide how open, inclusive, transparent, and accountable it wants to be. This is not to say that it is completely free to open or close its doors to all those interested in what goes on within the organization, critical or not. As Chairman Schwab said to us, the Forum may not have a nation-state-based mandate, but it can still be accepted as a legitimate actor. For this to happen, the organization, he said, needs to be appreciated as a transparent body:

> We need a more elaborate definition of a mandate. Not to see it as . . . not simply as being appointed by someone. There are other factors here. First of all, you have to show that you have a system of checks and balances. So . . . I built over the years a foundation board, which is independent. I mean . . . in the beginning certainly, they were more close friends of mine, but today I cannot tell Christine Lagarde [managing director of the IMF] to do something which she wouldn't like to do. [We all laugh at this idea, as if it would be a ridiculous thought.] The first factor is checks and balances. And . . . for our foundation board, the multistakeholder dimension is important. Half is business, half is not. So we avoid the situation that we become an advocacy organization. The second thing is to have as much, no, to have transparency in what you are doing. If I take Davos, we have . . . every fifth participant is a media person. And Davos is so well established that we wouldn't need, if I may say so, the media in such a great number to promote ourselves. But I think it is important that what we are doing is . . . open and accessible to those who are not participating.[38]

What Schwab describes in this quotation is that the Forum has proven itself to be a legitimate actor in spite of what he terms its lack of mandate. The legitimacy of the Forum is, in his account, based on the WEF being open and transparent. To his mind, the Forum has also been able to show that it operates by means of internal democracy, where it is not up to him to decide in the name of the organization. In the internal system of checks and balances, it is the WEF board of trustees that governs the organization. (Hence the remark about not being able to get Christine Lagarde to do something that she does not appreciate.) In addition, in Schwab's account, the organization can show a track record by which it can prove that it is useful for others outside the organization. This last aspect, he says, is not always easy to prove outwardly because much of the Forum's importance lies in achieving things confidentially. To prove his point, Schwab goes on to describe a confidential, diplomatic issue that the Forum was active in resolving, emphasizing that the WEF cannot be as open as it may sometimes wish to be. Both of us nod in an understanding of the need to be nontransparent with regard to delicate diplomatic issues.

What is transparent or not is, however, not a simple matter to decide. Transparency is not only about visibility; it is also about positioning, negotiating, and controlling perception and action.[39] Critical management scholar John Roberts notes, "The metaphor of shedding light is a gross simplification of the complex labor that is involved in the manufacture of transparency."[40] Contemporary organizations must continuously deal with and learn to master the balance between revealing and concealing, protecting some dimensions of their dealings while showcasing others.[41] How this is done and with what rationale and motive differ from organization to organization. Comparing the transparency of the WEF to that of the UN, for example, we see critical differences. Whereas the UN and other international organizations abide by publicly known rules on such issues as funding, representation and participation, media accreditation, and public disclosure, the WEF can decide for itself from case to case on most of these issues. The only official body to which the Forum has a formal relation to is the Swiss Federative Council, which governs its status as an international organization.[42] In its 2015–2016 annual report, the Forum writes that this report "as well as all institutional documents, are submitted to the Swiss Federal Government, which in law acts as the supervisory body for the Foundation."[43] The Federal Council, however, does not ask for public disclosure of, for instance, funding or activities.[44] The WEF's interest in being transparent is by and large built not on a mandatory rule but on its need not be to accused of being nontransparent—to cultivate its organizational image and reputation, or its "brand" (as it is termed in its staff "code of conduct").[45]

This form of ad hoc transparency, according to which the actor can choose what to highlight and what to place securely behind the veil, can be useful for many organizations. What is striking in the WEF case is that strategically combining transparency and opacity is a cornerstone of the Forum's activities, a major preoccupation among WEF staff, and a central cultural tenet in the organization. If it would choose to be more open, it would most likely undermine the appeal and seductive power it exerts on its invitees. As we learned in many interviews and conversations, the fact that the WEF is a closed and secluded arena makes it attractive for the participants, be they presidents of nation-states or corporations. Its seductive capacity resides to a large extent in the seclusion and secrecy provided. Invitees can sit down without the attention normally surrounding a meeting between heads of states and CEOs of large corporations. Moreover, some meetings that actually happen within the private framework of the Forum would otherwise not have taken place. Managing director Paul Richardson gave us this example of how the opaque and discreet form of governance works:

> You remember Cop15 [the 2009 United Nations Climate Change Conference] in Copenhagen? How everybody saw that as a failure? Well, one week later, all the key protagonists, apart from Obama, met in Davos. Without the political pressure. They met without any particular agenda. It was decompression. And our role? We, as organizers, pursue no particular agenda, but we provide space. And, after that meeting, Calderon [president of Mexico at the time] suggested to get a move on with what later became the Cancun Agreement. At the top level, there is an increasing demand for this kind of space. It works as decompression. Here, it is possible to say things that can't be said at top meetings.[46]

Especially the last part of this quotation indicates the importance of seclusion and opacity in order for the WEF to remain the key actor in global governance it aspires to be. At WEF, it is possible to say things that cannot be said in top meetings. Seclusion, privacy, and closed doors are at least as important for the Forum as it is to meet the norms of transparency and accountability. As organizational principles, these interests in many instances contradict each other. The abundance of blogs, reports, and films of events published at the Forum website, along with its stark security arrangements, are expressions of both these interests and the interplay of transparency and opacity as constitutive parts of the organization. The interplay provides the organization with a powerful and attractive allure and allows for the creation of agency in global governance. Sociologist Georg Simmel aptly described the essence of human interaction as "conditioned by the capacity to speak" but "shaped by the capacity to be silent."[47] By knowing when to speak and when not to and when to keep a secret, an actor can manipulate and even dominate the relationships in which the actor engages. In the WEF case, the interplay between open and closed also forms part of its euphemistic play with silence and speech. Broadcasting events from the Davos meeting, for instance, tells the world how open the WEF intends to be. What is not on display is the invitation-only part of the program, a large part of the Davos frenzy and the most interesting, politically sensitive part. In some respects, the Internet displays are mystifiers posing as demystifiers.[48]

Moreover, as Simmel explained, secrets function by setting barriers between actors, even as they offer the temptation of gossiping or otherwise breaking the silence.[49] The veil of secrecy, kept in reference to the demands of its high-end invitees, produces the same kind of interest in the organization as the secret societies that Simmel described. This is not to say that the Forum is a secret society. Rather, the kind of secrecy involved is an informal kind of secrecy, based on networks and trust, in the manner outlined by organization scholars Jana Costas and Christopher Grey.[50] The Forum knows how to manage secrecy discretely and use it in the interests of the organization.

The dynamic interplay or, more accurately, combination of secrecy and transparency that the Forum draws on for its mobilization is founded on and takes the form of discretionary governance: a form of governance characterized by low degrees of hierarchy and procedures.[51] This type of governance is not typical only of WEF, but of organizations such as the Trilateral Commission, International Chamber of Commerce, European Round Table of Trade, and the Bilderberg Group. Such global governance actors may be able to construct a situation in which they may have a substantive degree of freedom to act politically without referring to international relations protocol.

From this position, the WEF can choose freely whom to invite as a member of its communities, a guest at its meetings, or a member of the board and what to negotiate and what to make public. Pivotal for discretionary governance is not to put participants at any level of risk. It is therefore essential for the WEF to provide "a safe place," as the internal WEF lingo would have it—safe as the meaning of both security and seclusion. Therefore, all WEF meetings are surrounded by heavy security. Especially the Annual Meeting in Davos is protected by Swiss military police patrolling streets, roofs, and sky. Entering the secure zones is far more difficult than entering an airport. But more important, all WEF meetings are based on Chatham House Rule, meaning that what has been said there can be discretely talked about in other settings, provided that names of participants are not disclosed. Accredited journalists and researchers are therefore generally allowed only into meetings of less importance, meetings that are designated open and posted on the WEF website. A majority of the discussions is closed and not even mentioned in the official program. What is made public in Davos and other meeting places is consequently based on the discretion of the Forum. The rest is closed and restricted. Under such circumstances, the public is commonly left with issues that most agree with. Issues of more conflictual character and urgency are dealt with behind closed doors.

Transparency makes the Forum legitimate, while closing of doors makes high-end people interested in coming for deliberating behind the doors. The strategic combination of transparency and opacity is in this sense essential for establishing distance between the transnational elite and the broader public, and thus for the withdrawal of the elites

The secretive, secluded nature of the organization is pivotal to maintaining the allure and the seductive capacity of the organization. This is no coincidence. As organization scholar Gareth Morgan has noted, seduction is integral to organizational life:

> One of the major ways the organization functions as an addictive substance is through the promise it makes and holds out to every employee. The purpose of such a promise in the addictive system is to take people out of the here and now. This process moves the person from what he knows and encourages him to look outside the self for answers, security, and a sense of worth.[52]

Such is the space of action that WEF has managed to construct for itself. It is built on a corporate-funded, circumscribed, and liquid mandate, but it has the advantage of being private, based on discretion and the strategic use of seductive communicative actions, providing leeway for a number of actors with an interest in convening. Making strategic use of its assets and preconditions, WEF has been able to establish itself as a consequential organization in global governance without sacrificing much of its informal and secluded character. With the change of status that the Swiss state recognition of the Forum as an international institution entails, a key challenge is to keep the informal character. As Cassius Luck said to us, the Forum wants to be of importance, but at the same time, it does not want to lose its informal character because it has no intention to "build a big global bureaucracy." The change in status is not meant to change the character of the organization. "It's keeping it relatively agile, and it's making sure it can do what it does effectively in as many parts of the world as possible."[53]

The Allure of Zuckerberg, Trudeau, and Shakira

Seduction is the most subtle form of power and persuasion.[54] The key to successful seduction is the appearance of being an object of desire. Few are drawn to the person (in this case, the organization) that others avoid or neglect; people gather around those who have already attracted interest. The WEF works the laws of seduction by having the—allegedly—most brilliant, talented, and influential people flock around it.

Over the years, the Forum has been able to establish its activities as *the* community to be part of, both financially and politically. For funders, it is first and foremost a market matter. The position of our corporate informants was consistent: if you are not there, you do not count at the global market level. Most of our corporate informants vouch for the usefulness of their funding efforts and their participation at the events and in communities, which offer occasions for business negotiations and grants them a voice as political actors. For policymakers, the attraction of the Forum rests in its image of a global policy actor with sway. The Forum model speaks to the interwoven and networked nature of the transnational political space and provides other routes to engage in global policymaking. In addition, Davos opens opportunities for secluded political discussions, out of the media limelight. And so policymakers and business leaders make time for and spend money on Forum activities. The engagement of these actors defines the WEF as an actor to count on, endowing it with an agency and potency it would otherwise not have. The Annual Meeting in Davos is especially important in this respect. It is the showcase event of the organization. By making Davos a spectacular event, with huge media attention, the Forum attempts to create the appearance of a stable global actor in spite of its reliance on a liquid mandate—and in many aspects it succeeds.

We see the WEF as an enactment of this seductive capacity, based on euphemisms. Participants of all kinds, including media all over the world reporting from the events, construct a definition of WEF as an organization with important impact in the sphere of global governance—as a phenomenon that politicians, policymakers, and business leaders need to pay attention to and as an invitation that people need to accept. This enactment will have consequences. First, the more the "right" people are repeating this pattern, engaging year after year, the more the WEF will be institutionalized. The Swiss government's recognition of the WEF as an international institution further contributes to strengthening the status of the organization beyond the allure afforded by the participation of Zuckerberg, Trudeau, and Shakira and others like them. Furthermore, participants (including media reporters) will be interested in upholding the definition of WEF as an actor with the capacity to influence and have an impact on global governance in order to legitimize their own actions. Certainly, many of them may criticize the Forum off the record or talk dismissively of its relative lack of importance. Yet the overall picture of the Forum presented to the general public is that of an established actor in global governance that deserves to be acknowledged.

Fundamentally, the position that the WEF has constructed for itself rests on its discretionary governance. The capability of attracting the largest corporations to invest in funding the organization, drawing into its circuit the people it needs in order to construct political agency, and keeping its doors closed to prying eyes whenever needed, are all pivotal for creating a mandate, however liquid. To be sure, the discretionary spaces and form of governance that the Forum has created are also always under threat. Many of its funders and invitees, let alone many of those who are not invited, air critical views, and some dismiss the allure of the WEF altogether. To uphold the allure and discretion and the mandate to act as a global player in shaping politics is a continuous and painstaking effort. Nevertheless, based on this liquid mandate, the Forum has been able to construct a way of exercising agency and to be consequential in relation to other actors. The practices through which the Forum becomes consequential—in other words, how it achieves authority—is the theme of the next chapter. What initially may be perceived as mere chatter is, based on ethnographic insights, rendered intelligible and articulate as the specific form of discreet power that WEF exerts.

3 Setting Precedence

So we're trying to push some of the consequences of the work that we
do into the conversations that we have in these places, but obviously we
have to do it in collaboration with the folks we're working with. We can't
lead people on more quickly than they're willing to be moved themselves,
but we do have permission—at least, if people say to us, "How do you
become more competitive?" Well, our evidence suggests that you do it by
empowering women, by having good institutions, by having transparency,
by having rule of law. Those are the secrets of competitiveness research.
If you ask us, would we like everyone to go down that road? Well, the
evidence suggests it's a good idea. But can we force people to? No we
can't. You have to accept the countries and the governments that one is
given to deal with.[1]

Once again we are meeting with WEF's senior manager, Cassius Luck, in a hotel
lobby. This time it is in Cape Town in June 2015, when the Forum arranges its
Regional Meeting on Africa. We are asking questions about the importance of
the Forum having been acknowledged by the Swiss government as an international organization ("other international body"). Mr. Luck says that it means
little in terms of what the Forum is doing. It is still not a decision-making body
in the arena of global politics. It will continue its attempts to improve the state
of the world by talking, conversing, and communicating its messages, as it has
since its inception. In so doing, it will push for some ideas that speak to the
Forum's core values. As Mr. Luck declares, it cannot force people or governments to do anything. The route the WEF therefore must take is to submit, persuade, and seduce—not to make decisions for others to follow. Using the words
of sociologist Max Weber, the predicament of the Forum could be termed as a
lack of rational legal-based authority. Seen from this perspective, the appreciation of the Forum as an authority in the global political landscape appears as
something of a social enigma. How does the Forum operate to make strategic

communication—as opposed to legally binding decision making—a route to power and authority? Our answer to this question centers on the concepts of discretion, seduction, and communication. These are the basic ingredients in the discreet power of the Forum, by which it is consistently capable of constituting the will of other actors.

It is not unusual for critics of the Forum to infer that it is powerful because it has powerful supporting actors. Although the agency of these resourceful funders and supporters makes up a vital part of the precedence-setting capability of WEF, it is not analytically useful to use power to describe power. We need to show and understand how these actors are put into use by and for the Forum in the interest of exercising power. Moreover, such an approach runs the risk of reifying and mystifying the power of the Forum. As sociologists Bruno Latour and Michel Callon suggest, we are interested in finding, describing, and analyzing the "the processes by which an actor creates lasting asymmetries," keeping in mind that there is "no difference between the actors which is *inherent in their nature*. All differences in level, size and scope are the result of a battle or a negotiation."[2] In order to identify how powerful relationships are formed and stabilize over time, we therefore need to "locate them in the gestures and the works that they use to extend themselves."[3]

In this chapter, we describe the authoritative capabilities of the WEF in terms of communicative but discreet power. Based on ethnographic descriptions, we show that the activities of WEF are consequential precisely through its communication, in spite of often not being made public and in spite of lacking a legally based authority. Clearly communication is not a specific activity for organizations; it is the very means by which organizations are designed, created, and sustained.[4] Thus, communication is also the base of power and authority. In the WEF case, communication entails that precedence be set in global politics and markets, even as it provides routes that allow these options in other organizational settings.

Consequential Communication

In resolving the social enigma of Forum power and authority, we start by recognizing it as a broker operating between organizations, brokering ideas for global politics, business opportunities for corporations, and status for everyone engaged in Forum activities. A successful broker is an actor with the capacity to facilitate communication among actors, which may not otherwise have had the trust or the interest in being associated with each other.[5] Brokering may therefore be used as a central mechanism in mobilizing other organizations for change. Through brokering, the WEF offers itself as an allegedly neutral mechanism among various types of actors in an attempt to make these actors act in the public interest of the planet as a whole.

In empirical terms, we suggest that this brokerage occurs through communicative practices: the WEF construes itself as an open arena in which people from all walks of life meet to discuss global issues. But as we show in this chapter, this "multistakeholder arena," to use WEF lingo, needs a fair amount of construction, ordering, and decision making regarding topics, solutions, and invitees. Through these organized acts of brokerage, the WEF not only secures access to key resources in the form of information, knowledge, and economic capital, but also performs a crucial intermediary role in the transmission, translation, and mobilization of these resources, forming discourses and setting the agendas of other organizations.

Departing from the notion of power as suggested by sociologist Niklas Luhmann, we argue that the WEF succeeds through brokerage in distributing visions that are given precedence over other visions by establishing itself as a neutral, albeit highly resourceful, problem-solving mechanism.[6] Power is here seen as capacity built on social relationships that may or may not be exercised. The interesting aspect is not primarily the types of issues for which the WEF may be powerful, because that changes over time, but in what sense and by what means it constructs the capacity to make others endorse and follow its interests and suggestions, however nonunified, conflicting, and shifting these may be. Luhmann is partly in contradiction to the well-known Robert Dahl formulation that A has power if A can get B to do what B would not do otherwise, and more in line with Foucauldian reasoning regarding power as an act between free individuals.[7] Luhmann's perspective implies that power does not entail the instrumentalization of an already present will, but that it constitutes that will and can oblige it. Power fundamentally builds on choices and decisions. In the WEF setting, this translates into choices regarding all its internal and external activities, which, for the actors involved (including guests and funders), communicates precedence of options about what to go forward with and what to avoid. As the WEF communicates on such topics as who will participate in an event or what risks to avoid, it not only informs and articulates what its interests are and the reasons for those interests; it also communicates an understanding of what is important, pivotal, and in focus—and what is not. Thus, in communicating its choices, it not only presents its own view but, in a constitutive move, also performs this view and sanctions it by choosing it.[8] This is similar to what social anthropologist Douglas Holmes has revealed based on his studies of central bankers: central bankers engage in communicative experiments that predate critical events and continue to be refined during unfolding turmoil. They communicate experiments that do not merely describe the economy but actually create its distinctive features.[9] The information and utterances of the organizations involved in the Forum are, in the same vein, not merely reporting; they constitute the issues at hand. The Forum sets precedence to later choices, but only insofar as other actors will accept it. A key Luhmann insight has to do with the meaning of communication: it is determined only in retrospect and only when others are acting on the reports.[10] Thus, the difference that WEF actions may or may not make is observable only in later communication. Did other actors use any WEF communications in their constitutive and performative acts? As we demonstrate in this chapter, the answer to this question is repeatedly *yes*. Setting precedence for future choices, based on its own discretion in its own discrete, secluded arena lays the foundation for the discreet power of the Forum.

Insofar as the WEF is capable of setting precedence for political options for other actors, it upholds power in relation to them. In practice, this capacity is constructed in a reciprocal transaction between invitees of WEF communities and the organization itself. In the first move in this interaction, invitees make the WEF resourceful in economic terms and more broadly by attending meetings. The participation of the CEO of Dutch Shell, Queen Rania of Jordan, Chancellor Angela Merkel of Germany, former French president François Hollande, and less publicly known but high-ranking managers, officers, and entrepreneurs provides the organization with prestige and status. Mustafa Wallah, a senior staff member of the Forum, explains: "What works in Davos is to get the people excited about what they have committed themselves to—to get them to hear about the work, to leverage them, and to get them excited. When that happens resources flow in." In this way, the invitees are the original authority bearers, vesting the WEF with the authority of a political actor.[11]

In a second move, though, the WEF bestows status on the invitees, enabling them to perform in global markets and politics while furthering their personal interests. This rendering of status onto the invitees makes them more likely to want to return and—in a third move—more prone to act in line with what they believe the WEF wants. For analytical reasons, these moves are separated here, but they do occur simultaneously. A key point is that this structure predominantly relies on people rather than on their organizations, which facilitates the personal relationships between the WEF and its invitees. Compared to the power structure that sociologist James Coleman depicts, based on the replace-ability of people in the modern corporation, the WEF structure is premodern in this respect, placing people at the core.[12] Although these may be specifically chosen in order in order for the "communities" to have exactly the "right" peo-ple, coming from the "right" organizations, the WEF does not practice repre-sentation as we described in Chapter 2. All participants are chosen and invited as individuals, not as representatives of their organization. Yet organizational connections are certainly made clear; every badge indicates the name of the company, nongovernmental organization, or government the individual is as-sociated with. But individuals will not need to speak on behalf of that organiza-tion; they represent themselves. They will probably be discussing experiences they have because of their home affiliations, but in the eyes of the Forum, they will not be held responsible to bring the Forum's ideas back to their organiza-tions the way a representative would be expected to. In this way, the construct of the WEF network and the authority it achieves for itself is built on individu-als. Had it been built on representation, the third move of making funders and participants actively align to WEF constructs would have been much more dif-ficult to accomplish, as it is generally difficult for organizations of any type to accept the authority of another organization. And it would have been difficult to get CEOs and heads of states to participate. The situation is slightly different for individuals, however. They can bring their experience as WEF invitees back to their organizations and draw on it if they wish, without having to relinquish the authority of their home organizations. In the reciprocal moves between in-vitees and the WEF, the Forum retains the upper hand as long as it is important to the invitees to be invited again—as long as the WEF is appreciated as a de-sirable place for anyone who aspires to be part of the emergent global nobility.

Key to our understanding of the specific power relations that WEF forms with other organizations is the prestige and status that it has been able to con-fer onto invitees of the organization, in combination with the choices that its activities are built on. As sociologist Max Weber described it, status—the social estimation of honor—is essentially based on recognition, distance, and exclu-siveness. By "setting themselves apart by means of any other characteristics and badges . . . all these elements usurp status honor."[13] In so doing, individuals may obtain the right to be part of—however informally—a status group, which in turn may be the basis of political and economic power.

The reciprocity moves by which the WEF creates its authority in relation to other organizations is based on a number of the Forum's communicative practices: the event, the report, corporate politics, and diplomatic conversations. In the next section, we invite readers to follow us through these practices, as we present ethnographic descriptions and analyze how they are played out in the interest of setting precedence of options, performing the discreet power of the Forum.

The Event

Dubai, November 2012: In the Brain Trust

We have suddenly been granted access to the WEF Global Agenda Council meeting in Dubai, which Forum staff describe as the "brain trust meeting." Only around fifteen hundred of the "world's best brains" are invited to this highly exclusive meeting to brainstorm and set the agenda for the coming WEF Annual Meeting in Davos.[14] For a few days, they will all sit down in smaller groups—Global Agenda Councils (GACs)—each of which has its specific area of interest. By way of "thought leadership," the GACs are intended to generate initiatives of their own, with the goal of shaping political and business agendas, raising public awareness, establishing standards and best practices, and spreading their ideas through all possible channels.

We enter the beehive, as the Forum calls it—the room where all the GACs are having their discussions. It's a big room with some eighty small cubicula, arranged in the shape of the inside of a beehive. It is quite dark and, because it is coffee time, relatively silent in here. Water, tea, coffee, fruit, and candies are lined up along the wall where we enter. The room is large, and it is difficult to get an overview of all the cubicles. We split up. Christina chooses the GAC on global governance, suggested by Mr. Luck as an interesting group, and Adrienne chooses the informed societies GAC, which deals with four criteria that are critical to the development of informed societies: transparency, literacy, privacy, and empowerment of citizens. The aim is to identify and raise awareness on how various stakeholders can ensure that all citizens have access to reliable information to make informed decisions.

In the group that Adrienne has chosen, participants are just returning from having visited other GACs, wanting to inform themselves about what others are doing. When the group slowly reassembles, there are ten people in the cubicle. Adrienne presents herself to the group, explaining that she is there to study what the Forum does. The group members, four men and six women from business, governments, academia, and intergovernmentals, smile welcomingly.

The cubicle is shaped somewhere between a rectangle and an oval, with brown walls, several posters, water, and candy in a bowl. The session is reconvened by its chair, Ronald Tahara, a publisher described by the Forum as one of the one hundred most influential people in Africa. The group has plans for creating an index that measures how "informed" various societies are. In the other groups they had visited, people had generally been positive toward the idea and had wanted to contribute variables to the index. Mr. Tahara says, "The sense I get . . . when people come to us, they all want to put their stuff into our index. Surprise, surprise!" The group then questions if it is supposed to be the gatekeeper for the index or if the group would rather that it be open—a general framework that others can tap into. They discuss the issue but leave it unresolved. The group members are a bit tired and decide to break up. They turn the project over to Rebecca Wilder, a young woman who appears to be in her late twenties and is working on behalf of the Forum as the convener of this specific council. She is to write a draft memo for their session the next day, incorporating the key concepts that the index will build on.

Adrienne follows one of the group members, Marcus Graham, to his next session—a working group on solving global problems. Mr. Graham, a man in his sixties and a senior advisor to the Forum, is an internationally known entrepreneur and scholar—or "thought leader," as the WEF staff would call him—in the field of information technology, economy, and media. He is presented on the Forum website as a leading authority on innovation, media, and the economic and social impact of technology. In the working group— the only working group parallel to the other eighty-eight councils—Graham starts by showing slides, giving a historic overview of global issues, how they have or have not been resolved, and to what extent. He says that the institutions from World War II are insufficient today. This is where global networks could come into play; they are stakeholder networks that extend beyond any one state. Graham puts forth a taxonomy comprising knowledge networks, policy networks, advocacy networks, and operational and delivery networks. He describes how they all exist side by side and are not mutually exclusive. He is about to launch a multimillion-dollar research project on the potential of improving the state of the world, working together with the WEF and a think tank housed in a Canadian school of management. The mission of the project is to develop a new understanding of the broader public conversation around shared and sustainable prosperity, seen as an essential piece of democratic capitalism. This is the background for this working group, and Graham says that Klaus Schwab wants the project to become a book.

After this introduction, discussion begins, open for all attendees, and most of the people in the small room are participating. Mr. Graham receives relatively harsh criticism, primarily revolving around the concept of legitimacy. What makes these networks legitimate? How is it possible for a layperson to evaluate the legitimacy of the Forum? Graham argues, with some edge to his voice, that the WEF is legitimate, doing all that it can to be transparent about its funding and the way the organization works. A participant who usually works at the World Bank says that it is not certain that an organization such as the World Bank is more legitimate than the WEF. He argues that the World Bank is legitimate only because some other global institutions say it is. "So what's the difference?" he asks rhetorically. Graham thinks this is a good point, and some of the others nod in agreement. One of the chairs from another GAC, Ruben van der Horst, head of an organization of local governments for sustainability, claims that many of these networks are not multistakeholder groups and adds that the WEF is but a single stakeholder that invites others to join. This does not match Graham's idea of the WEF, and he underscores his position that the Forum serves as a multistakeholder network in everything it does. The discussion does not lead to any conclusion, and the group dissolves.

In the meantime, in an adjacent cubicle, Christina participates in the GAC on global governance. The goal of this session is to address governance structures and accountability mechanisms among stakeholders involved in public–private partnerships. The council also aims to study whether there are certain preconditions or specific environments that are considered best for partnerships to succeed, or if they can be successful in a broad range of areas. The background for this GAC is the assumption that the role of public–private partnerships is increasingly seen as an accelerator in achieving major global goals, particularly in the fields of development and humanitarian affairs in the UN and other international organizations. Such partnerships are recognized as having the capacity to set new norms and contribute to novel governance models.

Some twenty people are present in the room, including Peter Bond, a high-level director at one of the WEF strategic partner corporations. Mr. Bond, a man in his mid-fifties with an open, lively mind and a spirited glint in his eye, had played a major role in getting through to Klaus Schwab with our request for access to this meeting. The night before, he had expressed irritation at the disinterest of WEF leadership in assisting us in our research and had (at least we assumed he had) made a personal call to Schwab (or someone close to him) to plead on our behalf. Bond thought it would be beneficial in the long run for the Forum to allow us access. To deny us could only harm the idea of the open arena, he reasoned, apparently with some success.

Christina is seated between a female minister from Kuwait and a male senior manager of a US high-tech firm. Both are eager to chat, asking about Christina's reasons for being at the WEF, and they indicate positive interest when she tells them about the research project. The central question for this GAC occasion is: Who oversees the leadership of international organizations? The discussion revolves around the significance of procedures for keeping leaders and their organizations accountable and promoting transparency around leadership and decision making. The majority view is that international organizations vary greatly in the extent to which accountability and transparency are actually implemented. In order for international organizations and public–private partnerships to gain legitimacy, there ought to be mechanisms for checking these matters. Ideas are aired and written on the whiteboard, and notes are taken, but no consensus is achieved on how to move forward. "We have a big challenge ahead," Mr. Bond declares at the end of the meeting. "We need to report on this in a few months, but I'm not sure we can come to a sensible agreement."

In the evening, we join the summit party offered by the hosting government of United Arab Emirates. We have no time to return to our hotel to change into something more fitting for the occasion and hop on the bus outside the Mina A'Salam hotel as soon as the sessions end. When we reach the dinner venue and enter, night has fallen. It appears that we are intended to take a tour around some stalls in a heritage village showing typical folklore from Dubai. We start the tour—slowly, because it is crowded and quite dark. We enter one of the stalls in which two women, sitting on the ground and wearing traditional local dresses, are displaying handicrafts. They are exhibiting what we presume are handmade dolls dressed like the two women, in *battoula*—a masklike veil traditionally worn by Bedouin women. The *battoula* covers most of the face, leaving only eyes and cheeks visible. We are abruptly aware of our mixed emotions in relation to the whole situation and stumble out onto the pathway and continue the tour.

Suddenly we bump into Fabiano Abelli, one of our earliest informants from the Cologny headquarters. He and his assistant had been kind enough to open the doors for us when we first visited Cologny, setting up a number of interviews for us. We had run into each other a number of times in Davos, and along the way, he seemed to have lost patience with us. This time, as we bump into each other, he looks irritated and asks in passing, "Are you still around?"

Dinner, music, and fireworks follow the tour among the stalls. Adrienne is seated with Aart Goossens, the president of a Dutch civil society organization, who tells the story of his first meeting with the WEF ten years ago. He had been hesitant about attending because of the elite participants. Would he fit in? Would he want to fit in? When he came back, though, his organization was $4 million richer. Since then, he has continued to come, and he still finds it rewarding.

Christina learns from her dinner partner, Susan Doe, that the WEF is not yet as hyped among business leaders in the United States as it is in Europe and possibly in Africa and the Middle East. Ms. Doe is a senior executive at a high-tech company in Silicon Valley who has traveled a great distance to the meeting. Her reason for joining is entirely about networking and seeking business partnerships. She has the sense that the people at the meeting represent a selection of those she should be trying to get introduced to. In any case, Dubai is a convenient stopover for her on the way to Hong Kong and Shanghai, where she has business meetings planned.

The next day is the final day of the meeting. The mood is a bit slow, without the same frenetic level of card exchanges, but new connections are still being made. We chat by the coffee bar with Richard Stoner, a man in his thirties from the United States; he seems energetic and interested in getting to know us. That he has been chosen to be part of the brain trust is not surprising to him. He was invited because, he says, he started an elite university. Somewhat perplexed, we ponder this information. He is, of course, happy to be in Dubai as well because it gives him opportunities to develop his network. In our short chat over coffee, he summarizes what the event is about for him: a way of channeling his interests, meeting new people, and staying informed.

In the afternoon, we leave the human beehive and the form it has taken in Dubai. Over the past three days, we have been provided with an in-depth view of how the WEF brokers ideas for markets and politics: by choosing topics and questions to discuss and propositions to mold, based on the discretion of the Forum and combined with what is presented as a high level of expertise and political topicality coming from "the best of brains." Criticism is certainly heard among some of the invitees, but many feel inspired, and most, whether critical of the meetings or not, want to return—not only because they believe, or at least hope, that what they do during the summit and in the GACs they attend could be useful somewhere down the road, but also because it brings opportunities to be among a crowd of other people who have been defined as "brilliant." It functions as an act of status performance; to be chosen to be among the brilliant ones makes one appear brilliant too. Specifically, the framing of the event as the best of brains helps to stage this move toward high status. It constructs an effect similar to what philosopher Ian Hacking terms "looping."[15] When someone is classified in a certain way, other actors in its environment can use this classification, thereby starting a process of interaction between the classified person and the classification. Being among those chosen by WEF becomes, in a similar vein, a classification that vests the invitee—and the Forum—with status. These words of classification are not so much an attempt at reporting what is going on at the event as they are a reflexive attempt to build the image of brilliance with exclusiveness and prestige. It is status being seductively performed.

In practice, this is one of the fundamental and reciprocal ways through which the WEF is able to broker its ideas. Combining prestige with political topicality bestows invitees with a sense of individual importance, agency, and urgency, along with ideas, values, and priorities related to the contemporary political agenda. These ideas may or may not be employed in the organizations in which the invitees are active in their home environments. That is an uncertainty that the Forum must relate to. Moreover, it is not possible for the Forum to estimate how many or how often ideas are drawn on in other contexts, but it happens in various ways and forms, and it is much encouraged by the Forum. Top-level manager Cassius Luck described to us in the lobby of the Mina A'Salam Hotel while we waited for our security clearance that the WEF "encourages ownership" of ideas. Invitees are more than welcome to bring home some of the knowledge, ideas, and solutions developed in Dubai and at other events and to make use of them in their specific contexts.

In relation to the Dubai event, we had the opportunity to observe how this "ownership" was activated when we sat down with a group of GAC invitees in Stockholm a few months later. The people in the group were working in corporations or with the Swedish government; they had been invited to the Dubai summit in different capacities. Although they had not been in the same GAC, they had gathered now to discuss how they would make use of their experiences in Sweden. It was clear to the group that apart from exchanging information about what they learned individually, there could be synergies if invitees from

Sweden could orchestrate their efforts. This is not likely something the WEF had asked them to do, but by attending the meeting of this group, we were introduced to how the Forum functions outside the immediate summit. In this way, the WEF's initial precedence setting comes alive and is taken one step further. When invitees make use of ideas, values, and solutions that were developed at the events, the WEF's authority is expanded and the Forum is activated.[16]

The Report
Cologny, September 2012: Constructing Competitiveness
It is September 2012, and we are visiting WEF headquarters in Cologny for the third time for a new round of interviews. By now we are used to the fact that it takes considerable time to gain access to the premises. Armed guards from a security company secure the dark wall that surrounds it, and visitors must present identity and accreditation, which is then checked. Once we are allowed behind the wall, the Forum and its headquarters are generously opened to us. We are welcome to walk around the premises relatively freely, using the cafeteria and the many open meeting places or to sit down and work in between our scheduled interviews. The building is large; part of it is newly built in order to accommodate the steadily growing number of employees. Apart from a traditional oil portrait of Chairman Schwab, modern art is everywhere, mostly on the theme of globalization. One such sculpture is a line of small globes on pillars, beautifully placed in an area of sofas where staff members hold their regular meetings. On the walls of a long corridor leading from the original parts of the building erected in the early 1970s into the later parts, photographs recall the WEF's prouder moments. We spot former state presidents, such as Nelson Mandela and Bill Clinton, together with pictures of Bono and many others, usually caught by the camera at the Davos Annual Meeting.

On this afternoon, we sit down with Nikola Bayer, accompanied by her two colleagues on the competitiveness research team, Marie Gardinier and Vaiva Liepa. Because most of the WEF's internal work is undertaken in open office areas, with few private offices, we are now seated in a small meeting room. Ms. Bayer is casually dressed and looks to be in her thirties; she has an interest in such issues as national competitiveness, regional development, and benchmarking indicators. We hope that she and her team can help us to understand the role of reports in the WEF range of activities.

Every year WEF publishes approximately one hundred reports, with topics ranging from gender gap issues, through climate change, to education. The

Forum also publishes innumerable blog posts and comments about the daily news. Apparently publicized texts are critical for the communication system that WEF has constructed, a characteristic that the Forum shares with almost every other think tank, foundation, and research institute. We are intrigued by the extensive work invested in these reports. As a rule, they are printed with a layout that brings commercial advertising and public relations to mind. The reader is meant to be attracted to the content by graphs of contemporary trends, along with photographs of flawless women, men, and children and of landscapes, often with soft sunlight beaming in from the side. The written content is presented not so much in terms of troublesome issues but as opportunities or challenges. Selling the sizzle of a future ripe with options rather than a troublesome present is at the heart of these products, even when they are scrutinizing precarious issues. In terms of setting precedence, it is evident that the reports are based on such choices as the people who are to be selected as experts and what should be presented as knowledge, in order to make a difference.[17] The texts are part of the constitution of the organization and also meant to foster learning among its readers. They make a difference merely through their existence, but their impact is enhanced when they are picked up by other actors who will start a new line of decision making along the lines of what is presented in the reports.

The team of nine that Nikola Bayer leads produces the index drawn on for one of the Forum's true flagships, the *Global Competitiveness Report* (GCR). This report seldom contains pictures of beautiful landscapes, however; rather, it specializes in relatively technical tables, graphs, and diagrams. Drawing on a large number of variables regarding such issues as innovation, business sophistication, and market size, but also health and education, the idea of each report is to show how almost 140 countries fare in competitiveness. How does the development of India look in this respect, for instance, compared on a global scale and regionally? Chairman Schwab established the report and the index that it builds on in 1979 as a summer research project, Ms. Bayer tells us. "He came up with the idea to do a scorecard first and let it evolve into a ranking" of each country's competiveness.

The index is built on an annual survey, in which some fifteen thousand businesses, contacted partly with the assistance of 160 think tanks around the world, answer questions regarding what they perceive to be the most promising or problematic factors for doing business in their respective countries. In addition to the survey, Ms. Bayer's team collects hard data from each country, such as growth, deficit, and unemployment figures. The results of the survey and other data are displayed in the format of twelve "pillars." The intent is to not to make larger changes in the format of the survey because the primary value of the index is its benchmarking of national competitiveness over time. But Bayer describes this as "a constant struggle, because you know it's so interesting doing new things, but then you don't have the data." To resolve that issue, the team attempts to make larger changes in the index at regular intervals rather than minor changes along the way.

Ms. Bayer describes the index as something of a research project, a form of knowledge seeking that the Forum normally does not engage in: "The Forum is not a think tank of the conventional type, right?" She explains that because the Forum is known for its meetings, there have been internal discussions regarding the role of the report. Yet over time, she says, it has become clear that the report is "useful to frame the discussion at the beginning" of an event. The report does not "provide any solutions; they come into the discussion afterward. So we use it really to start the discussion."

In addition, the three team members we meet describe how governments and corporations in specific countries use the report, often in collaboration. The Forum obviously launches the report globally, but it is for the partnering think tanks in each country to organize national dissemination. And the team has many examples of how the report has been used nationally. Ms. Bayer explains this:

> There are a few countries that use it for their economic strategies. They use it basically to say, for instance, that by the year 2015 they will be under the mark of the top fifty. It was used in that way just to mobilize support in that country. So this was probably the most extreme use of it. . . . Then we have many countries that use it when they are low in the ranking on a specific variable, when it is used for discussions in the country to illustrate how bad the situation really is. It was used like that in Germany over tax reforms. You know they are one of the lowest-ranked countries on complexity of the tax system, and it was used in parliamentary discussion. These are kind of the highlights, because we see that it is used to change something—it's changing something—that it is used at the political level, that we have some impact on the real world.[18]

The cases she provides are described as good examples because they show that the report has induced change and has had "impact on the real world." In these cases, the report has lived its own life after the launch and has been picked up in conversations at the national level. The Forum may also help in various ways to encourage governments and corporations, for instance, to use the report in their national settings. Vaiva Liepa provides an example in speaking of workshops that the Forum organized in order to contribute to growth in sub-Saharan Africa:

> We got one case in Nigeria where we had a full-day workshop, bringing again public. . . . We had the minister of finance there, as well as a couple of other ministers, but he really highlighted the importance of the report and how it was put together, and they set up post-facto a national competitiveness council. I mean, it is one body that sort of brings competitiveness to the national agenda, and if it is set up right, it can definitely be a good vehicle for improving competitiveness at the national level.[19]

In quantitative terms, the *Global Competitiveness Report*, along with the many other WEF reports, comprises a large portion of the ideas it brokers and illustrates the way it brokers them. It is one of the main ways in which the Forum maps what is already, or is to become, political domains,[20] although it may not be precedence setting to the same degree as getting heads of states in the same room to discuss the follow-up to the Kyoto Protocol, as discussed in Chapter 2. Still, the report is one of the many channels by which the WEF attempts to influence global and national policymaking making through seductive communicative practices. To the extent that the report is read and acted on, as exemplified in Bayer's and Liepa's comments, it forms part of shaping a discourse through which some phenomena are constructed as competitive and others are not.[21] Moreover, as Ms. Bayer says, WEF funding corporations also make use of the report, which is high priority to the Forum. It is imperative that funders are kept happy, and if they find value in the report for business, that is good for the Forum. The Forum uses funding corporations for world improvement, and it needs them to take an interest in its products. Getting its one thousand funding corporations to act according to its propositions would entail a strong precedence-setting effect for the Forum. In line with Luhmann's argument regarding power as a mechanism for reducing complexity, it would mean that the complexity of decisions for contemporary business and politics is reduced as the Forum discreetly sets priorities on its choices.

At this point, we turn to corporate politics as an equally fundamental form of communication for the Forum—a form of discreet power that it may control to a much greater extent than the uses of a report.

Corporate Politics
Cape Town, May 2015: System Failure

When the taxi driver in Cape Town hears that we are there for the WEF meeting, the atmosphere changes quickly. He does not like the meeting, and he does not like WEF. To his mind, the meeting is bad for the people of South Africa because it will only make the rich richer.

As usual, we are on our way, uninvited, to a WEF event. This time it is the World Economic Forum on Africa 2015, held in Cape Town. Approaching the convention center, we spot signs posted on a lamppost reading "Africa Is Open for Business." "Who put these up?" we wonder. Because we cannot really defend ourselves by saying that we are merely researchers and probably not the bad guys the taxi driver believes us to be, trying to enrich ourselves at the expense of South Africans, we do not mind when he wants to let us off some nine hundred feet away from the conference center, in spite of pouring rain and our being a few minutes late for a scheduled interview.

The same morning we had met with participants who were staying at our hotel. The sentiment was a bit like that in Davos: people having apparently improvised small meetings in every corner—business meetings, we presume, as that is what our informants tell us they have come for. Patricia Beerhoven from Ghana, an enthusiastic woman in her thirties, is one of them. She is in the business of education and is in Cape Town with her husband, who is there for the regional industry meeting. For Mrs. Beerhoven, networking is the attraction of WEF; she can find new customers, make new contacts, and accumulate new ideas for her company. In practice, she says, her days will be spent listening to conversations such as the one where we met her, in which Graca Machel, minister for education and culture of Mozambique, spoke to young people and students from the Cape region. "Nothing new was said," Mrs. Beerhoven explains, "but it's all about networking." And to her, that is how WEF functions and what it is all about. She says that WEF makes things happen by getting people together doing the right things. It is a twenty-four-hour experience for her, with evenings used for cultivation in the broadest sense by developing contacts, enjoying a nice dinner, and going out dancing without talking shop.

A Nigerian lawyer, Desmond Magoro, with whom we chat later on the same day, gives us the same impression as Mrs. Beerhoven did: "WEF meetings are good for business." Mr. Magoro is participating at a WEF meeting for the second time. He attended last year in Nigeria, and now he has come to Cape Town.

He finds the meeting highly rewarding, mostly because he comes home with a number of new clients for the firm he is working for. His first interest in WEF arose when a friend told him about it a few years ago. Last year, one of his in-laws vouched for him, and he was accepted. We agree that this is the way things work; it is necessary to know someone who can vouch for you.

Hurrying out of the taxi, away from the angry driver, we are allowed into the security zone because we have an appointment inside the premises. We give our names and cell phone numbers to a guard from the Westin Hotel. He is dressed in a long black coat but not wearing the high hat some of the staff of the other hotels are wearing. We rush out of the rain into the lobby, where there is a security check but no checking of badges. The security machine is broken, and we are let in without having our bags screened. A man behind us, wearing a white badge, which means that he is an invitee, says with a smile: "I trust you aren't carrying a gun!" "It's all about trust," Adrienne replies. The three of us laugh.

We are to meet with Martin Lesoto, a senior WEF manager. We want to get examples of the relationship between the Forum and its funding corporations and discuss that issue with him. What does the Forum want with corporations apart from their funding? Is it possible that the Forum could make use of its funders as much as they make use of the Forum? If so, how? Because Lesoto has been working with Forum corporate relations in varying capacities since the early 2000s, he is the obvious person to talk to. Indeed, as we had already had a rewarding conversation with him once before in Cologny, we are happy to meet with him again. We remember that he had a reflecting and open way of talking; he had invited us to discussions and had helped us to understand the role of corporations within the Forum.

Waiting for Mr. Lesoto, we sit down in the lobby on a brown leather bench. Iced rooibos tea in small glasses has been set out for guests, and we help ourselves. Suddenly we notice security guards, partly recognizable by their comfortable shoes, placing themselves around the lobby. The atmosphere thickens. After a few minutes, Klaus Schwab and his entourage pass by, followed by his wife, Hilde Schwab, and his advisor Pat Tremblay, on their way, we assume, to announce the annual Entrepreneurship Award. Guards disappear, and the lobby is back to its buzzing, relaxed ambiance.

Christina walks to the hotel desk and asks for Internet access. The receptionist provides the information we need with a smile. We start checking e-mails to see what we may have missed and discover a message that

Mr. Lesoto is going to be a bit late. But all of a sudden he is there, dressed in a light gray suit and a blue tie. He smiles at us and we shake hands. We suggest the café in the hotel as a good place for our discussion, but he says that we use one of the downstairs rooms—a part of the hotel where we had not previously been allowed access. We're happy to see this part of the hotel because many of the agenda meetings take place there, so we gladly follow him downstairs, away from the buzzing of voices. After spending some of Lesoto's precious time looking for somewhere quiet to sit down, we find a room that is apparently between sessions. Two of the Forum's white armchairs for key speakers are placed side by side, facing the black rows of simpler participant chairs. Lesoto makes a joke about our now having the opportunity to sit down in one of the white chairs. We laugh while pulling out three black ones, forming a small triangle suitable for our conversation.

Holding our notebooks in one hand, we begin talking. Mr. Lesoto laughs when he understands that we have come all the way to Cape Town uninvited merely for this type of conversation and interview. Is he a bit impressed? Or does he simply consider us losers for failing to get an invitation? Adrienne asks if it is okay to use the cell phone for recording the interview. He agrees. As we begin, a man is testing the audio equipment. "One, two, one, two, testing, testing." Luckily this is accomplished quickly, and the three of us are left alone.

Three years before, we had met with Mr. Lesoto for a conversation in Cologny, and it is easy to start the conversation again. He tells us about the Cape Town event from his perspective. Until recently he has been senior director for the Global Strategic Infrastructure Initiative, but when we meet this day, he is heading the Forum's activities on Global Challenge Partnerships. With a half smile, he says that every three years or so, there is a change of some sort within the Forum and his new role in the organization relates to the Industry Partnerships Program, which is part of the Forum's next strategy, meant to serve it for several years.

At the Cape Town meeting, "the big agenda for me has been on infrastructure," he starts explaining. He has been running a project for three years, in which he and his WEF colleagues have been working with the African Development Bank, African Union Commission, and a number of corporations, such as African Rainbow Minerals, Agility, and Yara International (to name but a few of some twenty participating corporations), in order to develop African infrastructure. The initiative is part of the general intergovernmental plan,

PIDA—Program for Infrastructure Development in Africa—comprising fifty-one programs across the African continent that will, as Lesoto explains, transform Africa. The African Union Commission and other intergovernmental agencies developed the program, but it was meant to be implemented in close collaboration with the private sector. The public–private collaboration was initiated at an earlier regional WEF meeting, held in Addis Ababa, Ethiopia, in 2012, which drew on the Forum's funding corporations. The Forum has since worked with the project, he explains:

> We have been going through a process to funnel the fifty-one [PIDA] projects down to a set of prioritized targets. And the major milestone here, after three years, including taking of one of these projects down to national level, we actually went and ran a number of roundtables and worked with the governments in a big program called "The Central Corridor" that goes through East Africa and actually helped elevate for this project . . . to actually be . . . implemented. So that was a big effort. So this summit marks, three years later, the transition of the Forum's role to the NEPAD [New Partnership For Africa's Development] agency as having the mandate to implement, coordinate, the implementation of PIDA. And in that regard, also then launch the new phase of work related to the structure of financing in Africa. So that is one of the big things that I am focusing my time on in this particular meeting.[22]

The Forum was involved in the PIDA initiative for three years, helping to sort out the projects and launching the first one, the Central Transport Corridor, which is meant to link Dar es Salaam's port in Tanzania to the neighboring landlocked countries of Rwanda, Burundi, Democratic Republic of Congo, and Uganda. The corridor initiative was not taken by the Forum; rather, it was an agreement from 2006 between these five governments. But between 2012 and 2015, the Forum became part of the grand PIDA initiative in order to integrate private sector input regarding the direction and acceleration of "these infrastructure mega programs."[23] The Forum has had two roles in the project. It served as convener and organizer for the collaboration between intergovernmental authorities and the private sector and provided the initiative, with its member collaborators, to bring some forty companies and organizations into what WEF has called a "business working group." As Mr. Lesoto explains, this group has, with the assistance of the Forum, been looking into "infrastructure opportunities systematically for three years." But then he clarifies that the task of the Forum is not to do the project but to "catalyze, build and hand over." The

Cape Town Summit therefore marks the transition from WEF involvement to its behind-the-scenes involvement. In Lesoto's words:

> You know this is a twenty-year thing, so I think we will stay involved behind the scenes, just to sort of give some support. . . . It is a step down, so our resource can be moved . . . after three years of doing this . . . so now it is . . . time for our partners to step up and take over the ship. The legitimate intergovernmental partner has the mandate to officially do it. They should step up and start doing this.[24]

The Forum thus intends to step back, leaving the intergovernmental agencies and the corporations to continue the project. It is difficult, though, for the WEF to step down and merely act as a broker to the organizations. It has made itself useful, and with a hint of irony and a small laugh, Lesoto says, "The reason the Forum exists is because there is a gap in the intergovernmental system, so why would you expect that they can take over something? If there is a failure in the system?" He is not sure, therefore, that the IGOs that are taking over the task will be able to continue as hoped. Still, he explains, the Forum believes that it needs to leave the scene for the organizations with the mandate to build infrastructure.

The conversation ends when people start coming into the room for the next session. Lesoto dashes off, and we gather our things and go upstairs again for a cappuccino in the large hotel café and restaurant area. We reflect on how Lesoto pointed to the ways in which the WEF jointly uses the event and the project as precedence-setting activities. It becomes clear to us how the Forum is relating to corporations in its governance interest. On the one hand, it constructs an arena ripe with business opportunities. For a Nigerian lawyer or a CEO for one of the world's major corporations, for example, it makes sense to go to a WEF event as a convenient arena for doing business. That is even more the case for actors within the PIDA. On the other hand, corporations are also prompted to do "the right thing." The extent to which corporations do what the Forum hopes they will do varies, but drawing them into its circuits is the precedence-setting conduit of the Forum in relation to corporations. The Forum's role is not to implement political ideas and solutions but to broker for people from corporations—and in the PIDA case, also governments—inviting them to act according to WEF ideas. The form of power that the WEF constructs here does not entail implementing anything that any of the participating organizations do not want to implement (as in the Dahl power formula),[25] but it forms part of discreetly constituting the will of the participants. By participating in the PIDA project, WEF funders are acting out part of what the Forum sees as necessary on the global political scene.

The WEF is to be seen here as one of the apparatuses that drives global governance, within which are staged the shaping and directing of others in desired directions—and corporations are drawn on as a main agent in the mission to "improve the state of the world."[26] Corporations respond to and act out the precedence of choices set by the Forum. This is not to say that corporations form part of the WEF for altruistic reasons. Evidently, there are high economic stakes to bring home for the corporations seeking to get the contracts. Nor does it mean that corporations are obedient followers of Forum dictates. As Luhmann noted, organizational processes are fundamentally contingent; they do not come ready-made.[27] WEF attempts to prompt corporations into following WEF interests are wide open to failure, but also to success, insofar as they are picked up and developed by corporations. For the WEF, though, this contingency is not a problem. To the contrary, according to Forum logic, this is a win-win situation. Due to the sheer size of its corporate funders, it shapes the everyday life of billions of people. If they are interested in "doing good" and picking up on Forum ideas, developing them according to their own logic, they will change the world for the better while upholding and acting on Forum governance and discreet power.

Diplomatic Conversations—Off the Record
Davos, January 2013: Contesting the Arctic
It is Friday noon in the WEF Davos week, January 2013. We are waiting in the foyer of Hotel Cresta Sun for Professor Paula Shielding, an internationally renowned scientist whose main research interests are in the area of climate change. She has come to the meeting to warn about the consequences of climate change unless we take action. Ms. Shielding is a decisive-looking, dynamic woman in her forties, head of an esteemed university-based research institute. From Forum employees, we have heard that she is so popular within the Forum that they keep special track of her to ensure that she does not become tired of the organization. We have arranged this meeting in order to hear a researcher's view of WEF. As it turns out, the meeting gives us insights into the inner wheels of WEF events: "informal diplomacy" via this by-invitation-only session. Here the setting of precedence and discreet power of the Forum is played out in plain view.

Sitting in the foyer, we watch the invitees enter. A board member from Volkswagen AG (white badge with a blue line and a dot) is talking beside us. Suddenly a dashing figure comes in, looking flawless in a suit, like a famous movie star. This turns out to be Gjermund Bugge, prime minister of a Scandinavian country. Two assistants in well-cut suits accompany him. The foyer is slowly filled with other invitees, many in fur coats. Some of our informants from Dubai appear. But there is no sign of Paula Shielding. We wonder as we wait how we will be able to talk to her now. We will certainly not be able to follow her to the next stop on her schedule, which we know is packed with conversations and attendance at smaller or bigger events—strategically planned by WEF—or to less planned meetings such as the one with us, inserted between slots on the agenda. We decide to start lining up for the event that is about to take place in what seems to be a dining hall and a bar inside the foyer. We ponder the idea of following Professor Shielding as her assistants, but for that, we would need green badges, which we do not have.

Suddenly she is there. We had met her before, so we greet each other quite cheerfully just as the line for the event starts moving, and we tag along, conversing as we go. As we approach the door, Shielding asks a WEF employee if it is okay for us to join her, which, surprisingly enough, it is. WEF staff tell us they will look the other way as we enter. We are allowed to sit in the bar and observe the event, which turns out to be a private lunch for some twenty-five people, arranged by the WEF and the GAC, focusing on the future of the Arctic. "Private" here means that it is not on the public WEF program. "It's invitees only," a WEF staffer explains to us later. Beside us in the bar is a woman in her thirties, also apparently here for the Forum, but not participating in the lunch. In the Davos spirit, we strike up a conversation, and it turns out that she is married to one of the lunch invitees. Her name is Patricia Taylor, and she gives us her and her husband's cards. Before marrying a few years ago, she was a yoga teacher; now she accompanies her husband around the world. She plans to publish a children's book next year.

Lunch invitees are gathered around a number of round tables with white tablecloths. Baskets of bread are passed around. Glasses of mineral water are filled. We see chit-chatting, shaking of hands, the odd kiss on a cheek. From the interaction, we can tell that these participants do not know each other well, but many have met before. A man in his early forties rises and opens the lunch. He is Christopher Carter, a social scientist from a renowned US university. We quickly search the Internet and learn that he has written a book on global warming. He is now the moderator. He jokes that when the GAC group met last year, they had dinner, but that their topic must be higher on the agenda this year because they are closer to the congress center. (Later the same day, another invitee jokingly says that when they are allowed to have their meeting inside the congress center, the excitement will be gone, because "inside you can only say what you are allowed to say.") Carter continues, saying that the lunch is to be about real projects, real people, real investments, real challenges, and that they are here to bring a variety of perspectives, finding examples of how to handle problems in the area and setting out best practices. There are a few discussant leaders within the group, and they will initiate discussions by introducing their individual viewpoints. After these introductions, there will be conversation and lunch at each table, ending with a general discussion.

Mr. Carter calls on Prime Minster Bugge, who is seated at a center table. Cell phones and tablets are put away when Bugge stands up. He begins by saying that the Arctic is facing great changes and that is a good thing. These changes mean access to new natural resources. To his mind, these resources may be used under three conditions. First, the Arctic is not a legal vacuum; both national and global laws and regulations will have to be followed. This is the simple truth, he says: this is an area where there is legal regulation. Second, Bugge invites the lunch guests to put "people first." The region is not a white spot at the end of the map. People live in Greenland; that is their home, and they make a living there. "We have to respect their culture and remember that nature there is unique and fragile." Third, this uniqueness does not mean that there is a need for unique forms of—or exceptions from—regulation. This part of the world and the nature there will be exploited, but it needs to happen in a respectful way, applying existing regulation, Bugge stresses, regarding maritime worlds, for example. He finishes by saying that we should seize the opportunity but handle it with respect.

Bugge's comments are met with light applause. Now the meeting is turned over to Paula Shielding. She may not remind us of Hollywood, but she talks with the kind of authority that comes from years of research and publishing. She also underscores the many changes ahead in the Arctic. But she does not see them as business opportunities. During two weeks in June the previous summer, Shielding says, the ice melted more than it had ever before. She looks at the other lunch guests for a moment, continues, and says that this will have huge impact on business around the world, because what happens in the Arctic affects the entire world's ecosystem. If the world is not cautious, unpleasant surprises await around the corner. Her words receive polite applause.

Mark Hammer, until very recently the CEO of a major oil corporation, speaks after Professor Shielding. His message to the group is that the natural resources of the Arctic are enormous. If the world chooses not to use them, he says, that will also have huge disadvantages because it will be extremely costly to exploit other options. "Of course," he adds, "in the end governments decide, but the role of corporations is to take the lead, go ahead, and show the way."

Others now testify to the great opportunities in the Arctic. One CEO from another global corporation states, "I love the Arctic," along with the opportunities there and the development he can see coming. His company loves investing in the Arctic, and it loves respecting the population, he exclaims. He explains that they believe in the area for social reasons as well—that this is an area where the world will learn how to negotiate a peaceful solution in spite of so many interests.

After this round of short introductory speeches, luncheon is continued with table discussions. Christopher Carter moves from table to table, listening. Many of the participants like to debate. The sound level is rising. Laughter and clinking glasses. Ice cream with berries for dessert. We are not eating; we have not been served and are fully occupied taking notes. Fifteen minutes later, when discussions have halted, many others who have not presented take the opportunity to offer their perspectives. Carter raises a question discussed at his table: Are international discussions really moving forward as well as many actors claim? Bugge describes the discussion at his table: Would it be all right to start drilling for oil? His answer is that they will have to wait until they have found more common standards. Shielding urges the group to be proactive in the Arctic, and Hammer urges the Arctic Council (an intergovernmental forum for Arctic governance which has presence at the lunch) to decide who is in charge of the area in order to know who monitors it.

After ninety minutes, cell phones are switched back on, and tablets are pulled out again. WEF staffers leave the room for their next task. Prime Minister Bugge steps into a car with black windows. One of our informants from Dubai, Dieter Weiss from a global logistic consultancy company, a mild, cautious man in his fifties, is networking at the back of the room. We approach him, wanting to say hello, and hear talk of the next event on the Arctic agenda. Meetings such as these, with all the "right" persons in the room, are rare, so seizing the opportunity is vital. Shielding rushes off to the next nonpublic meeting that WEF has arranged for her. After a quick good-bye to Mr. Weiss, we follow her for a bit, talking about the lunch. She is upset by Prime Minster Bugge's willingness to give away the Arctic, asking only that corporations follow standards. Reaching the location for her next meeting at a nearby hotel, she is quickly drawn in behind locked doors, through which we may not enter. When we ask the WEF staffer at the door if we can accompany Shielding, he looks troubled, saying it is a closed meeting. As so often happens when we are researching the WEF, feelings of shame at our dismissal arise as the door closes. Nevertheless, we return to the village with a sense of deeper understanding of the organization, in particular, how it sets precedence and establishes its discreet power.

The Arctic lunch is an example of the diplomatic but highly informal brokering activities that WEF specializes in. We call them informal diplomacy because they focus on a public issue that has commonly been dealt with within diplomatic and interstate frameworks, but takes place at self-created interfaces of politics, markets, and science.[28] Post–Cold War changes have meant that nonstate actors forming part of diplomatic processes are not rare, and diplomacy is seen less as a field specifically designed for states and international politics.[29] The term *track two diplomacy*, pointing at attempts to gather influential persons to develop new answers for solving conflicts that may influence later events, covers a large part of these trends.[30] The WEF forms part of them.[31] It has, however, a more general outlook than track two diplomacy generally implies: the concept focuses on peace and conflict resolution, whereas the diplomatic activities of the Forum display a broader range of topics and may often be less coupled to formal track one diplomatic interventions. In the case of the Arctic lunch, WEF sets the frames for this lunch encounter, at which these various actors met. The lunch is but one of several occasions that this specific GAC hosts, together with the WEF, at which it sets the agenda for deliberations and decides who is to participate.

Importantly, the diplomatic aspects of the Arctic lunch are parallel to those of market interests. Participants at Forum meetings often air the significance of the WEF as an arena for "value creation," in the broad sense of the term. They are referring to the fact that engaging in the activities of the WEF and meeting other corporate and political leaders of similar status may not be instantly rewarding from a marketing point of view, but in the long run may shape discussions in a way that makes an impact on regulations and the structure of markets. Peter Bond, our key informant from the Dubai meeting, told us over dinner that he had been involved in WEF communities for a number of years and had attended the Davos meeting several times. He said that it was at the informal meetings in the interstices of the formal program that the more interesting discussions occurred. He told us of a time when his working group had gone out for dinner, and it was there that the significant breakthrough came about. "It is really the informal gatherings that are value creating," he said. In his view, the WEF can be used strategically in several ways to the advantage of the corporation through extensive networking. This example and the Arctic lunch are instances of deep lobbying, in the sense that networking can be strategically deployed to "create value" and push particular policy positions for oneself and one's organization.[32] Participating in WEF activities can function as a lever for both advancing one's career and furthering the ideas and positions of the corporation, in front of an influential audience. A continuous process of social networking and communication can change the ideological or business climate around an issue.

The Discreet Power of WEF

As Cassius Luck told us over coffee in Dubai, "The WEF is a shy organization. It is not interested in displaying its victories." This type of euphemism reflects the self-image of the Forum. The subtext of this comment is clear: WEF is resourceful enough, even without media impact and an external rule-setting capacity. It implies that the WEF has been able to construct power for itself as an actor in global governance without a legally based mandate and any external decision-making capability. (Schwab elaborated on this issue in Chapter 2.) It has achieved the capability of exerting some control over the actions of others on a global scale and making itself used by other political actors across the world.[33]

The location of power and authority constructed by the WEF is to be found in its proficiency as a seductive broker acting on its own discretion. By promising status and rich market and policy opportunities for its funders and invitees, it succeeds in attracting people and organizations to covet participation in its activities. These participants are the original authority bearers, but in reciprocal transactions they vest authority onto WEF.[34] The WEF, on its behalf, endows the participants with status, enabling them to perform in global markets or politics, even as participants' personal interests may be furthered. Key to its attraction is the provision of a discretionary space, secluded and secure, based on its choices and the discretion of its participants.

The Forum wants to make the world to a better place and acts intentionally to achieve this goal. To this end, it draws on a range of strategic communicative activities, from reports to summits, over corporate politics to nonpublic diplomacy. These acts set precedence for later choices. The Forum therefore does not merely provide space, as it euphemistically would have it. With respect to power and authority, it succeeds in diffusing its own interests by getting other actors to deploy it, despite a lack of a rational-legal mandate for making decisions for others and despite the fact that it does not overrule the interests of any other actor.

Setting precedence in global governance takes the form of communicated choices. This process is not merely about echoing utterances from its activities; it constructs options for other actors. In turn, these options may or may not be picked up by these other actors. Moreover, influence and impact are difficult to measure. The exercise of power is often indirect and winding. It is challenging for the Forum and the people and organizations it interacts with to show what and how much is actually acted on in other settings. By way of attracting what it considers the right people to talk about the right topics, proposing the right solutions, the Forum participates in shaping the discourse of global politics, markets, and diplomacy. It even contributes at times to proposing what later—in other organizations—becomes the formal agenda and the foundation for decisions and practices of these other organizations. The events and the reports presented here are examples of the way it shapes discourse, just as WEF participation in the PIDA project and the lunch discussion on the Arctic constitute foundations for practices in other organizations. What is noteworthy about the construction of WEF authority is its relational character. It is truly a case of extending power from one organization onto others, becoming powerful through and on behalf of other actors who make WEF ideas travel into other organizations.

This forming of the agenda, decisions, and practices of others appears on the surface not to involve conflict. But as political scientist Steven Lukes reminds us, lack of open conflict does not necessarily mean lack of conflict.[35] Lukes 2005). WEF staff and invitees certainly like to believe otherwise, yet conflict is strikingly apparent and recurrent around the Forum. As indicated by the severe security arrangements surrounding all WEF activities, particularly at Cologny headquarters, WEF is acting in contradiction to and in conflict with other actors who are not present—other uninvited actors. Sometimes these actors are waiting outside the gates, as in Davos, where activists try from time to time to make their voices heard, showing clear-cut conflict. But conflicts in relation to WEF are primarily of a looming kind. Helicopters hovering over

Davos, snipers hiding on the roofs, and the dark wall of the Cologny headquarters indicate ways of efficiently keeping out unwanted guests, just as it indicates conflict. The Forum has no interest in acknowledging these types of conflicts, however. The air of harmony that surrounds events and the day-to-day business inside the walls is part of the harmony discourse it aims to construct.[36] Moreover, an acknowledgment of conflict would mean that the Forum recognized its boundaries as an actor in its own right, having interests of its own—something the Forum has no intention of doing and carefully avoids. It wants to convey the image of a committed but nonadvocating organization, with no interest in setting precedence for some options over others. Essential in these attempts to achieve discreet power is the use of status. Status endowment comprises a substantial part of the attraction of the organization. In the next chapter, we delve deeper into the machinery of WEF status construction.

4 Status Machinery

We have been through a multiplicity of crises in the last few years. What we're hearing now in Davos is that we've gotta find a new path.

The situation has been stabilized, and we're on a slow, protracted way for improvement, but there should be no complacency.

You get blinkers. You're so focused on what you're doing that it's very easy to ignore things that are happening in the world, and then they catch you by surprise.

Dealing with so many challenges requires resilience.

If you wanna grow in this world, you've gotta be planting seeds in a lot of places, you've got be making things happen and try and do things.[1]

These five voices of business leaders, politicians, and WEF leaders introduce the highlight video compiled after the WEF Annual Meeting in January 2013. This was a time when the aftershocks of the financial crises were still affecting large parts of the world, climate change had risen high on the political agendas, and terrorist attacks were shaking the public and threatening international security. Together, the voices sketch a view of a world facing acute crises and severe challenges. They also address the need for resilience and concerted action. The world is at stake, but there is hope.

The theme of the 2013 meeting was Resilient Dynamism. The executive summary of the Davos 2013 meeting noted:

The Davos Agenda in 2013
We live in the most complex, interdependent and interconnected era in human history—a reality we know as the hyperconnected world. This reality presents a new leadership context, shaped by adaptive challenges as well as transformational opportunities. Yet efforts to rebuild confidence and restore growth remain vulnerable to looming political and economic shocks. Indeed, there is

no "risk-off" setting for the global economy, but leaders from the public and private sectors need to adopt a "risk-on" mindset to catalyse dynamic growth. Dynamism in this context requires successful organizations to demonstrate strategic agility and to possess risk resilience.

"Resilient Dynamism", therefore, is the focus of the World Economic Forum Annual Meeting 2013. The aim is to catalyse and facilitate global, regional and industry transformation as a trusted partner of our Members and constituents. For more than 40 years, the Annual Meeting has provided an unrivalled platform for leaders from all walks of life to shape the global, regional, industry and business agendas at the beginning of the year in Davos. These agendas are integrated into the design of the 2013 programme.

These quotations, typical for Forum discourse, tell the story of the world as tightly interconnected and at risk: no one can escape the risks around us. In this context, the Forum posits itself at the frontier of the invention of various models to deal effectively with the contemporary global predicament and as an advocate of a particular version of global morality and responsiveness and a platform for dialogue and knowledge seeking around complex and urgent global issues. As the top-level director Cassius Luck says, "Being an informal catalyst for change is our raison d'être."[2] In this role, the Forum presents itself as offering a unique approach, distinct from other international organizations. Across Lake Geneva from the Cologny headquarters, one can catch a glimpse of the UN Geneva building. Our WEF informants were eager to refer to the UN on the opposite side of the lake as "the Other"—an altogether different kind of organization: international, as opposed to global; bureaucratic, stalled, and representing a bygone world order. Whereas the WEF views the UN organizational form as not geared up to the task of facing global challenges, the WEF depicts itself as an actor with a more agile and dynamic approach to global challenges. The Forum aims to play the role of globalizer, paving the way for novel, network-oriented, and issue-based ways of governing the world.

The hype, urgency, and status bolstered around the WEF and its events may be seen as instances of a dramatization of political events and concepts. They are a way of bringing them to life, in the way that dramatic performances can bring the characters and themes of a play script to life, as the philosopher Gilles Deleuze would have it.[3] To portray political events and challenges dramatically opens up the possibility that they can be used in a pragmatic and optimistic engagement with the challenges the world faces—as articulated and visualized by the Forum. Significant events and people are invited on center stage. When

European Central Bank president Mario Draghi, invited to speak at the 2013 meeting, said that financial markets were experiencing "relative tranquility" at the start of the year and that all the indexes pointed to a substantial improvement of financing conditions, the central notion of resilience was brought to life, setting the frame for further discussion. In this sense, the Forum attempts to determine the conditions of thought on which actors subsequently act on the world.

The platform that the Forum provides is not an all-inclusive and open one, however, but an exclusive and closed arena, on which high levels of energy, seriousness, and topicality are produced. It is an arena of discretion and discreet power. The processes by which individuals are chosen to participate in discussing, debating, and advocating solutions to urgent global problems are meticulous. Their way of creating communities of expertise, cultivating a brain trust, and extending awards highlights and celebrates particular individuals, ideas, and actions and dismisses others. Furthermore, it works to distance the WEF itself and its selected invitees from the public, thereby strengthening status distinction and a withdrawal of the elites into secluded spaces. In this chapter, we look more closely into how this status machinery works.

Brain Communities

Strategic networking is a cornerstone for the construction of WEF's discreet power and capacity to be influential in global politics. By way of meeting participants networking, ideas, knowledge, and propositions are continuously in motion. As presented in Chapter 2, the WEF can in this way extend its reach and ability to act, by borrowing some of the agentic capacity of the actors in the network. A key component of this networking is the sense of being part of something bigger than the person himself or herself that is nurtured and the exclusivity that comes with this community feeling.

Forum staff often describe the WEF as "a community of communities."[4] Communities are, in essence, loosely organized groups of people joined together around issues. The "community of communities" metaphor implies that the WEF as a whole—the headquarters with staff, funding corporations, and members of working groups—is seen as one community, that is, an integrated whole. When we met WEF senior manager Martin Lesoto for the first time in Cologny, he described this aspect to us:

> There's a lot of talk about the Forum, about building community. I believe that's fundamentally what the forum does, and why we are able to engage. The projects, what we call the insight, even the events, those are all secondary. I mean,

events are crucial to building community . . . So for me it's fundamentally about building community.[5]

WEF employees refer to the construction of these communities as "networking." At the emic level this captures part of what our analytical perspective suggests: making use of formal and informal contacts to gain access to information, knowledge, and other people and spreading one's own ideas. At times, these relationships are formed without the WEF interfering—that is, it merely brings people together. Acquaintances are made over lunch and over coffee between sessions, during Davos nightlife, in clubs, and at cocktail parties. On countless occasions, we have been approached by people who simply strike up a conversation, not knowing who we are and by no means encouraged by WEF staff to do so. And we have maintained contact with some of these people in various ways, just as they cultivate their networks. These types of networks build on trust and are not designed by the WEF, although the Forum would have applauded the initiative had they heard about it.

Apart from the informal networking, the WEF also constructs and formats communities that are set up to form a basis for the organization outside its headquarters and regional offices. The board of trustees (formerly the Foundation Board) is one such community, established in order to support the Forum's mandate to serve as a representative group of key global stakeholders. In Klaus Schwab's words:

> The Board of Trustees reflects the multistakeholder concept on which the World Economic Forum is built and which is fundamental to our role as the International Organization for Public-Private Cooperation. In playing an active role in setting the strategic framework for the Forum, the board acts as a guardian of our independence and impartiality.[6]

The trustees are invited to participate in the Forum's annual meetings: the Annual Meeting in Davos and the Annual Meeting of the New Champions in China. They have privileged access to the regional meetings across the world and continuous access to the Forum's expert networks. The Network of Global Agenda Councils (GACs), the Global Leadership Fellows (GLF), the Young Global Leaders, and the Global Shapers are other such formatted communities. The GLF network aims to attract "outstanding individuals" to take part in the GLF Programme. It is run in collaboration with partner universities and involves work and learning experiences. Fellows may be offered the opportunity to hold a full-time position as a senior community manager at the Forum and to study for an executive master's degree in global leadership. The Forum of Young Global Leaders comprises more than seven hundred "exceptional young leaders who share a commitment to shaping the global future."[7] Conceived of as representing "the future of leadership," they are drawn from business, government, civil society organizations, arts and culture, academia, and social entrepreneurship and are enrolled in the network of young global talents. These young people go through a rigorous nomination and selection procedure, with rounds of discussion within the Forum and with trusted partners. Once selected, they are involved in virtually all WEF initiatives, meetings, and events for a time.

Apart from these types of communities, the WEF is also eager to organize affiliations through the construction of partnerships. As WEF staff informed us, any initiative launched on behalf of the Forum will commonly consist of a group of stakeholders who commit to undertaking a project. The aim of the projects is often to acquire new knowledge on a specific topic and, most common, to publish some form of report, thus making the content known to the relevant actors. These stakeholders are then seen as having formed a partnership, albeit relatively informally. There are rarely codified rules for the group, merely the norms relating to discretion, and the hierarchy regarding who makes decisions and talks in the name of partners is developed within the group. But the Forum monitors the partners, selects them, and decides on their conditions (their terms, composition, general content, and so forth).

The WEF communities are thus instrumental to the Forum, but they may also be equally beneficial for community members. For the appointed person, becoming part of a community, having been selected and deemed deserving of invitations, is to receive a voice. The appointee becomes someone worth listening to, someone who has deserved the trust of the Forum. As literary scholar and critical essayist Elaine Scarry pointed out, for a performance sentence to be taken seriously, it needs to come from the right individual: "A performance sentence spoken by the wrong person is not simply invalid but it does not take place."[8] Hence, appointing a member of a community not only contributes to forming the WEF network of communities; it establishes the individual as a person with a voice—the right and authority to speak on a particular topic and in otherwise closed-off places. Individuals invited to be part of the brain trust, recognized as "young global leaders" or "shapers," thus gain recognition and status. The use of such language—words of privilege, brilliance, and seduction—allocates political power.[9] It is also the means by which members are invited to construct and understand themselves as individuals and as members of a community of discretion.

These communities share some of the qualities that organizational scholars Marie-Laure Djelic and Sigrid Quack have attributed to professional transnational communities, in the sense that they are formed around a common—constructed or taken for granted—identity, maintained through active engagement of the participants, translating and sustaining a sense of belonging. Compared to the communities that Djelic and Quack analyzed (for example, the transnational temperance community and trade unions), the WEF communities vary in the extent to which they are "characterized by the mutual orientation of the member . . . [creating] a form of dependence between the members."[10] We found that many Forum participants may be active in the communities but without a dependence on the other members. Rather, their strongest relationship is with the WEF because they rely on their WEF liaison for providing them the identity and status of a WEF member. The WEF thus serves as a centripetal force, connecting individual community members to the organization.

The formation of communities of expertise is a way for the Forum to involve, engage, and define its wider environment and gain leverage from their work. By way of its communities, the WEF taps into the expertise of others, thus outsourcing part of their knowledge seeking to individuals outside the core of the WEF organization. By the same token, the WEF insources potentially valuable ideas and knowledge into its organizational core, where they are elaborated on, translated into the WEF vocabulary, or discarded. Through these double transfers, the Forum cultivates a particular form of transnational policy expertise—one that builds on status elevation, distinction, and discretion. The communities in the WEF network may be seen as forming part of what Diane Stone refers to as a community of "transnational policy professionals."[11] These actors, she writes, have "intrinsic governance capacities" to define problems and shape the climate of the debate.[12] The interlocking activities of these communities—the testing of ideas and crafting of knowledge, the writing of reports and policy statements—shape the political and business priorities of the Forum—its employees and participants. Such interlocks constitute an important resource for all parties—for the funder corporations, as well as for invited individuals and the WEF itself.[13] They channel resources in the form of strategic contacts, information on business priorities and challenges, assessments of critical trends, and financial resources. Most important, these interlocks provide a basis for extending the capacity of the WEF to act.

The communities that the WEF establishes to deal with global challenges are in fact organized in a fundamental sense. In accordance with organizational scholars Göran Ahrne and Nils Brunsson, they are constructed by way of concerted and decided, as opposed to haphazard and evolving, activities.[14] The Forum carefully scans, checks, evaluates, and decides on the composition of the networks, thereby extending its organizing capacity and its agency above and beyond its own organization. It creates a partially organized network.[15] This organized network comprises a hierarchy of members who can speak and make decisions in the name of the organization once the content of its messages has been checked. There are norms for members to follow, and members are monitored to ensure that they are following these norms. Members may be sanctioned (positively and negatively) in relation to these rules.[16] These organizational processes provide a degree of stability and predictability to the otherwise loose networks around the Forum, bolstering its collective agency and voice.

The Badge

For an outsider, the Davos gathering may look like a big get-together for anyone who matters in the world. But it is a far cry from an open assembly. A strict hierarchy of access rules the meeting in Davos, just as the meetings in other places orchestrated by the WEF. Access to some key places in the meetings is strictly for a few dozen invited heads of state, the CEOs of global corporations, and the heads of a rich plethora of international organizations. Badges testify to the cost of the entry ticket, the degree of access granted, and the weight of that individual's presence. It takes some time and effort for those new to Forum events to recognize the variety of badges and their significance. Badges, among the more important status symbols that the Forum deploys, signify one's position in the community hierarchy. The badge is thus a signal in a status system, in which distinctions of badge color, along with other minute distinctions in clothing and accessories, become the basis for social judgment (Photo 4.1).[17] The strategies of social pretension at play during WEF events are intricate and significant.

The most exclusive badge, which grants access to informal meetings behind the scenes, is the white badge with a holographic sticker. Technically, the purpose of the hologram is to distinguish for the benefit of the Davos security people who is allowed into the Informal Gathering of World Economic Leaders (IGWEL). The IGWEL, it is said, remains one of few occasions where international politicians can meet informally, off the record, to talk about their chal-

PHOTO 4.1. Our badges from WEF Summit on the Global Agenda, Dubai 2012. Source: Garsten and Sörbom.

lenges and aspirations. This type of badge is usually given to senior government policymakers, government ministers, and a select group of WEF employees. WEF's permanent staff are recognized by their dark blue badges, in the same tone as the logotype. Volunteers working with them wear light blue badges. There are other white badges too. The white badge with a blue line is given to official invitees: panel speakers and presenters invited to Forum events who are expected to attend sessions and contribute to public and private debates. Editors-in-chief and senior financial columnists may also receive these coveted white badges. The white badge with a blue line and a dot is given to Strategic Partners—funders of the Forum events. The plain white badge may be given to spouses of invitees, who often accompany their partners skiing and to parties. Reporting members of the press, that is, journalists writing on what is happening rather than participating in the panels, receive orange badges. Some media people have access only to public sessions and are otherwise restricted to media areas. The technical media teams are recognized by the purple line on the bottom of an orange badge. Technicians, who work in great numbers behind the scenes to stage the event, wear purple badges.

For the status-conscious attendees, the color coding of the badges provides quick and useful information about the badge owner's relationship to the Forum. It signals the weight of that person's invitation, the degree of access provided, and the role he or she is expected to perform at the event. A white hologram badge may make security personnel, journalists, and waiters more attentive, gracious, and service minded. A purple badge usually goes without notice. In sociologist Erving Goffman's dramaturgical terminology, badges signal who is to appear front stage and who is delegated to a backstage role.[18] Technicians, drivers, and other service staff may, to use Goffman's term, be considered "nonpersons" and have discrepant roles. They are the ones who appear both front stage and backstage but are not considered part of the performance. The audience and the performers do not acknowledge their roles, and they are viewed in some aspect as outsiders. The fact that most of the time, we had no badge signaled that we were not even in the play. The one time we were granted badges, during the Global Agenda Council Meeting in Dubai, they were white badges with a blue line and the title "Media Leader," which identified us as official invitees.

Sporting a badge is thus quintessential for displaying status and distinction and may serve as a signal of membership in one of the WEF communities. As sociologist William Goode shows, status distinctions rely on the reputation created by myriad rankings, evaluations, and feedback in daily life, by groups and organizations, which will affect those under scrutiny.[19] In order to create personal esteem, individuals and organizations may draw on their membership or belonging to groups and organizations—effective for both policymakers and business leaders.[20] Again, the status order constructed and formatted by the Forum works both ways. As much as the individual participant may develop her or his esteem, the Forum on its behalf draws on status orders for both delivering its messages and securing its position as a broker of ideas of consequence. By closing the gates to people who are not recognized as part of the group of world leaders, it confers social honor and status on those who are invited. The status hierarchy of badges reinforces the seductive quality of the organization and generates attraction and desire in potential participants. The badge is an important "object of desire," in psychoanalyst Jacques Lacan's view—an almost unattainable *objet petit*—and a stamp of approval by the gatekeepers for those who have it.[21] Indeed, it works to attract leaders from all corners of the world to meet other leaders who have also qualified. For one to be among the selected few, knowing that, like all the other participants, one has been carefully scrutinized and judged to pass is to rest assured that the ties nurtured within the WEF may work to influence the future agenda in the direction one desires.

At the other end of the desire to be part of the superior group is the feeling of shame—shame for not having or not yet having obtained the qualities needed to be part of the allegedly superior community. Between the invitees and the un-invited exists a social divide. The uninvited cannot boast that they were almost part of the Forum. Either they are or they are not. The divide is upheld by the Forum in the interest of keeping it exclusive and to nurture the idea that the in-vitees are "the best." Seclusion is a trademark of the Forum. The feeling of shame that one may experience anew with rejection or failure to be invited to a Forum event or community derives from a constructed sense of importance and status endowed on those who have been selected—an effect of being excluded and not deemed worthy. In this sense, the Forum has managed to create what anthro-pologist Ruth Benedict called a "shame culture," based on social exclusion pro-cesses that make people feel they *are* inferior.[22] The dismissive gaze, the smiling rejection, and exclusion from the verbal references "to the most brilliant" and those who comprise the brain trust conjure up feelings of being inferior, that is, not brilliant enough, and therefore unworthy of a badge. There is a noticeable tendency among WEF staff to display their privilege by way of subtle cues, such as a touch of condescending scorn in remarks made to outsiders or by display-ing indifference to questions asked.

As ethnographers, we lived with this feeling of shame throughout our fieldwork, only occasionally and randomly taken into favor. We have thus ex-perienced what the construction of membership may entail, in the sense of inclusion into or exclusion from a community, the power of seduction and re-jection. We have been treated with openness and politeness and with indiffer-ence and disdain. As Robert Greene has worded this experience, "Seduction, like warfare, is often a game of distance and closeness."[23] And, we might add, of inclusion and exclusion.

Starstruck

Forum meetings are replete not only with experts and the occasional Nobel laureate, but with artists, celebrities, and members of royalty who have been invited to appear in various roles. The selectivity exercised by the Forum con-tributes to the hype around the selected few. Mustafa Wallah, whom we had interviewed in Cologny and now met up with in Davos at the close of the meeting in 2013, was excited: "Davos is a complete circus. We all kill ourselves be-tween December and January. . . . This year was like last year but on steroids! We had more high-level people and stars than ever!"

Charlize Theron, actress and founder of Charlize Theron Africa Outreach Project, kicked off the first night of the Annual Meeting in 2013, when she spoke at the Crystal Award Ceremony. The award honors artists "who have used their talent to improve the state of the world." Hilde Schwab, Klaus Schwab's wife and his close associate, is often charged with leading the ceremo-nial artistic awards events. At the Annual Meeting in 2017, she explained the role of artists in the global community:

> Artists are bridge-builders, and role models for the global community. They
> are challenging assumptions, bringing new perspectives, and they seek to in-
> spire collective action. There have been over 80 winners, recipients, of Crystal
> Awards over the decades. From musicians to film-makers, from writers to ar-
> chitects, all of whom have been recognized for their commitment to advanc-
> ing inclusive progress on issues like peace-building, social inclusion, education,
> health, food security, environment, and sustainability.[24]

As in many global corporations of some repute, artists are often drawn on to enhance the hype and allure of celebratory events. We also find actors, film directors, photographers, painters, and writers at the WEF business meetings. Through these crossovers, the Forum may take advantage of celebrity names to attract attention, thereby leveraging their status and reputation. Celebrities may also take advantage, extending their renown by having been invited, and possibly even given an award. Anthropologist Brian Moeran has said this is the cultural and economic logic that fuses top business leaders and politicians with star celebrities. Both camps exchange favors in a "name economy."[25]

Many well-known artists—musicians, actors, writers—have made it to Forum events. Bob Geldof, Irish singer-songwriter, author, and political activ-ist, was invited to the post-Davos Nordic Summit Meeting in Stockholm in March 2013, which we attended. This meeting was stimulated by the Davos Annual Meeting as a follow-up meeting, initiated by Swedes who had partici-pated in Davos and felt a need to set something in motion in their national en-vironment. Geldof's appearance, although it probably had a magnetic influence on the invitees, also infused some criticism into the meeting.

The meeting was held on the premises of a renowned think tank in the center of Stockholm. Around two hundred people had been invited and were seated at round tables. iPads were loaned to participants to facilitate note taking, interactive response, and tweeting via the screen. The opening address was delivered by a Scandinavian, a senior manager of a funding corporation. In reference to the financial crisis, he asked rhetorically: "Is the worst over?" A presentation on how to stay competitive in the global market ensued. The moderator underlined: "The voice of business must be heard. Politicians need to understand. There is no recovery without growth." He went on to note the opportunity this event presented to make new friendships and to urge everyone to participate actively in the discussions.

Bob Geldof soon took the stage. Moving around as if preparing for a song in concert, he exclaimed: "We have failed. We have ruined the world. Perhaps we have turned a corner, but it's delusional. These are outmoded logics. We must think afresh, new. Davos is the summit of summits. . . . We confuse summits with action, they're not!" He went on to criticize the tendency of invitees to be caught by the "euphoria of being in the in-crowd":

> Davos Man is essentially a hypocrite, a pedant, and a windbag. Why do we pay attention? And here, we discuss this non-event. . . . It makes me puke. That's the truth. . . . Capitalism is all about opportunity. And individualism has become an expression of capitalism. Individualism only works when we act collectively. . . . In this asymmetric world, instability is inherent, and Davos is yet another event contributing to this asymmetry. So, let me not hear of the wisdom of old men.

Here Geldof, an invitee, turns his recognition of being selected into a position in which he critiques, and even mocks, the pundits in the WEF community. He uses his position to point to what he perceives as empty talk by poohbahs at nonevents. This criticism is a recurring theme in the media, particularly around Davos meetings. Geldof's mockery of "Davos Man" brings to mind the anthropological notion of Big Man, coined by Marshall Sahlins.[26] Although the context of the Big Men is very different (Melanesia and Polynesia), Big Men share certain traits regardless of context. One of them is particularly relevant here. Big Men (they are rarely women) may not have formal tribal or other authority (through material possessions or inheritance of rights, for instance), but they can maintain recognition through skilled persuasion and wisdom. A Big Man has a large group of followers from his own kinship or social group and from others. He provides his followers with protection and assistance, who in return give him support, which he uses to increase his status. In essence, the making of Big Men and their followers is a status machinery.

Coined by political scientist Samuel P. Huntington, the notion of Davos Man was meant to refer to members of the global elite who perceive themselves as international or global.[27] The term has gained a negative connotation beyond that of high-level attendees of the WEF Annual Meeting in Davos to denote ruthless high-flyers in finance, untouchable political big shots, and any invitee in a high-profile position. It also signals the gender bias of the WEF events, at which women are still in the minority (28 percent in 2017).

Minions and Mistresses

Forum events have a seductive potency that goes well beyond the circles of global leaders in business and politics. Plenty of other kinds of actors are drawn into the magnetic allure of the WEF. The Davos Annual Meeting has been termed "a glorified dating agency" in the social media by a Swiss banker and former attendee.[28] The reporting press also tends to include in their coverage the "horizontal markets" that exist around the meeting core, including drugs and transactions of representational and sexual services. There are rumors of other dodgy business transactions, such as bribery and corruption occurring in and around the meetings. Whether these reports and rumors are true or not is beyond our knowledge. Nevertheless, we have seen call girls at parties, accessible for service offers, and picked up by invitees. On occasion, we were mistaken for being call girls ourselves, as we hung around in hotel bars and restaurants, attempting to perform our role as ethnographers by talking to participants.

The Annual World Economic Forum Meeting in Davos has also been referred to as "the tycoon equivalent of sleepaway camp, except the bug juice is Moët and the campfire stories all involve globalization."[29] Male invitees are rarely starved for female companionship (meaning female companionship other than their peers—invited female participants). Participants may bring their spouses (most often wives), but they may also bring along mistresses. Officially recognized spouses may receive the plain white badge; minions, including mistresses, may or may not be given specific badges, with red and yellow stripes. There are also other hangers-on: aspiring mistresses, call girls, and wannabes (and at times ourselves). Wannabes are not identified by any color of badge but are left to hang around the premises, hoping for a chance to be invited to a party or other intimate gathering. Escort agencies openly advertise their services online in English, with reference to Davos. Prostitution is legal, though regulated, in Switzerland, which facilitates the business. Advertised services vary from agencies promising discreet but glamorous partners to escort important people to important events, on the one hand, to agencies that list sexual services in clinical detail, on the other hand. Young party girls who can speak English are said to be particularly in demand. The escort business adds another element to the seductive and discreet power of the Davos meeting and points to another variety of networking and another form of discreet services and spaces, at the margins of the official.

One occasion at which the margins of the Forum community were made visible to us was at a Russian party, staged on the outskirts of the meeting compound, outside the wired-fence area, in Davos in 2012. We happened to pass the large white tent marked Ekaterinburg EXPO 2020 on our way back to our lodging. We had spent a long day at the Open Forum, hanging out near the meeting, talking to participants, and conducting interviews, and we had walked up and down the streets of Davos in an effort to get a grasp of the meeting surroundings. Tired and cold, we headed back to rest. As we passed the tent, a man approached us and handed us tickets for the Russian Night that was to take place the following night. He encouraged us to come, which we did. How could we resist being invited to a social event that might be informative for us?

When we entered the tent the next evening, two young Russian-speaking women handed us each a package of gifts: white wool mittens, a traditional Russian shawl, a key ring with a Russian doll, and a coffee table book in Russian. We accepted the gifts, hung our coats, and entered the party area. In the large open space, Russian disco music was pounding from loudspeakers. We could barely hear each other as we tried to talk. We approached the bar and were offered a glass of champagne. As we turned our eyes toward the dance floor, a number of incredibly tall and spiky blondes in exceedingly high heels, wearing short skirts and mittens from the gift packages, were moving about indifferently, dancing with men in suits. There were few female meeting participants around, and it soon became clear to us that the women had been flown in for purposes other than contributing to panels—as escorts. The party never really took off, and after about an hour of hanging out, we left.

The fact that about three-quarters of the participants and badge holders at WEF events are men in their mid-fifties and that the extraofficial and discreet services outside the program are provided primarily by women in their twenties, points to a significant gender and power imbalance surrounding the WEF community. Those in an established core of male leaders in the community tend to be recognized and acclaimed. Younger women and others considered unqualified tend to be excluded from the community. This is an uncomforting issue for the Forum, which claims to be working consistently to include "people from all walks of life" and to work toward the empowerment of women.[30] The Forum, and not least Klaus Schwab, is well aware of the gender imbalance, and there is an ongoing attempt to rectify the balance, making "the voice of the young" and "the voice of women" heard.[31]

Gatekeeping

The process of constructing communities starts with finding people to invite as participants at events. At WEF headquarters, staff members who vouch for the credibility of individuals and the information and political or ideological positions they bring to the network enjoy key roles and become gatekeepers, determining who meets their standards and who is admitted. The gatekeepers are arguably highly influential in defining problems, shaping the agenda, and enrolling organizations and individuals. And finding the right person for each panel, project, workshop, or party is one of the main tasks at WEF headquarters. Mustafa Wallah explained to us in Davos 2013, "Getting the exactly right moderator for a panel is pivotal to the success of the event." Other staff informants have told us that some invitees have become great disappointments, not meeting the standards of functioning as a moderator or a regular participant. In practice, this has meant that the original plan for the event—constructing a new community or partnership—could not be completed. Therefore, it is of great importance for both parties—the Forum employee and the invitees—that the invitees perform according to expectations at meetings.

Using one's network of colleagues to find the right person is the most trusted way to search for potential invitees. In sociologist Mark Granovetter's terms, the strength of "weak ties"—relationships that are relatively tenuous and where contact is more sporadic than regular—is that they may be successfully used to spread information, advance one's interests, and build cohesive communities.[32] In Cologny, we met Mr. Wallah's colleague, Diana Gordon, an energetic and forthcoming woman in charge of staging Forum events, who explained the process of finding a moderator:

> I think that, on many occasions, we tend to use moderators that we have already worked with before. But we obviously need to freshen up the pool of moderators, so we do try new moderators. Usually it's by word of mouth; it's through networks, through our colleagues who have been at conferences, through our own conferences, through recommendations . . . a lot of desk research. With YouTube and videos and everything that's available these days, it *really* has helped to evaluate whether you feel that someone has the qualities of a good

moderator. So, in some cases yes, we do try to use new moderators, but we would always try sort of smaller activities or smaller sessions first rather than the large sessions. But we choose . . . we also work with a number of media leaders, but in particular those that are ready to push the envelop in terms of the format. . . . So it's a real combination of word-of-mouth, through the networks, but then also research and looking for people.[33]

For all of the people who are found interesting enough, a process of due diligence is undertaken in order to ensure that the person and his or her organization is acceptable for the Forum. All in all, this is a time-consuming process. Peter Berg, a timid young man in his mid-twenties with cautious manners, is a member of the Global Leadership Fellows community. He tells us that he spends a large part of his working hours finding the right people for the groups he manages. He describes the process as a strange mix of a large amount of freedom for him to find the right people and a highly developed bureaucracy, where layers of staff need to approve and sign before he is able to send an invitation to someone he knew from the beginning of the process would be invited.

Crucial to a return visit, to become an affiliated member, is to be seen as constructive and able to think creatively without being considered too radical. This is how Diana Gordon describes what, in her mind, constitutes a failure in finding the right person:

CHRISTINA: So, do you, like, regularly get disappointed? You take someone in and you think it's worthwhile, and then they're not?

DIANA: Not regularly, but there are always people that we think, like: "Okay, well that maybe served its purpose for that particular . . . but it's not someone we would necessarily want to continue to engage with," but again, for various reasons. It could be that . . . they are brilliant, all of them, brilliant people, it's just that, you know how available were they in the preparations? It's one aspect that we really have to take into consideration. And how willing were they to really understand what the mission and the vision of the Forum is, and not just bring their own idea to the table? How good are they, and not just . . . obviously, they are amazing thought leaders . . . but how well are they able to articulate their ideas on a panel? All of these kinds of criteria have to come into play.[34]

As Ms. Gordon noted, a major point in coming back is to understand the "mission and vision of the Forum," indicating that it is not enough to be brilliant, as she says; one must also fit the Forum's views on what is important with regard to content and format. Criticizing the Forum is fully possible for the average participant if he or she still expresses some kind of trust in the organization. Expressing more fundamental criticism is difficult but not impossible. It may work for a person who is either famous, like Bob Geldof, or very young, like members of the community of Young Global Shapers. In general, though, not complying with the basic ideas of the Forum means that the person (and that person's organization as well) will be seen as not complying with the ethos of the Forum and left out of the network. What this ethos is and how it plays out in practice is transferred from WEF employees to participants in the process of planning panels, seminars, and other events. For every session, there is an internal evaluation in combination with what is described as anecdotal evaluations, through which responses from other teams and colleagues are sought. In addition, there is a constant form of monitoring taking place, through which staff discuss with participants and colleagues how well a moderator or panel participant has functioned. Diana Gordon had this to say:

> To be honest, we do a lot during the event itself. We get a lot of, and we have a lot of, direct feedback and information. People are very willing to be open and share what their perspectives are, so . . . but again it's ad hoc, it's anecdotal. It's not a very thorough and consistent feedback, so that's where we need to get to. But we also rely on… our colleagues' feedback, the messages that they get from their constituents as well, so . . .[35]

As Gordon mentioned, affiliation and membership in the Forum community are subject to continuous evaluation. After the end of a member's served term or after this person participates in one specific event, the WEF decides whether he or she will have the opportunity to stay on and serve in another working group or return for another event. Many of the participants aspire to return. Some of them have whispered in our ears that people will be afraid to tell us what they *really* think about the event and the Forum because they want to come back. These informants underscore the fact that from a personal perspective, it is important for one's career to be part of this network, to meet all of these people whom they otherwise would not. And as our informants in the Geneva office claim, participants want to be able to add to their curriculum vitae that they are part of the network; they like to have the words "World Economic Forum" related to them. "You would not believe the effort we have to put in telling people that they *can't* come," Peter Berg at headquarters tells us, referring to people who try to invite themselves. "Much more [effort] than saying that people can come." And those contacting the WEF requesting invitations range from heads of states to CEOs, journalists, and researchers—others like us.

Participants who are found to be compliant with WEF standards of what constitutes productive participants may be invited again. Internally, recurring guests are highly valued because they make day-to-day work life easier, while serving as prerequisites for the stability and longevity of the communities. We have met several people who have been "working with the WEF," as they usually put it, for a decade or more. Therefore, employees at the Cologny headquarters working with events, initiatives, and projects keep the participants they can invite under close supervision. They are seen as "belonging" to a particular member of staff, a relationship that can be an internally valuable asset. It is a patronage of sorts. When moving from one position to another within the Forum, employees also bring their contacts. Furthermore, if group X has found a new person to invite, group Y cannot invite the same person. Moreover, there is a hierarchy in relation to these people, meaning that if a person is talking more to the core of the general theme of an event, that trumps another potential invitee. As various staff members explained to us, keeping track of invitations is necessary because there is an inherent risk of overusing some people, making them prone to rejecting further invitations. At one point, Rita Lesley, a senior WEF manager, told us that she could not use Paula Shielding, a longstanding invitee and member of a WEF community (whom we met at the Arctic lunch described in Chapter 3), at the Davos panel she was preparing because another WEF manager already "owned" her and had first claim on her participation.

These norms illustrate how WEF invitees become key assets in the Forum's interest of organizing for authority in global governance. By finding and drawing on these individuals (most commonly working on behalf of other organizations) and using their aspiration to be invited, the Forum is able to construct agency beyond itself, all based on its own discretion. Membership, monitoring, and sanctioning become pivotal, albeit relatively informally.

Silencing

The Global Agenda Council networks and other communities organized by the WEF produce a large number of reports each year. They are intended to document the thought processes of the working groups and inspire solution seeking on a number of issues. They provide accounts of existing states of affairs, challenges, and potential and proposed scenarios. The reports rarely, if ever, present the voice of a particular author; instead, the voice is that of the Forum and its designated community. Forum staff undertake editing and provide final censoring before publication. There is thus a sense in which potentially opposing views are silenced by the organization's core. Membership in a community brings with it lessons on the discretionary demands of the organization.

These discretionary demands are also noticeable in oral presentations at Forum events. We have occasionally heard how members of communities who have been invited as speakers in Davos have had their slides edited by Forum staff. One informant told us that a slide had been removed from a speaker's presentation because it gave an unfavorable image of one of the funding corporations. Informants often found it difficult to talk about the silencing of their words and views and would twist and turn uneasily in response to our questions. Academics enrolled in the WEF community, mostly in Global Agenda Councils, have been unwilling to talk to us about the WEF in general and about their role in particular. The topic of academic freedom and the potential claims to alignment made by the Forum has been particularly touchy.

Journalists are another group that may be affiliated with the organization as a kind of member. Their reporting on the events is also monitored and even silenced to the extent possible and when relevant. A correspondent for Swedish public radio said in an interview that he was locked in the congress hall when he was trying to report on outside demonstrations:

> I was working, alongside my colleague NN, when we suddenly heard the sounds of riots outside—what must have been the sound of teargas grenades. We set off in order to see what was going on, but we were stopped by guards who very firmly told us that no one could leave the building. I was locked in! For the first time in my life as a journalist, I was locked in. We were not allowed to come out for as long as the riot was on. We tried to talk to the guards, asking them why, but they only said it was for the protection of participants. Then we showed them our badges—where it said that we were not participants, only journalists—but that didn't help. As the guard said, we had only been given these in order to come in, not to be let out! I was so mad. This is clearly unacceptable in a democratic country. And we got an apology later from the press officer at the Forum, who said that they had nothing to do with this. That it was the police management who had made that decision.[36]

The incident that the correspondent describes, which he also related to radio listeners in Sweden, is not unique. The WEF's efforts to influence and control media reporting are well known in media circles.

On one occasion when we were officially invited as participants by WEF staff to a media dinner in Davos, we were told other stories of editing and silencing. The media dinner is a WEF event staged annually to acknowledge the reporting of accredited media professionals. As Cassius Luck said in the welcome speech, the WEF holds this dinner as a way of "thanking attending media for the job that had been put into reporting the event." His job during the Davos event was a demanding one, and now, toward the end of the event, he looked pale and exhausted, his voice broken and weak.

During dinner, it became clear that the Forum had longstanding relationships with some of the reporters. One journalist we spoke to, Beatrice Kallis from a major European media house, told us that she had "inherited her right to come and report from the Annual Meeting" from somebody at her company, and she explained that she wanted to continue returning. Therefore, she swiftly told us that she did not want her critical views of the WEF to be known because it was important for her to return. During dinner, a WEF employee came by and asked what Kallis has reported from the event. Anything in particular that caught her attention? Afterward, she turned to us saying that she saw this polite interest as a way of checking that she had not written the wrong things, which she had no intention of doing. It seemed to us that her reluctance to report criticism was not only to remain on good terms with the Forum; it appeared that she did not consider it an important issue. She was balancing her individual interests with a journalist's core ethics. Still, she may have reported in a different way had she not seen it as important to come back and had the Forum not checked on her.

Through all its knowledge-seeking activities, reports, and media dissemination, the Forum works on making certain dimensions of its work accessible and visible. At the same time and through the same processes, it works on producing silences. There is a double, or rhizomatic, dimension to the logic of practice at the Forum, in which status elevation, inclusion, openness, and voicing go hand in hand with dismissal, exclusion, opacity, and silencing.

The Aspiring Class

The World Economic Forum and its communities are in many respects a status machinery. With intentions to act as a catalyst for change and to improve the world, it works continuously and diligently to create networks of talented and capable people who can assume these challenges. Because the mandate of the Forum is liquid rather than official, it needs to build its position and authority by means other than those that conventional intergovernmental organizations use. By building its vast network, the community of communities, the Forum is able to extend its agentic power and expand its organizational base and diplomatic reach.

The many communities of the Forum offer their invitees various types of membership. Membership is tightly controlled by WEF staff, however, and continuously overseen. As we have shown, the eligibility and performance of members are monitored and sanctioned in various ways. To stay on the books, as it were, one needs to learn to abide by the norms of discretion and subtle adherence to the cultural codes of the organization. Those who are selected and manage to maintain a long-term working relationship with the Forum constitute an aspiring class—people who believe in their capacity to contribute positively to the world. They share an aspiration: to be part of the new nobility of the most brilliant, the best of brains. In this context, status markers, such as the badge, function as signals and proxies as to one's position in the landscape of the aspiring class.

The aspiring class, or the new nobility of transnational policy elites, is not altogether easy to delineate. Some caution is needed in describing staff and community members as a class—as a distinct category of people occupying a specific hierarchical position in society and sharing access to certain resources. They do share certain distinct characteristics, however, which make it reasonable to talk about them as an aspiring class. They tend to have been educated at one of the Ivy League universities, Oxford, or Cambridge, or at some highly ranked business school; are from the United States or Europe; and are predominantly white, male, and in their fifties. The Forum nurtures and reinforces the idea of them as "brilliant," "the best of the best," "the brain trust." Needless to say, to be chosen is highly coveted among all the groups that the Forum aspires to include: business, policy, academia, arts, civil society, young people, and women.[37]

Looking more closely at the composition of the WEF meeting participants provides a clear indication of imbalances. In the period 2011 to 2013, the percentage of male-to-female meeting participants was 80 and 20, respectively. Over the years, the ratio of female participants has grown slowly but steadily, and in 2017 it reached 28 percent.[38] In the period 2011 to 2013, 23 percent of the female participants and 27 percent of male participants had a PhD degree, and 56 percent of the female participants and 51 percent of the male participants had a master's degree as their highest degree of education. The alma mater of a large proportion of them, almost 40 percent, was one of the top ten ranked universities in the world. The average age was 56.5 years.[39]

The WEF community is not only a discretionary space, but also a congested and competitive space, to which only the select may gain entrance. Being among the chosen, participating in the working groups and panels, is a stressful experience for many. They are expected to exhibit top performance and to meet the high expectations of the Forum. Nevertheless, the WEF community exerts a degree of attraction and seduction on potential and actual members. It is a magnet for aspiring leaders and policymakers for the status acknowledgment accorded: for the hype of media attention; the topicality of meetings; the chance to meet with celebrities in business, politics, and the arts; and for the career boost it may entail—in short, for the recognition of being selected.

What is seen as desirable also tends to be that which has been established as allegedly superior, established by way of reference to pragmatic or symbolic power. Through the recruiting of elites as participants, the anchoring of practices in a modern dramatization of the world at stake, and a celebration of individual agency, the WEF continues to position itself as superior. And it confers status and superiority on individuals chosen to be part of it. This position is, however, not stable. Because of the in-built instability of the status order, because it can wane, it is a trait that makes participation even more desirable. It often becomes important for participants to guard the gates of participation almost as much as the Forum itself would.

Sociologist Leslie Sklair has said with reference to an emerging transnational corporate class: "There is no transnational dominant class that acts in secret to impose its will over every facet of life for everyone in the world and with complete success."[40] A transnational class may well be dominant in certain ways in certain spheres, however. This is what we see happening in the WEF community and beyond. Weber's distinction between class and status adds further distinctions here. In Weber's view, class and status are part of a broader multidimensional schema of stratification. Status groups always imply some level of identity in the sense of some recognized "positive or negative social estimation of honor." A status group, he continues, cannot exist without its members being in some way conscious of group membership: "In contrast to classes, Stände (status groups) are normally groups."[41] In this sense, the WEF community would constitute a status group. In the broader transnational context, members have also acquired influence beyond mere group identity and status; they have established an organizational platform and a mandate (however liquid) from which they may leverage influence and discreetly gain impact in policymaking and politics. They thus have the degree of comprehensiveness and control that Sklair would deem necessary to qualify as an emerging—or in our words—aspiring class.

The aspiring class also looks toward the future in cultivating the next generation of global leaders. In various forms, it draws on the lives and careers of young professionals as a way organizing the future. Peter Berg and his colleagues from the WEF leadership program and the so-called Young Global Shapers are prime examples of this attempt. In the next chapter, we analyze the role of anticipation that these young people are set to play.

5   Mobilizing for the Future

"Improving the state of the world" is the World Economic Forum's motto for its activities, epitomizing its interest in organizing the future. The intent is not merely to take care of what exists but to develop, progress, and change into something yet unknown. The underlying assumption, as in politics in general, is that there will be a future world with attributes not entirely dissimilar to those of today, and this future will encompass change over time through ongoing experiences, both anticipated and unexpected.[1] As previous chapters have shown, attempts to improve a time to come take many forms within the Forum.

In this chapter, we look at the role of the social imaginary, as articulated by social anthropologist Benedict Anderson, in providing a common set of background assumptions for the people involved in the WEF community.[2] We analyze the activities that are distinctly formatted around the future—mobilizing the young and presenting future scenarios. In the spirit of Ulf Hannerz, we look at Davos culture as an attempt at constructing a cosmopolitan culture around "a vaguely demarcated set of meanings and meaningful forms," in which the crafting of geopolitical future scenarios and educating the future generation are key ingredients. [3] While most activities within the Forum rotate around a horizontal axis and intent, attempting to spread the message of the WEF horizontally into other organizations, these activities have more of longitudinal perspective. Still, forming their actions on the basis of seduction and discreet power, the emphasis here is on preparing for the future as it unfolds. Instead of governance, markets, and diplomacy, the central terms here are *young* and *risk*.

Young People and the Forum

As we have already shown, the funders of the WEF—the corporations—are invited to send their representatives to the Annual Meeting in Davos and other events. Other than that, the Forum has no built-in mechanism of representation. It is essential for the Forum that it may exercise its right to choose what it deems as the exact right participants at its activities. In order to make a balanced mix among those chosen, the Forum attempts to cover "all walks of life." Overall, the goal is to have equal representation of participants from business and nonbusiness. Within these two big slots, quotas are created in order to ensure that no group is accorded too small or too large a presence. As Forum staff told us, this is not always a smooth process. The paying guests— the corporate funders—want as strong a presence as possible, whereas the Forum is interested in broadening the range of invitees as much as possible in order to be the multistakeholder arena it claims it is. Internally, this creates a situation of constant haggling, with each unit trying to bring in as many of its guests as possible.

In order to shape the harmonious mix it seeks, the Forum especially aims to integrate young people. As we noted in the Introduction and Chapter 4, the ordinary meeting attendants, the "leaders of excellence," are typically male, from the North, and notably not young. For several reasons, the Forum recognizes that leaving young people out is not good enough—partly since it challenges the social legitimacy of the WEF in the eyes of the public. The Forum also recognizes that it may miss out on important learning opportunities and connections to social changes and processes that it would want to be part of, propel, and capitalize from. As Chairman Schwab described to us during a conversation in Dubai, the Forum has created a number of subcommunities through which it intends to bring in young people and make their voices heard within the Forum.

In this chapter, we provide ethnographic insights into the integration of youth within the Forum, elaborating on two questions. What is the relationship between the younger generation and the Forum? Who gives what, and who gets what? We look closely at the way agency is provided to the Forum by its young invitees at the same time as status is conferred onto these young people. We then describe the discourses around these young people. Obviously they are presented as representing the future, but more particularly, what are the young believed to do for the Forum? And how do youth within the Forum live up to these aspirations?

The Voice of the Future

Sitting in the networking area at the Swissôtel in Istanbul, we are talking to
Fadil Badinij. He has been invited to the Regional Forum Meeting on the
Middle East, Northern Africa, and Eurasia in early June 2012. We had not,
but we ventured to go anyway. Badinij is a civic society organizer, looks to
be in his fifties, and works in the United Kingdom with young people at risk,
challenging them to start their own businesses. To his mind, the WEF event
is too much about business, and he appears to be fed up. That is why he is
now hanging out in the networking area, stretching out on the sofa, instead
of attending sessions. He stresses that the good thing about coming here is
that he will be bringing home a few names for his network. One of them is
Anwen Abdelnour, who is sitting beside him. She is from the United Kingdom
and works in the cultural sector; she appears to be in her late twenties and is
part of the newly established Young Global Shapers community within the
Forum. To her mind too, there is a great deal of business being conducted
at the event. She tells us of a Forum culture in which all participants present
themselves with a business card, although she says that she does not mind
this. More problematic, in her view, is the fact that much of what is said in
sessions does not constitute news for her—she has already heard about them.
Anwen Abdelnour, together with other Shapers, had met with Schwab and
complained about not having enough young people on panels. The Chairman
had defended the organization by saying that it was necessary to invite people
who are now in decision-making positions, and they are typically not young.
In spite of her criticism, Anwen is basically happy about the Shapers' initiative. She has met a number of people she would never have met otherwise, and
WEF has taken her to places she would otherwise not have been. She describes
Shapers at the event and in the London hub (to which she belongs) as a tight
group. They see each other as friends; connect via Facebook and other social
media; help each other out with job opportunities; and some of them even go
on vacation together.

The idea of the Shapers, as Anwen Abdelnour sees it, is "to get involved, to
offer our more youthful perspectives on things and to learn from those more
experienced." And "I feel like I certainly did all of this," she writes to us a few
weeks after the Istanbul event. "I think they also want us to connect with the
existing WEF community; global leaders and business members. I, and we,
also did this and it certainly fits in with what I want from being a Shaper."[4]
This was also what Schwab told us when we met in Dubai at the Forum's brain

trust meeting. He underscored that WEF is not merely about corporations and CEOs. The WEF also needs to let other voices be heard in order to stay true to the multistakeholder model. The model cannot include only business, civil society, and politics; other voices need to be heard too: those of the young, women, experts, researchers, and people of faith. That is the reason for the creation of the Shapers group—or community, as the Forum calls it.

The Istanbul meeting was an early event in the history of this particular group. At that time, there were about 1,230 Shapers in 170 so-called Shaper hubs, but they constitute a growing group within the Forum. In mid-2016 almost six thousand young people were part of over 450 hubs spread across the world. A short introductory film posted on the Forum website describes the initiative as a way of connecting to the "millennium mindset," which is seen as collaborative and hopeful. We are "naive in a good sense," one of the Shapers says, and "tapping into that generation can help you reconnect with that idealism that is hard to find on a day-to-day basis." The Forum presents them as coming from "all walks of life," but sharing "a spirit of public entrepreneurship in the public interest." Managing director David S. Aikman, in charge of the initiative, says "the insight from this global network [is] to make the biggest possible difference in their own community."[5]

When we reconnect with Abdelnour in 2014, she has not been able to participate in the Shaper community for a while because of changes in her life, but she is still part of the London Hub, which is one of the larger ones, and she is still content with the opportunity to belong to the Shapers group. In 2016, about fifty Shapers are mentioned at the London hub website, globalshapers.org. But the website suggests that the activity level within the Hub is low. It had initiated two projects in 2013, both related to a weekend in June during which a number of Shapers met with three charities with the intent of "taking them to the next step of their journey."[6] It was described as a huge success:

> Over this one weekend—fueled by Chipotle Burritos, beverages and a great atmosphere at the Boston consulting group—the team of around 25 new and founding Shapers was able to come up with various solutions to the issues that the organisations faced. Partnering with facilitators from Make Sense, the weekend was a spectacular success.

After this event a number of news items were presented in 2013 and early 2014, one of them narrating when the hub met with Schwab, and some blog posts. After that, silence.

The same fate is detectable within the Giza hub. It has been easy for this group to assemble people, but it proves more difficult to muster activities. We met this group in Cape Town 2015 at the regional meeting on Africa. WEF staff at the airport had told us we could hop on one of its shuttles, taking us to the hotel, and we were waiting for it to leave when a group of young people embarked, clapping their hands, singing, and eager to make contact. This turns out to be the Giza hub of the Young Global Shapers, as Abdul-Badi Issa tells us. Issa, a man looking to be in his late twenties, promises that we will hear from this group throughout the meeting because they will ensure that they are heard. He tells us that he is originally from Cairo but now resides in Lebanon, where he works as the leader of an Internet-related project sponsored by a high-ranking American university. The aim of the project is to spread knowledge about the Arab world and improve connections between this region and the rest of the world. The journey to Cape Town was paid by the WEF, although he must fund the stay at the rather expensive Southern Sun Waterfront Hotel through his project. For Issa, the trip to Cape Town and his other trips as part of the Shapers group is completely worth the time, effort, and funding because they make it possible for him to meet with interesting people and have interesting conversations, "such as I am having right now with you guys." Before every meeting, Issa tells us, he spends time going over the participant list, marking all the people he is interested in talking to. For this event, though, he did not have time to do this because he just came from another WEF meeting in the Middle East. For him, the WEF is "all about talk." It is a platform for talk, which may mean traveling to other places and engaging other organizations and people.

In response to his questions, we tell him that we have arrived at the meeting in Cape Town in our capacity as researchers financed by the Swedish government through the Swedish Research Council. We are here, we tell him, to understand what the Forum is about and how it succeeds in doing what it is doing. Issa laughs and says that he would like to understand that too! "Understanding what the WEF does, I mean . . ." We laugh together at the perceived vagueness of the WEF. As we approach their hotel, we exchange business cards and shake hands with the rest of the group, promising to stay in contact. Alas, we never stumbled on them again in this meeting of fifteen hundred people.

According to the activities listed on the Giza hub web page, though, the activity within the hub is low. Two years later, we find two updates from earlier on (2014), saying that the hub was open for applications and one news report showing that two Shapers had been interviewed regarding job creation and the Global Shapers community. Other than that, there are no updates. One may think that most of the activities of the hub are either undertaken in relation to events, like those that Issa described, or they do not show up on the web page. In either case, about twenty Shapers are named on the website, but no news and no projects are reported apart from the first ones inviting people to apply to be part of the group.

It is primarily since the early 2000s that the Forum has attempted to attract young people, beginning with the Forum of Young Global Leaders (YGL) program that started in 2004. Since then, this program annually selects and elects a limited number of people under age forty who are seen as outstanding young leaders. The Forum writes that each year, thousands of candidates are proposed "through a qualified nomination process and assessed according to rigorous selection criteria." The one hundred to two hundred people who are selected have "a record of extraordinary achievements" and have demonstrated a commitment to serve society at large "through exceptional contributions."[7] They are welcome to be part of the Forum over a five-year period and may take part in most Forum activities. Those chosen are presented by the Forum as "a dynamic, diverse, global community of the world's most outstanding, next generation leaders, who commit a portion of their time to jointly share a better future and thereby improve the state of the world. Young Global Leaders represent the future of leadership."[8]

In 2016 the WEF counts 949 of these young and extraordinary leaders, half of them recruited from business and half from what is termed nonbusiness.[9] People such as Daniel Ek (founder of Spotify), David Karp (founder of Tumblr), Lerato Mbele (a presenter at BBC World Service), and Crown Prince Fredrik of Denmark and his wife, Crown Princess Mary, are among the chosen ones. The Forum motivates the formation of the group with reference to the future. The challenges facing the next generation are "more daunting and intractable than ever and cannot be mastered with the current set of strategies, institutions and attitudes."[10] For this reason, the new generation fills a need within the Forum to "engage in global affairs to shape a more positive, peaceful and prosperous society."[11] The fundamental idea for the group is to develop "authentic relationships with peers" in order to "empower positive change," helping each other to make the "transition from success to significance and strives to move from a collection of successful individuals to a community of collective impact."[12] The group is also to represent the coming generations at Forum activities, thus embodying the voices of the young.

The impact of the YGL group is presented at the WEF website through a number of initiatives that have been established based on the group itself. In 2016 seven initiatives were presented as mature, in the sense that "most of them now have an established not-for-profit organization"—like Thirst, an organization that is trying to raise awareness of the global water crisis and saving 1 billion liters of water (www.thirstforwater.org), and Deworm the World Initiative, which is working with governments to develop and implement school-based deworming programs (www.evidenceaction.org). Six of the initiatives presented have not yet advanced as far but are still in motion.

The Global Leadership Fellows Program (GLF), another group of younger people within the Forum, was initiated in 2005. This three-year residential trainee program is dedicated to developing "the next generation of world leaders."[13] The Forum receives six thousand applications annually, and only twenty to thirty new fellows are accepted.[14] Given the large number of applicants, the accepted fellows are both academically and professionally accomplished when they enter the program, often sporting parallel exams and having already worked for governments, multilateral organizations, or businesses. The program dean, Gilbert Probst, states that the program is "a finishing school for leaders after they have completed their studies."[15] By 2015, 170 fellows had graduated. The fellows are intended to contribute 80 percent of their working hours at the Forum headquarters and 20 percent to formal training during the program, although some fellows say that the working time within the Forum is actually 100 percent, since they are expected to uphold their WEF tasks parallel to formal training. [16]

Chairman Schwab describes the program in terms "of an absolute need for global leaders who have a systemic view of global affairs," claiming that "the Forum, precisely for this purpose has created the program for Global Leadership Fellows in order to secure for this need."[17] The program leads to a master's in global leadership. For the Forum, this group is "at the core of the Forum's strategic aspirations, which are to foster visionary leadership; promote greater accountability towards the Forum's communities and stakeholders; to promote impeccable intellectual and moral integrity; and to inculcate the Forum's commitment to serving the public interest."[18] As associate director Juraj Ondrejkovic describes the program, it is not merely "developing leaders for the Forum but leaders who can make a difference now and in the future outside the Forum."[19]

The GLF program is thus intended to reflect the underpinning values of the Forum, investing these in a new generation of what are hoped to be leaders in organizations around the world. These values do not primarily concern market liberal values, but more the core ideas of the organization regarding how to engage. The fellows are taught to be leaders in the Forum's sense of the word, engaging in politics in the form of soft diplomacy and discretionary governance. The fellows, interviewed for a Harvard Business School case study, underscored this position; they emphasized the multistakeholder perspective and the importance of "soft power" in the format of "soft skills," diplomacy, and the construction, leading, and galvanizing of communities, as central characteristics for an influential actor.[20]

Peter Berg is a Global Leadership Fellow. He and the others in the program have administrative positions such as senior community manager or manager of the global action council on health. In these capacities, they commit many working hours contributing to the establishment of a WEF meeting, such as the ones in Davos and Dubai. When we meet Berg in Cape Town, he explains to us that he saw the GLF position as the logical next step in his career. He had been doing the same work in a similar but smaller organization at a national level. After the three years with GLF, which had just begun at the time, there is a possibility that he would stay on in other positions within the WEF. Nevertheless, he anticipates that it will be a bit difficult to stay on, given that such positions are rare. Moreover, he says, the intent of the program is to educate future leaders, meaning that the WEF actually supports their leaving for other organizations after completing the program. Berg also talks of the sense of community that is created among the fellows. Many of them share housing in Geneva and get to know each other relatively well over the years. He says that almost wherever he goes in the future, he will be able to find someone from the GLF community who is working in some government authority, civic society organization, or business. Berg places a high value on being a member of the GLF community and feels fortunate to be there in spite of all the demands.

As of 2011, half the graduated GLFs had remained with the Forum; the others had assumed positions at such organizations as the International Monetary Fund and World Business Council for Sustainable Development and in the Nigerian government.[21] As one of the program managers said: "We educate future global leaders for all kinds of organizations and situations."[22] As a result, the program extends far beyond the Forum's reach and its possible influence by creating a group of influential alumni around the world.

Youth, Future, and Change

The various constellations of younger people within the Forum are the result of organizational efforts to relate to a group of people who would otherwise not be part of WEF activities. They are presented in various constellations formatted by the Forum as "young" and "extraordinary." As is customary in organizing young people, no one really knows what being "young" entails, because "every definition of and description of youth is necessarily meaningful and comprehensible only within that discursive field where it is constructed."[23] In the WEF setting, "young" primarily means not being part of the ordinary group of members and invitees, with a mean age of fifty-seven years.

The need for young people is motivated by an interest in drawing on the energy and knowledge of this group. As was made clear in the Global Shapers' organizing efforts, young people are seen as carriers of specific characteristics: naiveté, energy, and contact with the future. They are doing things that older people are not—activities that the WEF feels compelled to tap into—and they will grow older and replace today's seniors. These other activities speak to possible futures, pivotal for the WEF to pick up on.

But the motivation for and the incorporation of younger people may be interpreted at a more latent level as well. In modern societies, young people have come to embody our desires and fears for the future.[24] Drawing on the symbol of the young has, at least since the early 1900s and since the 1904 publication of *Adolescence*, the classic work of psychologist and educator G. Stanley Hall, meant evoking a sense of societal change, for better or for worse.[25] Young people in the social worlds that Hall depicted and in the research on youth that draws on his work epitomize both a fin-de-siècle and a la belle époque expression. Fundamentally, this double perception of promise and threat is still related to interpretations of times to come, to the future. Young people as a category are treated as both scary and promising because they are seen as forerunners of the future. The future aspect is thus a key motivator for the organizing of, and the study of, young people. Young people are treated not merely as signifiers of the contemporary, but also as evocations of tomorrow and of the future in a broader sense. As in so many other political and social instances, the young often become lead players in narratives of the future. Cast in positive or negative terms, these narratives represent a colonization of the future, built on contemporary fears and desires.[26] Both desires and fears, however, are productive forces that propel action. Drawing on "the voice of the young" therefore expresses both hopes for and misgivings about the future.

The various groups centered around the young express desires to organize the future through young people and to legitimize contemporary Forum activities. The brochure presenting the Young Global Leaders calls them the "voice of an optimistic future, an energetic catalyst for change."[27] In the brochure, future fears are not described in terms of young people failing or at risk, a common trope in discourses on youth. To the contrary, the young people the Forum organizes are all described in such positive terms as "excellent" and "promising." And because the Forum needs young people to extend its capacity to mobilize for change, it is imperative to benefit from the power of mobilization of young people. In Forum terms, this mobilization is often depicted as "entrepreneurial" in spirit and activity.

Brothers and Sisters in the WEF

Within the WEF framework, young people are drawn on to legitimize the organization and its activities. Because the organization lacks both an external mandate and a mechanism for representation, it needs to show that people from all walks of life are invited. The young people who gladly commit time and energy to the Forum provide legitimacy to the WEF and assist in the acquisition of ideas that otherwise may have passed it by. This is highly valuable for the Forum, or it would not go to such lengths to obtain the participation of young people. At the same time, the energy and money invested in these arrangements are statements about the strength of the discourse on young people. An organization such as the WEF would have a hard time achieving legitimacy without some young faces. Their participation may not have much bearing on the core activities of the Forum: discretionary governance, soft diplomacy, the traveling market fairs it organizes in such places as Davos, or its regional meetings. Still, the Forum needs the young people to be there in order to safeguard it from the criticism of Anwen Abdelnour, her fellows, and other actors around the globe who find the Forum to be a place for old, white, rich men—not appealing enough regardless of their wealth, prestige, and status.

The aspiration that young people should be part of any official political arrangement is now an established part of at least Western discourse on citizenship, in the same way a contemporary political organization needs to be transparent.[28] The fact that it took WEF as long as it did to react and act in relation to the discourse on youth and transparency is a telling factor about its development as an organization. For decades, it was primarily positioned and used as a forum for business—even after the name change from the European Management Forum—and in practice not in need of relating to other societal discourses. Since the early 2000s, however, the Forum has strived for acceptance as an internationally reputed and trustworthy organization and has therefore started to accept and relate to outside claims for legitimacy. In this status striving, organizing younger people into networks and communities is energy and money well spent.

Conversely, at least some of the people calling themselves Global Shapers or Global Leadership Fellows are receiving a touch of the status that comes with a WEF identity or, at the least, a WEF entry on their CV. For some of the Young Global Leaders like the crown prince and princess of Denmark or Daniel Ek, this may not be required or sought for, but for many others, it may contribute to their careers. First, as is easily observable at the Shapers' web pages, being related to the WEF means a positive addition to their professional identities. Although they are accomplished in many ways—ambitious and usually highly successful in their careers—being publicly recognized as a WEF Shaper by this highly prestigious organization adds value. It is not certain that the prestige and aura of the WEF will rub off on all of the thousands of Shapers. But most likely, many of them seek this prestige, and for some of them, it probably happens.

There is another dimension in the relationship between the Forum and its younger invitees that should not be neglected: the brotherhood and sisterhood aspect. As one of the Shapers from the Alexandria hub writes on the hub's Facebook page: "Once a shaper—always a shaper!"[29] Certainly there is a great deal of hope and high aspirations in this exclamation. In a few years, these groups may be scattered, and little left but an entry on a CV and memories. On the other hand, some experiences will probably remain. This is most obvious for the group of GLFs, the fellows who work for three years at the Forum, sharing some important years at work and in shared housing. After the program, they will work in other global organizations, drawing on what they have learned within the Forum. Even this group may forget that they are affiliated to a WEF community, but it may well be that they—like many other people of their age set who have a common identity—maintain close ties over time, passing through a series of age-related status changes and following each other through life.[30] The term *age set* is most commonly used for tribal societies, but it is fully possible to apply it to a group with such close ties as the fellows have. In this case, the Forum's intention of drawing these young people into communities may have the intended consequences. As the title "fellow" indicates, the program brings young people into the organization. At the same time, the fellows become organized in relation to each other as part of a fellowship. They are therefore organized in two ways: as fully affiliated with the Forum, indicating that they will follow its norms, and as partly organized members within the fellowship, the norms of which they will also adhere to.[31] Moreover, as the age-set concept indicates, this will be a relationship that continues over the life course.

Drawing on young people in order to organize the future is an attempt to colonize the future. As Pierre Bourdieu reminds us, the word *young* is never innocent.[32] The frontier between youth and age is fought over in all societies, as is the meaning of what being young entails. In the narrative of the Forum regarding young people, they are described as naive, manifesting the dreams of the Forum as entrepreneurial and working for a greater good. Although only the GLFs have the position as interns, the narrative speaks of them as apprentices of the Forum. The idea is that by the time they graduate as "global leaders," they will be speaking the WEF lingo and drawing on its discreet multistakeholder practices. By organizing them as their affiliated members, with stronger or weaker ties to itself, the WEF seeks to shape the mind-sets of the young so they will reflect the value base of the Forum and hopes that they will bring these values into the future as they age. Like Trojan horses, they will carry the Forum values with them into the future while they are active in other organizations.

WEF as Futurologist

Mobilizing the voices of the young is one way to mobilize for the future. The Forum has also constructed a broad base as a projector of futures in the format of forecasts and prognoses. The annual *Global Risks Report* is the Forum's forecasting flagship, and "one of the fundamental activities that the industries and communities will have to take on," as by declared managing director Rita Lesley when we met her in Geneva.[33] The production of the report is supported by partnering corporations (in 2017 it was the Marsh & McLennan Companies and the Zurich Insurance group), and it benefits from collaboration with academic advisers, for instance, the Oxford Martin School and the National University of Singapore. The report describes a large number of projections of future risks and how they are interrelated, and it analyzes the contexts and structural predicaments of these risks. Along with the report, a short video on the Forum website presents a general understanding of the risks. The tone of the video is not alarming, but it is not merely descriptive. Ms. Lesley, who comes across as a proficient and focused woman in her thirties, tells us that the intent of the report is to frame the Forum's own future activities, but also to raise the flag early on for creeping risks, in the hope and anticipation of getting ahead of risks before they turn into shocks:

> So, the *Global Risks Report*, with its ten-year output, instead of actually experiencing the shocks physically, is meant to sort of enlighten people that this is something that you might need to think about, because it will have implications on your own society. And if it does, how would you actually better manage it?[34]

Lesley says that the report is intended to function as a diagnostic tool, with the purpose of finding the solution space and asking pertinent questions: What kinds of action can we take? What kinds of tangible interventions can we make? How can we make sure that the risk management process is beneficial and not counterproductive?

As the future cannot be observed, future scenarios such as those in the *Global Risks Report* are an interesting hybrid of fiction and fact, or at least something that could be treated as fact.[35] Identifying risk is a way of expressing the link between the perceived contemporary and an imagined future, and the identification of risk has come to be a core feature within the industry of futurology in later years. As an academic field and political practice, futurology was dominated by the forecasts and prognoses carried out by industrial think tanks and military interests beginning in the early 1960s; the Hudson Institute and the RAND Corporation in the United States were followed in Europe by the Club of Rome. Fundamental to the rise of future studies was the belief that prediction was not a product of fantasy but a field of reason.[36] After the fall of the Berlin Wall, there was a new wave of scenario planning. In the new situation, relief, hope, and anxiety were aired, often in the format of questions regarding what the future might bring. A small but lively intellectual industry rose to the challenge, creating scenarios for the emerging new world.[37] As the world turned, after 9/11 there was a heightened interest in identifying risks and scenario planning. The *Global Risks Report*, launched in 2005, is an example of the proliferation of these activities.

Crafting the *Global Risks Report*

Apart from texts, the common future scenario also builds on statistics, pictures, and graphs.[38] The WEF risk report is no exception. It is perceived as impressive, with text and graphs intertwined in the narration of future risk. Somewhat different from common scenarios is the fact that the WEF draws on evaluations from business, academia, and media—not merely on work done by the WEF itself. Basically the risk report is built on a survey the Forum undertakes, through which people from WEF communities can communicate what they believe to be coming risks in the next ten years. It is mainly the participants in the Global Future Councils, presented by the Forum as its brain trust, who are the survey respondents, together with people from the member corporations, and the other types of experts identified by the Forum—scientists, politicians, thought leaders, and civil society leaders, for instance. In addition, in later years, the some thirteen thousand CEOs participating in the annual *Global Competitiveness Report* have been asked to indicate what they perceive as the five main future risks.

Rita Lesley describes the complexities of the report in the following way:

> So we've got fifty global risks that we look at as a set, and then we conduct a perception survey over summer to fall every year, and then coming out from that, we sort of identify the key emerging themes in peoples' minds about the potential high-impact, high-likelihood risks for the coming ten years, and then we extract it into three different cases. It's almost like telling a story around these risks.[39]

In this process, Ms. Lesley and her team first work on the set of risks that will form the basis of the survey. When we meet her, there are fifty identified risks, but the number changes over time, she says. It had just expanded from thirty-seven risks in order to balance the risks internally. She explains that this was done because "some were much more macro, like climate change, and others were more like micro, like flooding, but we try to keep it on the same order as much as possible, so there is comparability." Later, the number would change again. In 2015 there were twenty-eight risks and in 2017 the number of risks had increased to thirty.[40]

The risks are constructed internally by Ms. Lesley's team, but are assessed by the WEF groups mentioned above, as well as by people connected to these groups. Drawing on these people framed as experts, the Forum describes the report as the outcome of an expert-based survey:

> We position it as sort of an expert perception survey, so it passes the mark of what the Forum thinks passes for an expert. We do turn to the Global Agenda Councils [renamed Global Future Councils in 2016]—it's mandatory for council members to respond to it—to the industry experts who are also part of the

community, and the same for the regional teams, meaning sort of the governments and international organizations. So the primary pool of sample is definitely Forum affiliated. The secondary one is not a huge pool, but it's the one that hasn't necessarily officially worked with the Forum, but in terms of risk work, we've identified quite a few people who are very interesting, who we are then trying to bring into the Forum. You know, we've got quite different processes to bring them on, so they're not quite there, but their opinions and perspectives are very valuable, so we do engage with them too.[41]

The criteria for being presented as a risk in the survey are set by the WEF itself. Rita Lesley explains: "Each risk will have global implications, in the sense that it affects more than one region and more than one industry, and it would be something that cannot be solved by one stakeholder." These risks can be of two sorts: coming about as a shock, like the financial crisis in 2008; or underlying factors amplifying the shock. In the case of the financial crisis that would be the "sort of structural issues around the financing incentives, or there might be structural issues around how the financial market is organized," she explains. These risks are not seen as static; they can all be put on or removed from the list at any time. If the creeping risk of ineffective antibiotics is mitigated, for instance, it would be removed from the list.

The Forum group that works on the report is relatively small: when we met with Lesley, there were only seven members. But as she explained the group is assisted by a large number of people around the world. The role of the team is to determine what to present in the report, decide how present it, and ensure that the information is valuable. As Rita Lesley says, "We can't really be repackaging old news, but at the same time we can't be too far out, because otherwise it becomes science fiction." Thus, the construction of the risks report is a balancing act between at least two issues affecting the work. One issue is the danger of missing something that later turns out to be a significant risk, affecting the lives of many people, simply because it is not mentioned in the channels that Lesley and the team have established. A second issue is to address a risk that many people consider not to be truly global but merely something that some actor wants to bring into the discussion. There is, of course, a strong interest among many actors to get their specific concern into the analysis and rated as a risk by the WEF. Since it is key that the WEF does not appear as taking sides in political issues, however, it is of great importance for the team to keep the risks that end up in the report as neutral and nonpolitical as possible.

Accordingly, an important part of the team's work is to validate and evaluate the importance of risks raised by their many contacts, so as to be in accordance with the mission of the WEF and yet noncommittal. Lesley explains:

> All the experts that we talk to have one agenda or another. So for us, it's also the agreement of the Forum to make sure that we're balanced and not inclined towards one risk or another, so we do try to make sure that we're looking at it more from a neutral background. We consult a series of experts to make sure that we're not actually listening to one set of people, with one set of ideas that really gets pushed through. So we do really try to maintain that neutrality as we actually select them as well.[42]

Moreover, identifying the risks shall by others not be associated with advocating for specific solutions. The Forum sees itself as raising awareness; it is for others to draw conclusions on how to act, as well as to act. More recently, though, the Forum has worked on missioning the concept of risk as interpreted within the Forum. One example is shaping a "risk culture" in the region of Latin America. As Lesley says, this is all about explaining risks and inducing leaders in the region to take action:

> First of all, it's also about explaining the risks in the regional context. So we need to make it relevant in that Latin American context, and for people within Latin America there are different country contexts. So we need to translate the global risks into the regional, and also the country level. Then by doing that, we also need to get the key decision makers drawn into the fact that this is something that they need to deal with, and that the country really needs to start working on it. We're working on sort of a series of dialogues for the Latin Americas, to really test what methodology is going to be the most applicable, and most effective. So this is pretty much the work in the pipeline right now that we're doing with them.[43]

The Forum thus intends to provide a product that is as neutral as possible, while at the same time propagating to mitigate the risks. Presenting risks, however, is not possible without some form of underlying and guiding values; otherwise the collection would appear haphazard. Furthermore, as is clear from the shifting number of risks over the years, risks are constructed in a value-based context that changes over time. By the same token, in order to map and explain the nature of the risks, larger structural forces need to be identified. To identify and communicate a risk, the Forum needs to explain some of its fundamental characteristics and describe the risk in context. The Forum has, in its own words, gone from "risk identification to thinking through risk interconnections and the potentially cascading effects that result."[44] These interconnections are established based on a narrative about what caused the individual risks. Beneath the narrative, there is an ontological understanding of what risks are and how they are related.

Futurists in general come in many fashions, offering utopias and dystopias, acting as fearmongers warning about the end of time or as positive brokers of ideas, solutions, and projects.[45] In the WEF risk scenario, risks are primarily understood as opportunities. Underlying WEF projections and imaginations of what the future will appear like is primarily a sense of hope. The projections are typically presented with appealing wording and layout, and in easily accessible language and scant in-depth analysis. The key message—as more generally in the large bulk of WEF reports, blogs, news updates, and so forth—is one of problems that can be solved, not of troublesome futures. The future appears ripe with opportunities. Issues are presented but tightly aligned with the promise of ways to handle them. The *Annual Report 2012–2013* tightly couples the sense of urgency with the promise of opportunities:

> We live in a fast-moving, highly interconnected world, yet our existing systems, structures and formal institutions no longer suffice. Pressing global problems can arise quickly and without warning. At the same time, new and unprecedented opportunities for global growth and positive change are emerging, ready to be harnessed for the future of humanity.[46]

The promise of growth and future markets is never far away in the WEF context. It is an integrated part of the WEF narrative and closely related to the idea of aligned values that we presented in the Introduction, emphasizing that there is no issue without a solution that markets supported by governments cannot solve. In the same vein, risks are, according to the Forum, to be treated as new beginnings.

The Metaframe

The metaframe for the narrative that the Forum tells and retells in the *Global Risks Report* and its many other products is a story of global future risks linked to the expanding interconnectedness of the world. Accordingly, in the WEF narrative, risks exist in and by themselves, but because the world is seen as increasingly interconnected, risks become multiplied in unprecedented and daunting ways. Klaus Schwab wrote in the Preface of the 2015 *Global Risks Report*, "Across every sector of society, decision-makers are struggling to cope with heightened complexity and uncertainty resulting from the world's highly interconnected nature and the increasing speed of change."[47] In addition, he uses the term *hyperconnectivity* repeatedly, indicating that "over the past years, the speed of transmission and the strength of interconnections have been increased" to the state where communication has become a problem.[48] Risks such as climate change, geopolitical uncertainty, rising inequalities, increasing nationalistic sentiment, and lack of regulatory mechanisms are thus understood to be sharply intensified because of their interconnectedness.

At the policy level, the main identified cause for problems related to interconnection and hyperconnectivity is the lack of a shared view on behalf of governments, business, INGOs, and NGOs. Since the inception of the *Global Risks Report* in 2005, the intent has been to foster a shared view on the most pressing issues. Schwab writes that "the shared understanding of challenges is needed as a base for multi-stakeholder collaboration, which has seen increasing recognition as the most effective way to address global risks and build resilience against them."[49] The concerns about the future can therefore be mitigated by way of WEF getting all the significant actors to share its view of contemporary challenges.

The interest of fostering this shared view is related to the fundamental idea within the Forum that it is possible to construct images of the future and risks that leaders from all walks of life could get to know, agree on, and act on. Essentially the Forum believes that there are solutions that will benefit everyone in a win-win way. In the espoused view of the Forum, there need be no winners, no losers, and no power relations. It is a model devoid of power and conflict, built on assumptions of trust, mutual understanding, and consent—in other words, harmoniously aligning economic and social values through consensual relationships.

The alignment of economic and social values has been part of the WEF from the time of its first meeting in 1971. It has since been worked on and argued for in various versions. As we noted in the Introduction, the WEF launched the so-called Davos Equation in the 2000s in order to emphasize the bond between the economic and social worlds. The equation presented the idea of symmetry beyond what at first could be seen as radically diverging tendencies and interests. Underlying the equation is the understanding that economic growth can work in tandem with a responsibility for the social and natural environment. With the goal of building and sustaining economic development, the WEF wants to promote ways to mitigate global social risks, promote health for all, improve social welfare, and foster environmental sustainability. In this vision, economic growth and social and environmental sustainability are brought into alignment.

The metaframe conceptualizing economic and social values as inextricably intertwined is worked on within all Forum settings. As evident in its statement that the Forum is "the International Organization for Public–Private Cooperation," it wants to play a role in the alignment of different and ostensibly divergent interests and values. In the 2000s, the concept of global corporate citizenship was added to the conceptual portfolio as a way of describing the entangled nature of market and society priorities.[50] Within the Forum, the notion of corporate citizenship is commonly understood to be tightly connected to the multistakeholder approach, expressing the interdependence of all stakeholder groups.

Organizing the Future

In the 2020 vision for the WEF that Schwab put forth, the future and the contemporary are entangled and speak to the Forum's future:

> Global challenges can never be met alone. Their complexity and interdependence must be addressed by integrated and interdisciplinary action—from business, government and civil society.
>
> To succeed, such cooperation requires a robust international framework: one that transcends the traditional barriers of politics and economics; one that brings different organizations and individuals together to form true public–private partnerships, and one that has the trusted organizational capability to pursue pragmatic solutions.[51]

In the Forum metaframe, a true public–private partnership is the solution to the daunting complexities haunting contemporary global society. The international framework that the Forum wishes to construct starts inside the dark walls of the Forum headquarters building. As Schwab presents it, it is the only organization with the capacity to address these complexities. The Forum intends to expand, globalizing its activities in order to establish a local presence around the world. In the view of the Forum, to meet these complex challenges, leadership is called for. The Forum has a special calling to respond to these challenges.

For the WEF, as for most other think tanks and policy-oriented organizations, the future is not completely open. As a fundamentally political organization, the Forum advocates specific choices for the future—choices that are aligned to its value base. Clearly this is not how the Forum would present its activities. Rather, it wants to be seen as providing tools for others to make informed choices. But the WEF does more than merely offer tools; it takes action in defining and articulating a preferred version of the future. And judging by its finances, the media attention it receives, and the credibility given to the organization by the presence of top-level politicians, business leaders, and governmental bureaucrats, it does so with a measure of success. WEF activities, its efforts to organize young and exceptional people and its socio-economic scenarios, will likely have consequences for what is possible to think and suggest in terms of policymaking.

Through its activities, WEF articulates and opens up a specific horizon, to use historian Reinhart Koselleck's term; here it is a figurative and analytical device to negotiate the relationships among experience, everyday life, and the past and future.[52] The sense of the future at the WEF is generated through tensions between experience and expectation, between identified risks and possible solutions. Their increasing divergence opens a horizon toward which agency can be projected and the authority and influence of the WEF may be leveraged. This horizon is envisioned from headquarters by the shores of Lake Geneva. It is based on the one-world perspective aptly described by sociologist John Law, relying on a self-contained myth of "Northern" beliefs.[53] Epistemologically, this myth entails that no account is required of what comprises the understandings, analyses, and descriptions possible.[54] Based on a one-world perspective, accounts of the state of the world and its future are presented as natural and realistic, not as based on political choices. In contrast, deviations from the main one-world narrative are reduced to ideology or poor knowledge. Postcolonial understandings of the multiplicities of ontologies that cannot be included in "our own" is absent in WEF's conceptualizations of present and future.[55] Staff, funders, and invitees may individually express such a postcolonial view, but it is not inherent in the understandings of the Forum. The Forum speaks with one voice only. The Forum narrative speaks of the market mechanisms and processes of globalization and technological advancement without analyzing the causes of the social order.

At heart, future-oriented communities of young people in tandem with risk and future scenarios are ingredients in the aspirations of shaping the world in a specific direction. They articulate a particular form of "anticipatory knowledge,"[56] geared to contribute to the shaping of political priorities and agendas, reflecting WEF's central values and priorities. Its future communities aim to shape the youth who have been made part of the Forum so they will carry the narrative of multistakeholder deliberations further. The risk scenarios aim to shape perceptions of what constitute global problems and how they might best be addressed and governed. In this way, they contribute to the anticipatory governance potential of the WEF: governance geared to integrate imaginaries of the future into regulatory processes. The scenarios for possible futures developed in this context inform new ways of building resilience to risks and threats of various kinds through close collaboration with its funders: the largest transnational corporations in the world. From this perspective, the WEF's future activities beg central questions about whose futures are being aired, articulated, and perceived to be resilient and whose futures remain mere potential. This is the theme of the next chapter.

6 Political Sway

After Donald Trump won the US presidential election in 2016, Canadian journalist Naomi Klein wrote that the result was to be blamed on "the Davos class," a hyperconnected network of bankers, tech billionaires, elected leaders, and Hollywood celebrities, having a ball at a party that Trump voters in their hearts knew they were not invited to.[1] Somewhat ironically, Trump was reported to use the elitist argument for not going to the Annual Meeting at Davos (which he at the time had never been invited to).[2] In both these reports, "Davos" is proposed as a driver of global elite projects.

As previous chapters have shown, the WEF certainly convokes global nobility. But what kind of political project is it advocating? Forum spokespeople would say that it is impartial, merely acting as a catalyst for change and not drivers of any specific change. Earlier research, as reported, for instance, in geographer David Harvey's *A Brief History of Neoliberalism,* commonly demonstrates that the Forum is a driver of a neoliberal project.[3] Our analysis shows that while these reports are accurate, the description gives only half the picture—and it may be stressing the least important part of the Forum's political sway. While never giving up on its defense of capitalism, the Forum over the decades has gone from promoter of free trade to critic of no-fettered economic globalization and promoter of social developments. Importantly, what has not changed is the advocacy for letting corporations into politics. The allegedly nonpolitical vision of the Forum turns out to be a highly politicized project, not merely in its content but by reframing the very forms that political actions and politics may take.

The aim of this chapter is to unfold the sometimes messy and conflicting political underpinnings of the Forum. Based on our analysis of core texts from the Forum (such as articles written by Klaus Schwab, internal historical overviews, and annual reports), we describe the assemblage of political ideas and positions articulated by the Forum. Our view is that the Forum advocates a specific form of neoliberal thought combined with third way social democracy, and a particular version of a set of ideas regarding the role of business in politics. Together these ideas underpin a postpolitical paradox in which conflict is seemingly turned into consensus, at the same time as the all-inclusive multistakeholder model turns out to be a mechanism for elite distinction. This is the political sway of the Forum.

Political Composition

In academic circles, WEF is commonly portrayed as an organization promoting neoliberalism. Some scholars describe the Forum as "the most paradigmatic example of neoliberal structuralism,"[4] and yet others portray the organization as one of the institutional forms that advance the hegemonic project of globalizing capitalism and a prescription for neoliberal governance.[5] Indeed, when comparing WEF reports and texts to the oft-cited description of neoliberalism proposed by David Harvey, we find traces of the neoliberal framework expressed. Harvey writes that neoliberalism is

> a theory of political economic practices that proposes that human wellbeing can best be advanced by liberating individual entrepreneurial freedoms and skills within an institutional framework characterized by strong private property rights, free markets and free trade. The role of the state is to create and to preserve an institutional framework appropriate to such practices.[6]

The emphasis on free markets, free trade, entrepreneurship, and a government that supports these types of practices is at the core of the WEF assemblage of political views and its advocacy. In a selection of 285 WEF reports from 2000, 2005, 2010, and 2015, we ran a few simple calculations, counting words and statements.[7] We found the word stems of *entrepreneur*, *innovation*, and *markets* over 15,160 times in these reports. The word *solidarity* was mentioned 22 times and *cooperation* approximately 1,300 times, reaching its height in 2010 with the publication of the Global Redesign Initiative report, *Everybody's Business: Strengthening Global Cooperation in a more Interdependent World*, where *cooperation* appeared 388 times. Furthermore, for most of the challenges and risks introduced by the Forum, the solution advocated includes core neoliberal ideas. When talking of global population growth, for example, more technological development is called for: "Preparing for a world of 9 billion people requires the foresight to invest in scientific research and develop breakthrough technological solutions."[8] And in relation to climate change, the need for "shifting in" the private sector is stressed, again in combination with technological advancement:

> For this reason, the new climate regime should have a very different geometry than its predecessor. In addition to top-down elements such as binding national commitments, other mechanisms and initiatives are needed to stimulate a shift in private sector behavior more directly and rapidly. Governments must create clarity about the successor to the Kyoto Protocol in Copenhagen but they should also build a complementary enabling architecture capable of accelerating progress within the private sector over the next five to ten years in those areas with greatest potential to lower the carbon intensity of economic growth, such as energy efficiency, technology development, low-carbon infrastructure investment and deforestation, especially in developing economies.[9]

In addition to the pressure for technological development, the WEF has been a strong advocate for free trade and reducing trade barriers since it began in 1974. In discussions of the 2008 crisis, trade was acknowledged as the reason for the economic downturn and the way to recovery:

> There is no doubt that, in the same way trade has contributed to spreading the downturn across the globe, it can foster the nascent recovery. Policymakers can support this process by reducing domestic barriers to trade. By doing so, governments will benefit not only their own economies, but also those of their trading partners, thereby contributing to a virtuous cycle of recovery. In recent years, market uncertainties have also highlighted the importance of smoothing the path between buyers and sellers and reducing the cost and uncertainty of the transaction itself.[10]

In reports, blogs, speeches, and statements to the press, the neoliberal approach is embedded in the propositions advocated by the Forum to effectively deal with any issue. Saying that the WEF is a neoliberal outpost thus captures some of its political content. This contention needs to be qualified, however. Geographer Clive Barnett has rightly observed that there is no such thing as neoliberalism.[11] What exists are versions of neoliberalism. Interestingly, the WEF version is a social democratic one.

Third Way Social Democracy

Broadly seen, the political alterations of the WEF have come in two shifts, leading to the specific version of neoliberalism it has come to promote. The first shift is recognizable in the late 1980s. Political scientist Elisabeth Friesen notes that in spite of a fundamental interest in safeguarding capitalism, prior to 1989 the Forum took existing rules and regulations as a given, showing no engagement in neoliberal advocacy.[12] Change was on the way, however, and by 1990 the "Davos consensus" was in place, reassembling the Washington consensus, hailing neoliberal policy prescriptions of privatization, deregulation, and economic restructuring. But as early as the mid-1990s, the WEF started to send other signals, criticizing unfettered globalization. In an opinion piece, Chairman Schwab and a close colleague at the time, Claude Smadja, critiqued unfettered globalization:

> Economic globalization has entered a critical phase. A mounting backlash against its effects, especially in the industrial democracies, is threatening a very disruptive impact on economic activity and social stability in many countries.[13]

The argument addressed high-speed capital transactions: how they lead to a competition among states and to a "creative destruction" (using Schumpeter's 1942 concept), with a pronounced emphasis on the destruction.[14] According to Schwab and Smadja, it was obvious that "the head-on mega-competition that is part and parcel of globalization leads to a winner-take-all-situation meaning that those who come out on top win big, and those who lose, lose even bigger."[15] To their minds, what was needed was partly to convince people that globalization has tremendous possibilities and to come up with coherent, effective, and sustainable approaches to help people cope with these structural adjustments. In this version, the neoliberal credo was still relatively strong. Schwab and Smadja talked not of regulation but of changing people and nation-states in order to be flexible and adaptable in the new situation.

Over the years, the tone changed in favor of a combination of market competition and state-based regulation. Capitalism continues to be enshrined in the principles of free markets and guaranteed ownership, but the political position of the WEF began taking the form of a composition of neoliberal axioms regarding entrepreneurship, free markets, innovation, and ideas regarding social rights recognizable from social democracy and socio-liberalism.[16] As Klaus Schwab expressed it after the 2012 Annual Meeting, "The ideology of a free but socially committed and fairly regulated market economy was never questioned in Davos." He then continued, speaking of the Nordic model:

One of the criticisms of capitalism centers on the widening gap between winners and losers, due to the so-called turbo-capitalism that is a result of global competition. In this context, the so-called Nordic model demonstrates that a high degree of labor market flexibility and social welfare systems do not have to be mutually exclusive—indeed, they can actually be combined to very good effect. This type of economic policy also enables countries to invest in innovation, childcare, education and training. The Scandinavian countries, which underwent a similar banking crisis in the 1990s to that which we are now experiencing in other Western economies, have shown that by reforming regulation and social welfare systems, flexible labor and capital markets really are compatible with social responsibility. So it is no coincidence that these countries are now among the most competitive economies in the world.

It is indisputable that an ideology founded on personal freedom and social responsibility gives both individuals and the economy the greatest possible scope to develop. To ensure that this capacity for development is fair, better regulation and safeguards are required—above all for capital markets—which also necessitate global coordination. In this sense, capitalism is now called upon to make the necessary adjustments for it to remain a key pillar of our free market economic system, but also for it to adapt to today's circumstances and to be the servant rather than the master of a socially responsible market economy.[17]

The political outlook of the WEF that Schwab describes is based on "personal freedom" and "social responsibility." As WEF would reason, this is what will promote development; to ensure this, "better regulation and safeguards are required," and capitalism must adjust to these requirements. Schwab is somewhat vague about what he refers to as capitalism in these writings. Still, this reformed and better version of capitalism, embedded in social relations of equity and society, comes close to what sociologist Anthony Giddens termed the third way of social democracy:[18]

Classic social democracy thought of wealth creation as almost incidental to its basic concerns with economic redistribution. The neoliberals placed competitiveness and the generating of wealth much to the forefront. Third way politics also gives very strong emphasis to these qualities, which have an urgent importance given the nature of the global market place. They will not be developed, however, if individuals are abandoned to sink or swim in an economic whirlpool. Government has an essential role to play in investing in the human resources and infrastructure needed to develop an entrepreneurial culture.[19]

When we counted word frequencies again from the 285 WEF reports, a more complex picture emerged, reminiscent of third way arguments. Several words are mentioned thousands of times: *government* 7,750 times, *political* 2,403 times, and *environment* 5,078 times. Moreover, reports and documents that were published on the WEF web page in fall 2015 made it clear that neoliberal ideologists such as Friedrich von Hayek and Milton Friedman would probably be dissatisfied to learn that they were rarely mentioned within the Forum by staff or by participants publicizing themselves in reports and on the WEF website. If neoliberal exponents are mentioned, it is rarely in a positive way. The most typical referencing reads something like, "We have come a long way from Friedman." Keynes is more often referred to than Hayek and mentioned more positively than either Hayek or Friedman. Marx is mentioned more positively than the neoliberal gurus, albeit usually jokingly, as if it is funny to use his name in the WEF setting. Moreover, the state is a key actor, and an esteemed one, in all WEF statements. Even in the statutes for the WEF foundation, the role of governments and intergovernmental organizations is accorded a specific paragraph, stating that it fully respects the essential role that governments play. This acknowledgment also captures WEF reasoning regarding politics and markets.[20] Instead of a "primacy of politics," which would have been the classic social democracy point of view, there is a "primacy of markets," but with an important ideological add-on, claiming that markets have to be embedded in state regulation.[21] These changes in the views of markets and states, on behalf of the WEF, and social democracy we may add, can be seen as parallel and, in part, symbiotic with alterations of stances on neoliberalism. Hans-Jürgen Bieling writes that neoliberalism in its general interpretations has, partly as a response to economic and political changes, gone from a phase in the 1970s of an "aggressive neoliberalism," through a phase during the 1980s and 1990s of "euphoric neoliberalism," to a third stage of "disciplinary neoliberalism" during which social democratic regimes have consolidated the neoliberal framework by strengthening corporatist forms of socioeconomic cooperation.[22]

Thus, focusing merely on the free markets and entrepreneurial aspects of WEF political content ignores half the message conveyed, making it difficult to see what is unique and how the unique forms part of what is in vogue, as seen from a broader perspective. The form of neoliberalism that the Forum promotes has been both deepened and altered over time in the direction of third way social democracy. In practice, there is a strong resemblance between third way social democracy and WEF neoliberalism. The head-on neoliberal struggle against the welfare state and social regulation has been abandoned and replaced by more cooperative strategies, in the direction of a market- and competition-oriented reform of the welfare state.[23]

The issue of gender equality is an interesting case in point in relation to the issue of embedding markets in regulatory, government-based grids. Since 2006 the Forum has issued what it terms a Global Gender Gap Index (GGGI) as a framework for capturing the magnitude of gender-based disparities. The rankings are designed to create global awareness of the challenges posed by gender gaps and the opportunities created by reducing them. The report aligns with the Forum's general interest in broadening its outlook beyond mere corporate interests. During the years, the reports not only show that closing the gender gap is of economic value for both corporations and governments, but also draw on the moral argument of equality. "Women represent one half of the population and it is self-evident that they must have equal access to health, education, earning power and political representation."[24] As international political economist Juanita Elias has suggested in her study of the GGGI, the advent of a post-feminist agenda is characterized by the incorporation of feminist positions into political and institutional life.[25] The WEF incorporation of gender equality is, according to this perspective, related to the unfolding of the practices of neoliberal governance and the need to mitigate the consequences of unhampered economic globalization. The WEF interest in gender equality is part of "rollout" neoliberalism, in which third way social democracy is a prime example. That is, the urge for combining economic and social interests represents both the frailty of neoliberalism as a political idea and the deepening of the very same idea, but partly dressed in new clothes.[26]

In regard to the political sway of the Forum, it has been argued that both center and social democratic politicians had to adapt to the neoliberal consent that the Forum had been part of establishing.[27] What we see is that over time, it changed its political discourse in line with the embedded market view of such center-oriented politicians as Tony Blair, Gerhard Schröder, Göran Persson, and Bill Clinton, who have regularly participated in Forum activities. It is critical to remember that the political practice of the Forum is one of give-and-take. As we showed in Chapter 3, it is based on reciprocal processes, where status and agency are cocreated. The political tycoons come because it provides them with the prestige of being let into the Davos elite. Still, many of them most likely understand their worth to the Forum. In order to remain of consequence, the Forum needs to keep the attention of the top political players and certainly attempts to both listen to and incorporate parts of their invitees' political messages.

Redirecting Politics

WEF would shun any typification, specifically political ones. A core Forum value is flexibility in interpreting political context so as to serve its mission statement of "improving the state of the world." As Klaus Schwab underlined at the recognition by the Swiss state of the Forum as an international organization: "Such an open platform for cooperation has almost limitless potential."[28] This means that it may combine the elements it finds most productive: there is no other position to which it is true in the logic of the organization. Flexibility and pragmatism are core values for the organization, more so than political ideology or specific political issues. To be sure, it is likely that funders have some limits as to what they will accept from the Forum. Balancing funder interests is, however, a constant issue within the organization, and so far, it is clear that it has been able to construct its own flexible but highly political path. What is not up for discussion is the concept of multistakeholder dialogue. In all its contemporary communication, WEF underscores the fact that since its inception in 1971, it has had one overarching idea: the multistakeholder approach:

> The idea at the core of the Davos meetings was to create a platform where managers could meet their stakeholders and discuss their mutual responsibility. According to the stakeholder approach, the management of the enterprise acts as a trustee for all stakeholders—not merely for shareowners. It is based on the principle that each individual is embedded in societal communities in which the common good can only be promoted through the interaction of all participants—and business success is also embedded in this interaction.[29]

Apart from saving capitalism from political attacks and disruptive crises, the fundamental Forum idea since its inception has been to create a space for a range of actors—a space in which people from "all walks of life" may discuss what is conceived of as the most pressing societal issues of our times. As we discussed in Chapter 2, providing a secluded space for political and corporate leaders to deliberate is at the core of the organization's interest and a key component of the WEF allure. The significance of this space was accentuated in the wake of the financial crisis in 2008. The articles Klaus Schwab signed in the years following the crisis had the multistakeholder dialogue as the central message. In an analysis of the financial crisis, Schwab wrote, "Our objective is to find answers that are not only holistic and systematic, but also take into account all of the stakeholders in our global society."[30] The same message appeared the next year:

> The state alone cannot manage all the global problems today. Solutions to global problems can only be found if there is a partnership of all actors—business, science and civil society. What we need, therefore, is a renaissance of the Stakeholder Principle—but at a much higher level. Governments, enterprises, universities, NGOs: all of them are Stakeholders of our global future.[31]

The same message occurs over and over again. When envisioning the role of the Forum in the years to come, Schwab posits it as the only organization that can properly meet global challenges:

> Global challenges can never be met alone. Their complexity and interdependence must be addressed by integrated and interdisciplinary action—from business, government and civil society. To succeed, such cooperation requires a robust international framework: one that transcends the traditional barriers of politics and economics; one that brings different organizations and individuals together to form true public-private partnerships, and one that has the trusted organizational capability to pursue pragmatic solutions. Alone among international organizations, the World Economic Forum provides this collaborative global framework.[32]

From a political perspective, Forum activities and the striving for multistakeholder dialogue can—at least since the redirection in 1987, when the European Management Forum was turned into the World Economic Forum—be read as a search for finding an answer to the longstanding question of how markets are to be seen and treated by politics. Are markets to be free from political intervention? In the first years of the new WEF, parallel to the boom of the Washington consensus (implying a neoliberal understanding of the relationship between markets and politics) and market-based policies on a world scale, the organization favored answers that more one-sidedly underscored market-based solutions to societal issues and the liberalization of markets. As we have shown in this chapter, though, this policy direction changed as public critique against the detrimental influences of globalization was more loudly aired. Schwab and Smadja were as early as many trade unions around the world in their critique of untamed economic globalization.

A central aspiration tied to neoliberalism and Third Way social democracy concerns not only the content of politics but the form in which politics is done.[33] In accordance with stressing markets as the core of both economic and social development, market actors are also conceived as relevant participants in policymaking. The often-referred-to trends toward increasing partnership-based forms of governance and the blurring of boundaries between the public domain and the market domain are a consequence of this reconceptualization of who or what is a relevant policy participant. This redirection of politics reflects a concern held by neoliberals and social democrats alike regarding the risk of state failure and the need to involve relevant stakeholders in political and policy processes. The WEF may be seen as contributing to the refashioning of politics along these lines. In the WEF version, politics—albeit in the broad sense—is done in a format that differs from the traditional format, based on elected politicians representing various constituencies. In the WEF format of politics, the organization makes its own choices regarding who may participate—whether CEOs, state leaders, or church leaders. The content of the WEF version of politics—saving capitalism—is thus but one part of the WEF's political message.

The Political Multistakeholder Model

Klaus Schwab's 1971 book, which we described in the Introduction, is essential to the formulation of the multistakeholder model as it is practiced within the WEF.[34] In it, Schwab analyzes how the modern enterprise in mechanical engineering may survive and prosper. These ideas were refined two years later in the Davos Manifesto of 1973, a treatise signed by the participants at Davos that year. At the core of this model is the "principle that each individual is embedded in societal communities in which the common good can only be promoted through the interactions of all participants."[35] In line with classic liberal interpretations of society, formulated, for example, in classic liberal economy and politics, communities are understood in this discussion as conglomerates of individuals, more or less loosely organized and joined together around issues. Seen from this point of view, the neoliberal part of WEF politics, with the interest in downgrading state intervention, is paired with an emphasis on nonstate government. The partnership-based program of the WEF is seen as fully expected from this perspective.

The marriage between neoliberalism as a political -ism and the multistakeholder concept does not rule out proximity to third way social democracy. To the contrary, the governance structure that WEF promotes ties in well with third way social democracy. When Tony Blair used the concept of stakeholder society in introducing New Labour, his interest was not merely to change the content of politics but also to find new ways of doing politics for a social democracy that believed that its older concepts were long due for a change.[36] The launching of the stakeholder society aimed at ensuring that every individual citizen had a stake in society and a voice in the way it was to be run. In order to reach that aim, New Labour meant that firms should be reorganized so that all stakeholders—shareholders, consumers, and employees, for example—would be able to participate in decision making. These decisions should be as moral as economically rational. Burkitt and Ashton noted in an early exploration of New Labour economics:

> New Labour's stakeholder economy is largely founded on the concept of social responsibility which is so central to communitarian economic thought. It hinges upon the idea that many interest groups may be said to have "a stake" in certain activities, not necessarily because they have a financial interest in them, but because they are affected by them. These stakes should be recognized by those whose actions may impinge upon them. Individuals should recognize that their behaviour can have repercussions upon society. They should act in a responsible way that does not damage others and also repay the costs expended by society on their behalf—for higher education, for instance. Stakeholder firms must act with responsibility to their stakeholders—employees, customers and surrounding geographic communities.[37]

There are striking similarities between New Labour's stakeholder society and the WEF multistakeholder concept. This is not to say that either party—WEF and Labour in Britain—shared and explored each other's views by necessity, although that is fully possible, as Tony Blair has long been a regular guest at the Forum. Nevertheless, not only do both concepts stress the importance of community as opposed to conflict; both also stress responsibility and the moral aspects of economy. As we showed in Chapter 3, a central part of the consequences of WEF activities is its ability to educate and foster its funders into corporate citizenship. From this point of view, the multistakeholder concept can be interpreted as a third way social-democratic redirection of politics, talked of by actors on both Left and Right. Moreover, both camps touch common ground in the use of the stakeholder concept as firmly resting on a technocratic notion of society and politics.

The multistakeholder concept is truly a political concept that argues for a particular conception of how politics is to be done. Accordingly, each challenge recognized by the Forum is identified as immanently containing the one way forward that will fit all. There is thus a strong positivist belief in the possibility of finding the one solution, based on unequivocal empirical evidence, that will work for all actors involved.[38] If the right people assemble and deliberate, they will be able to find the answer the world is looking for. Pivotal here is the role of business as stakeholder and actor in politics. This role does not materialize without conflict, however.

A Postpolitical Paradox

We are quiet, sitting on the WEF shuttle to the Swissôtel in Istanbul in June 2013. Along with us on the minibus are two young men about to start their workday at the regional event we are heading to. They are not Forum staff but have flown in to oversee the audio system of the regional event. We are quiet because they have informed us that they have been instructed not to talk to participants.

This is our first day in Istanbul, and we do not know what awaits us. Our nervousness increases as we approach the hotel. Men in uniforms carrying automatic weapons surround the hotel area, and it is fortified with sandbags. It looks like a battlefield. We are not accustomed to this level of securitization and uneasily grasp our handbags. Will they point these weapons in our direction when they realize that the shuttle is used as a Trojan horse for two social scientists? But the driver simply drives the shuttle through the barricades, and we enter the hotel. Later the same day, we incidentally end up in an elevator with Klaus and Hilde Schwab, riding with two armed guards. Silently we consider giving an elevator presentation of our project, but the ride is brief and we are overwhelmed by the presence of the guards protecting the Schwabs, so we are quiet.

This glimpse from Istanbul speaks to the security level and the conflictual character of the Forum (Photo 6.1). We have recurrently witnessed and experienced this as a ramification for our fieldwork in more or less direct forms. In Davos, walking in the close vicinity of the Steigenberger Grandhotel Belvedere, we spot snipers on the roof and are stopped by armed Swiss military police. For some reason not communicated to us, we are made to wait before continuing our walk to the café where we are heading. A pair of what looks

PHOTO 6.1. Layer upon layer of security in Davos street life during the week of WEF Annual Meeting 2011. Source: Garsten and Sörbom.

like middle-aged skiers beside us, carrying their alpine gear, wants to cross the street. The military police apparently have no time or intention of communicating their message: they push the couple against the nearest wall and forcefully hold them until a car with tinted windows has passed. Later, in the line to the Open Forum in Davos, conflict arises as a young man argued for his right to wait for a friend. Suddenly the guards overpower him and physically throw him out of the building. These incidents occurred instantaneously. Entering the scene two minutes later, it would be difficult to believe that violent conflict had just transpired.

Conflict and *politics* are two words that the Forum would not use to describe itself. In its own conception, it does not engage in political pursuit, and its quests for improving the state of the world do not involve conflict with other actors. Yet its appreciation of enterprise management as accountable to all stakeholders means a redirection of the idea of politics. It indicates a far-reaching interpretation of where politics is to be undertaken, discussed, advocated, interpreted, and formatted. The institution of politics in modern societies has been understood in terms such as *parliament, government*, and *political parties*. These arrangements and the concepts related to them have been, and still are, accurate, even though new actors and arenas have been brought into politics both nationally and internationally, going from typical government procedures to various forms of governance. However, the global multistakeholder arena established by the WEF challenges the government view of politics—not only by being far from parliaments and governmental buildings, but also because it is based on a private initiative and interest without the mechanism of representation. As we showed in Chapter 2, it is the funding corporations that mandate WEF rather than a public constituency. The politics formed as part of WEF activities is, in a sense, the opposite of the politics of governments. Moreover, in contradiction to governmental politics, it attempts to be nonpolitical and based on harmony seeking. Indeed, a moral component in the WEF version of politics echoes social anthropologist's George Lakoff's contention that politics is inherently moral.[39]

Political scientist Chantal Mouffe takes issue with the consensus model implicit in the reformulations of the nature of politics from later decades. Mouffe describes how the consensus model postulates the possibility of win-win politics, suggesting that there are solutions that are beneficial for everyone in society.[40] For Mouffe, the "excess of consensus" is potentially socially explosive: "Democracy is in peril not only when there is insufficient consensus and allegiance to the values it embodies, but also when its agonistic dynamic is hindered by an apparent excess of consensus, which usually masks a disquieting apathy."[41] According to Mouffe, it is a typical liberal illusion that we can have pluralism without antagonism, as that would entail losing what politics is fundamentally about. In insisting on the conflict dimension of the political, Mouffe argues that politics needs to distinguish between us and them in order to handle existing and unavoidable conflicts in society.

Employing Mouffe's argument, we suggest that WEF conceptualizes its activities as in harmony with the rest of the world, in search for solutions that will benefit all. In the Forum discourse, the search for common denominators is far more common than the recognition of conflict. Likewise, the solutions that the Forum offers suggest a win-win situation. The us-versus-them distinction, so crucial in much political thinking, is substituted by notions of partnership and collaboration, as in the WEF narrative, there is no basic antagonist between state and market, social accountability and business. By insisting that corporations are only one stakeholder among many, the power of corporations to have an impact on social, cultural, and environmental aspects of the surrounding society is acknowledged but downplayed.

WEF may, in this sense, illustrate a preference for what Mouffe later termed "the post-political consensus": the refusal of the antagonist dimension of politics.[42] As Mouffe shows, politics was long based on two conflicting traditions of politics. In the liberal version, politics was based on the interest of individual liberty and pluralism, whereas in the democratic tradition, ideas of popular sovereignty and equality were at the core. These traditions stood in an adversarial relationship, a state of relations that was generally accepted as legitimate. This is no longer the case. In a time of postpolitical consensus, Mouffe argues, politics is not acted on as a strife between conflictual societal ontologies; rather, it becomes a game played out in the register of morality.[43]

The WEF and the multistakeholder model is a constitutive part of this form of postpolitical consensus. Interestingly, however, discourse and practice are decoupled within the Forum, as discourse is geared toward finding the solutions that will fit all, abolishing the possibility of dissent and including the world as its constituency. In practice, however, the Forum is always in conflict with the world that is not allowed in. It constructs distinctions between those who are let in and those who are not. The us-versus-them dimension that Mouffe calls for is reinstalled in the midst of this conflict-avoiding arena. That is the postpolitical paradox of the WEF: dissolving the us-versus-them dimension by employing a win-win concept, at the same time as this dimension is brought to life as a result of its elitist ideology and practice. Bringing corporations into politics defies longstanding notions of politics, and it takes its toll attempting to do so.

Conclusion

A New Narrative for Future Globalization?

In March 2017, Klaus Schwab wrote:

> The world is at a historic crossroads. Market extremism, often labeled neoliberalism, which has shaped our national and global policies for the past three decades, has become a toxic fuel for the stuttering engine for global growth. It has also generated polluting side effects that are no longer tolerated by large portions of society.
>
> Yet market-driven globalization has lifted over a billion people out of poverty and has been an overall driver of improved standards of living. In its present form, however, it is no longer fit for purpose in our current—nor particularly our future—context.[1]

According to Klaus Schwab's—and the Forum's—understanding, the world faces severe and acute challenges, not because of market-based capitalism but because of the inadequacies of implementing a market-based system of development. Corrupt practices and speculative financial practices have several negative consequences: they distort the fairness of markets; transform production processes; emphasize automation, capital, and innovation over manual and, soon, intellectual labor; and pose serious threats to the preservation and regeneration of our environment through excessive use and erosion of our natural resources, seriously disrupting the functioning of the global market. Market-based capitalism in its contemporary version has lost its legitimacy. According to Schwab, "We need a new narrative for globalization"—one that recognizes the significance of innovation and competitiveness as main drivers of economic development but also seriously considers the need to implement adequate and trustworthy principles to maintain a viable social contract. In Schwab's words, we now have "a historic window of opportunity to shape technological break-throughs, such as artificial intelligence and gene editing, in the service and for the benefit of humankind."[2] The central vision of the Fourth Industrial Revolution is to radically transform the way we produce, consume, communicate, and live. In Schwab's perspective,

> It [the Fourth Industrial Revolution] will redefine the relationship between citizens and the state. It will provide us with great opportunities for enhancing the lives of individuals and societies. It will allow, if we get it right, a much more human-centered approach, fostering not only material satisfaction, but also genuine individual and societal well-being for all. . . . The promise of a better future lies in acting together as stakeholders of a technology-driven global transformation process, with the objective of building a more modern, inclusive and human world.[3]

In Schwab's and thereby also the Forum's view, the goal is to work toward "long-term solutions based on dialogue, and endorsed by the commitment and willingness to achieve the best outcome in the shared long-term interest of all stakeholders."[4] The World Economic Forum attempts to serve this purpose as a catalyst and convener. The organization positions itself as a central actor in the new multipolar global order—an actor that works to combine the forces of market-based capitalism with social responsibility and the empowerment of individuals.

Our mission has been to understand the ways in which the Forum operates as it works toward its vision through discreet power, seduction, and discretionary governance at the transnational level. The ultimate challenge for the Forum resides in the fact that it lacks a political mandate to pursue its aims and must rely on the power of seduction, persuasion, and discretion to advance its interests. This form of soft power relies on credibility. For the Forum, credibility is mainly about offering a narrative about the future world order that is visionary, attractive, and based on solid expert knowledge. As political scientist Joseph Nye points out, credibility is a delicate matter, in the sense that it is destroyed if an actor is seen to be manipulative or if the information that actor conveys is perceived as propaganda.[5] On the other hand, if the actor eschews attempts at imposition or manipulation, it may be seen as pursuing nothing but dialogue, and hence lacking in potency; again, credibility is lost. The Forum places the bar high when it positions itself as a major catalyst for change in the new world order. The Forum aspires not only to reflect the global order and the global predicament, but also to be at the frontier, set precedence, provide new models, and trigger global change. If it fails to deliver, it may be seen as just more elite talk.

The Forum deploys significant resources to build its discreet power base. First, it relies on the financial sponsorship of its strategic partners, the core groups of large-scale transnational corporations that contribute substantial amounts of money as a sort of membership fee into the Forum. Second, it relies on the reputation and standing of the participants at its meetings and working groups. By selecting what it perceives to be the best brains, the most brilliant contemporary thought leaders, and by identifying future leaders, it creates an aura of credibility, expertise, and potency around its communities. Third, it offers an alternative organizational platform in the established global architecture of nation-states, international organizations, multilateral organizations, and profit-seeking corporations. It extends its agency by borrowing the decision-making capacity of its partially organized network. Although this platform is, in a sense, marginal and without formal power, what takes place in this interstitial zone may still have significant consequences. Nye puts it this way: "There is no contradiction between realism and soft power. Soft power is not a form of idealism or liberalism. It is simply a form of power, one way of getting desired outcomes."[6]

The Forum is thus an organization with a cause, but one that is lacking the formal mandate to pursue that cause. To obtain leverage and achieve credibility, legitimacy, and authority, it relies on seduction as a basic mechanism of power. Successful seduction, as author Robert Greene tells us, "begins with your ability to radiate some quality that attracts people and stirs their emotions in a way that is beyond their control."[7] The exclusivity of the Forum—the fact that participation is open to a select few, and that most discussions take place behind closed doors—constitutes an attraction around the WEF and its events. Apart from frustrating outsiders and onlookers, angering them or inducing in them feelings of shame for not having been allowed in, exclusivity also adds to the sense of significance and allure of the Forum. Greene says of the symbolic power of the theater curtain:

> Onstage, the curtain's heavy deep-red folds attract your eye with their hypnotic surface. But what really fascinates and draws you in is what you think might be happening behind the curtain—the light peeking through, the suggestion of a

secret, something about to happen. You feel the thrill of a voyeur about to watch a performance.[8]

Clearly, the exclusivity—and the imaginations of what goes on behind closed doors—of the Forum ultimately creates alluring and magnetic effects. It helps attract attention to the Forum and its activities. The Forum may, through its exclusive character, enhance perception of its goodwill, or "benignity," a willingness and capacity to improve the world. The exclusivity may also confer a bit of charisma onto the organization as a place inhabited by brilliant, competent, and resourceful leaders. Somewhat paradoxically, then, grand-scale narratives, such as the one that Klaus Schwab presents in the previous quotation, however important they may be in framing issues in particular ways, require seductive strategies to mobilize other actors in the desired direction.

How Is Global Politics Possible?

As we have reiterated throughout this book, researching the WEF has been no easy task. We were generously accommodated at the Cologny headquarters but frequently rejected when attempting to approach the events. The process has been discouraging at times, to say the least. But two things have kept us going. First is the fundamental understanding that what we are experiencing also bears witness to the way the organization treats the rest of the world—the noninvitees. We found it necessary to keep going, to keep raising questions and pushing boundaries in the interest of understanding and explaining what the Forum does. Second, we have been strongly motivated by our theoretical curiosity about what global politics actually might entail. How is global politics possible?

The WEF itself is one answer to this question. Movements, standards, multilateral agreements, various forms of state- and nonstate-based diplomacy provide other opportunities. But the WEF is a forceful actor of increasing importance, reflecting the larger trend of growth and diffusion of corporate-funded think tanks, nongovernmental organizations, foundations, and policy research institutes around the world—all with the intent of molding global politics. As we have shown in previous chapters, the Forum has a peculiar organizational form even as it resembles other organizations working in similar ways. Idiosyncratic in its funding situation, in its broad public outlook, and in the size of the network it organizes, the WEF has a unique setup.[9] The combination of discreet power, seductive strategies and discretionary governance is not unique, however, but a key component in many similar organizations.

The Forum has no mandate granted by nation-states, nor is it a decision-making organization that can achieve authority in relation to such other actors as nation-states, corporations, and intergovernmental organizations. Yet it does exercise authority in the sense that sociologist James Coleman used the term.[10] It influences other actors within the fields of markets, policy, and diplomacy. In regard to markets the activities of the Forum have consequences for how they are organized; sellers and buyers are attentive to the discourse of the Forum, learning ways to be socially responsible market actors. Expectations placed on a good market actor are clearly articulated by the Forum, and funders attempt to follow these propositions, with varying degrees of interest and success. The case of Volkswagen, a WEF funder and "strategic partner," indicates the limitation of the Forum's authority. The Volkswagen scandal of 2015, in which the company cheated the pollution emissions test in the United States, is an obvious violation of what the Forum advocates. Still, Volkswagen remains a valued WEF funder and partner. Yet many cases have demonstrated how funders align themselves to Forum standards, as exemplified by the Program for Infrastructure Development in Africa project presented in Chapter 3 and the project undertaken by longstanding WEF funder Pepsi Cola to reduce water use in its plants. These projects speak to the way the WEF may also be succeeding in its political intent to shape the actions of its funders. The most useful resource in its repertoire is the fact that global corporations judge it to be valuable—to be economically rewarding—to be part of the WEF community. Obviously, for many corporations—in the weapons or tobacco industries, for instance—engaging in WEF activities may not be a high priority. The position is mutual, because it would go against the WEF ethos to include such organizations; the WEF would not like to have them associated with its name. As our corporate informants suggested, however, and as implied by the fact that a selection of the world's one thousand strongest corporations have chosen to fund the organization for decades, having the keys to Davos is a significant ambition for many global corporations.

In the world of global policymaking, the Forum creates an arena for policymakers to draft policy proposals and gain leverage for these. It creates and exercises its authority by conferring status onto others, who then reciprocally award status to the Forum. Decisions about who will be invited to specific WEF events are made internally, according to the criterion of "excellence." Yet other dimensions enter into the decision-making process: personal network connections, educational achievements, and geopolitical location. A man, born and raised in Europe or the United States, with a diploma from Oxford, Harvard, or a similar high-ranking university, one who is well connected to others like him, and who has previously attended WEF events is a more frequent participant than are people with other backgrounds. The skewed socioeconomic and gender balance of the participating crowd contradicts the Forum's narrative: that its events and communities include people from all walks of life. The invitees may come from different societal spheres, operate in different markets, and represent different political views, but they do not represent the full spectrum of social positions, perspectives, and priorities. That said, it is clear that many more people are knocking on the doors of the Forum than the few who are chosen and that status is conveyed by being among those few who were not sifted out. Not even a prime minister or president of a nation-state can count on an invitation, and definitely not on a reinvitation. Consequently, most of those who do end up on the invitation list will do their utmost to be good participants who perform according to expectations. The best way of doing that is to be productive "in the WEF beehive"; demonstrating in other settings the use of ideas emanating from the Forum communities; and linking one's participation in an event to further actions. It is a quid pro quo process through which the Forum gains leverage and recognition as a key organization in global affairs, and whereby participants gain status by being recurrent WEF invitees.

Finally, the Forum has achieved authority in the world of diplomacy precisely because of its discreet, secluded, and private character. In contrast to conventional international diplomatic practices, the WEF is not circumscribed by protocol, in the sense of being rule based—having rules stipulating how activities should be performed. There is protocol, however, in the sense of diplomatic etiquette. Adherence to the Chatham House Rule is one such norm, as is loyalty toward one's WEF community. Moreover, the Forum is skilled in managing secrecy, hindered only by the norms of transparency regarding public displays of its practices. The Arctic lunch presented in Chapter 3 provides insight into to the ways the WEF may work in these matters: an event based on invitation only, at which heads of states discuss what to do with the Arctic with a handful of corporate leaders and with the occasional academic. Although no decisions are made over lunch, they may well be made down the line—within the Arctic Council, for instance. The meeting also sets the stage for articulating a discourse, forging shared understandings and joint settlements. At these types of events, diplomatic and market efficiency may be even more important than participant status. Corporate leaders may find it highly efficient to meet top-level politicians and other actors within the secluded and nontransparent WEF realm. Providing a space for public diplomacy, and, indeed, for market diplomacy is a significant resource for the Forum. This in turn confers a degree of authority over those who wish to participate in these types of conversations.

Is the Emperor Naked?

In the Hans Christian Andersen tale "The Emperor's New Clothes," it is a longing for inclusion and distinction that motivates the emperor to parade in the nude. Apart from the two cunning imposters and the emperor himself, who is concerned about losing face, it is only the child at the end of the tale who is not afraid of being "excommunicated" by acknowledging that the emperor has no clothes. Similarly, in the WEF case, we need to acknowledge the power of aspirations to be included in its ranks, to be recognized as superior. Just like the naked emperor in the tale, a WEF without courting nobility and press is merely a Swiss foundation with no capacity for decision making. Yet it is treated as though it had clothes suitable for an emperor—or, less metaphorically, as if it were an organization that all types of actors must attend to. If corporations, prime ministers, artists, and high-ranking scientists would treat it otherwise, it would be truly naked.

This is the fundamental predicament for the Forum. The corporate-based funding and mandate it relies on may come with good economic and social returns, but it challenges the organization's longevity and legitimacy. Corporations can opt out from funding when they wish. The Forum needs to be on its toes to keep attracting its funders, which means that it must continue to attract high-level people. It is through its discreet power, global seduction, and discretionary governance that it manages this complex situation and comes out on top. The individuals whom the Forum organizes in its expanding networks are tempted by the status recognition that the WEF offers, the prospects for lucrative business opportunities, and an expanded set of connections that may be advantageous in future arrangements.

This instability and the networking character of the organization are bewildering to those who tend to equate power with decision making in the realm of nation-states and multilaterals. Throughout our journey to understand the Forum, we have encountered many skeptics who have aired the idea that the Forum is all about talk. Indeed, as we experienced firsthand, the core of WEF practices *is* talk, not formal decision making. The discreet power of the WEF and many other organizations like it is shadowed by incessant talk. This must not hinder those interested in the Forum from seeing it as consequential, since it may have an impact on the decisions of other organizations. Sociologist Niklas Luhmann rightly points out that communication is at the core of social life, and the actor that successfully organizes communication in its own interest and in its own favor is able to shape further social circles by setting precedence for coming options—not primarily by forcing other actors but by making these choices appear to be the reasonable ones, thereby constituting the will of others.[11] The choices the Forum makes in selecting participants, issues, and solutions will be communicated and drawn on in other settings. Power in the discreet format of the Forum is thus shaped and performed by relating to other actors, relying on their agency and their interest in continuous communication with the Forum. The Forum is an illustration of the paradox of power according to organization scholar Stuart Clegg, meaning that the power of an actor may be increased by that actor's delegation of authority.[12] This is a two-way process, based on the outsourcing and subsequent acceptance of authority in a relationship, entailing the engagement of other actors as the carriers of WEF ideas and the authorization of these other actors to expand the agency of the WEF.

The elusive character of the WEF does not imply lack of organization, as in self-emergent networks. Much of it takes the form of a network; it is lighter on its feet than the traditional political organization.[13] But the basis for the authority and power that the WEF exercises is that it *is* organized.[14] The concept of communities that the Forum draws on and the arena metaphor used in relation to the multistakeholder concept imply a mild agency restricted to providing opportunities and space.[15] The construction of networks, or communities, is a response to this predicament, and the choices of words (such as *community*, *arena*, *open forum*, and *safe place*) are best understood as deliberate euphemisms,[16] drawn on in the interest of disconnecting the WEF from traditional forms of politics and power. Such euphemisms play central roles in the self-promotion of organizational interest and agency, partly by displaying sensitivity to partner concerns by avoiding expressions that can be perceived as critical of particular political views or that may marginalize social groups.

The Forum is not merely a highly prized and well-versed convener of events. It works to strike a balance between showing actorhood and facilitating the actorhood of others.[17] The Forum cannot decide what invitees, funding corporations, nation-states, or multilaterals should do. Through its organized network, it may however exert a degree of influence and power by deciding who can participate, setting the norms for good performance, and monitoring the actions of people within the network. Certainly there are emergent, less organized aspects of this network: socializing in Davos nightlife, setting up camp outside the meeting fence, or arranging independent meetings in other places. The point of the organized network is that it transcends the WEF as a single organization and extends its agency far beyond its headquarters and its events. It lays the basis for its highly discreet global form of governance.

Discretionary Governance and the Withdrawal of Elites

The story of the Forum and global politics is one of power, seduction, and discretionary governance. In practice, it takes the form of meetings in many places around the world. Meetings in conference centers, but also in hotels, cafés, libraries, restaurants, or wherever else the WEF-aspiring class can meet is where this form of global governance is actualized. The form of global politics that the WEF organizes is a type of networking politics, as identified by international relations scholar Diane Stone.[18] There is a component of openness in the events that the Forum version of politics builds on. The Forum continuously reports and publishes part of what it is doing. But as described in Chapter 4, many of its activities are secluded and securitized. In comparison to the conventional form of politics undertaken in public national and international contexts, this form of politics entails a withdrawal of elites to places ordinarily unknown to the general public, out of their reach and that of the media. Moreover, it is a form of politics that involves actors who are not elected by any constituency, but one in which the constituencies will have to live with the potential consequences of these activities.

The networking politics that the Forum promotes is based in several respects on the discretion of both the Forum and its participants. The Forum chooses who can be there, altogether at its own discretion. And in order to be an appreciated participant, to be reinvited, an invitee must be discreet yet active. It is good for participants to make use of what they have learned at events, yet this must be done without publicly revealing the exact content of discussions, solutions, and ideas aired. Finally, the Forum attempts to control what transpires outside the organization. As we showed in Chapter 6, it may have political flexibility at the heart of its ideological core and it may talk of its many partnerships, but in the end, the Forum has a strong say on what can or cannot be said as part of the organization; it produces both silence and voices. Not only does it have final decisions in editing the publications, standards, rankings, and blogs emanating from the organization, but in many instances, it also decides what is discussed at the allegedly open arena. Contributions are monitored to avoid critical opinions that funders and other significant stakeholders might hold.

Despite the component of openness in the events that the Forum version of politics builds on, this form of politics thus entails a withdrawal of elites. It may be that this is the only form of politics that an organization such as the Forum could organize. If it opened up for broader participation and operated under less seclusion and in less opaque forms, it would not exist for long. It is precisely its discreet and closed character, the elevation of a globally aspiring class, and the status distinction that comprise the ingredients of its authority and create opportunities to pursue political matters. Moreover, this legitimizes the withdrawal of the policy and business elites who are engaged in Forum activities. This form of politics works to introduce wedges between those who are invited and thus given voice, and those who are not invited and left unheard.

As linguist and philosopher George Lakoff reminds us, politics is inherently moral.[19] The Forum has indeed taken the stand of a morally responsible actor, with the intention of doing good. It has grown into a political actor, endorsing fundamentally liberal democratic values and standing up for civil rights, mobility, and welfare. The noninclusive and discreet character of the Forum challenges, however, the very vision it has established: improving the state of the world. The fact is that only a smaller group of the elite is invited to participate in discussions and deliberations at Forum events and the lack of transparency in criteria of admission means that liberal democratic practices are in peril. Political scientist Wendy Brown has suggested that it may be that neoliberal reason undoes the political imaginary it promises to secure and reinvigorate. To pursue its vision of "improving the world" and to engage "people from all walks of life," the WEF will have to reflect on the practices by which these are pursued.[20] Even other actors interested in participating in the WEF network or otherwise interested in the ways in which it constructs its version of global politics need to appreciate these potential consequences of WEF workings.

A Historic Moment

The WEF has often been accused of protecting and defending the global economic order—and its interests in this order—in the face of major political and social upheavals. In recent years, citizens around the world have vented their frustrations at traditional political institutions. In 2016, voters in the United Kingdom, Colombia, and Italy delivered shock referendum results, showing that citizens are desperate to express their sense of disenfranchisement. Citizens also voted in favor of populist political figures such as President Trump in the United States and President Duterte in the Philippines. The British European Union (EU) referendum in favor of Brexit is the tip of an iceberg of EU disenchantment. Nationalist and Far Right political parties, neoconservatives, and isolationists are gaining voice in many parts of the world, including France, Germany, Hungary, the Netherlands, and Sweden. In many countries, trust in established political and welfare institutions is low and falling. Runaway economic inequality, with income gaps between the extremely rich and the poor that continue to grow, has further fueled people's frustration. In this context, the enhanced role of corporations in politics and the increased reliance on private–public partnerships between business and political elites is often viewed with mistrust as a form of collusion that blurs the line between politics and the market and consolidates the establishment of elites.

These developments point, among other things, to a will and a need among people for broader political participation and economic empowerment. Yet many people are experiencing restrictions on their basic freedoms of expression, association, and assembly. Civic public space is in many parts of the world circumvented. Press freedom is increasingly curtailed, human rights are threatened, and political participation is undermined—even in respected and established democracies.

One way of understanding this situation, which, ironically, the WEF has participated in setting in motion, is to see it as a postmodern transformation similar to "the great transformation" described by Karl Polanyi.[21] When the Berlin Wall fell, Francis Fukuyama famously claimed that we were witnessing "the end of history."[22] The WEF formed part of the neoliberal wave following the fall of the Soviet Union. As has become apparent since, the history of ideological clashes did not end there. Rather, history seems to be repeating itself. The promotion of self-regulated markets and laissez-faire policies from the beginning of the Industrial Revolution, along with countermovements to tame markets, which Polanyi analyzed in terms of a "great transformation," corresponds well to contemporary transformations.[23] The setting in motion of economic integration and liberalization of market regulations after 1989 has led to growing intra- and interregional trade, coupled with the diffusion of technology, capital, and free market values. These alterations have lifted some people out of poverty; for many others, it has meant even greater impoverishment. In the early 2000s, the alter-globalization movement took center stage as a form of collectivistic countermovement to what was conceptualized as a rise to the bottom among countries in the neoliberal world order. The WEF and the Davos meetings were prime targets in these mobilizations. In a few years, the movement grew silent, partly subsumed by the WEF itself. In its place, almost a decade later, came a protectionist backlash led by such politicians as Donald Trump, Rodrigo Duterte, and Victor Orbán, unleashing a globalization of rage and undermining liberal principles of globalization.[24]

In this context, the role of the Forum is ambiguous. On the one hand, the Forum has been a driver of economic globalization. It is precisely the agendas, social practices, and norms it has embraced that are now inciting the illiberal political furies that are unfolding. Moreover, the Forum is part of the problem, as it forms partnerships between business and nongovernmental organizations, drawing political leaders and top academics into its tight circles—a secluded and opaque organization that excludes the majority of people from participation and representation and a new transnational class of elites who aspire to change the world to be consistent with their personal interests. As sociologist C. Wright Mills observed in his classic description of the organization of the power elite in the United States during the 1950s, "even the outermost fringes of the power elite—which change more often than its core—consist of 'those who count.'"[25] On the other hand, the Forum aims to provide an alternative space for political and business discussions, promote novel ways for "people from all walks of life" to meet and to be empowered, and a "safe place" for political leaders to deliberate and discuss in their promotion of peaceful solutions. It works to promote responsible leadership in future generations around the world. And it may be that these spaces truly are needed for global issues such as climate change and global migration to be dealt with at a transnational level. Troublesome as it may be, democratic organizations such as the UN may require less transparent spaces—the WEF, for instance—in order to find common denominators worth pursuing.

The WEF changes with the world order around it. It is a prime example of the growth of a world society in the sense that sociologists John Meyer, Gili Drori, and Hokyo Hwang use the term: an organization built on the expanded notion of agency and purpose, promoting other normative visions of a new world order.[26] Furthermore, it illustrates the organized attempt to build workable ideologies of social responsibility and control in a world where nation-states have lost much of their role as carriers of ideology, government, and community. In this context, the Forum appears as a nongovernmental site for the production of political ideology and vision, normative propositions for voluntary governance, and the articulation of translocal communities. With recent economic and political developments, however, the role of the WEF in the world has also shifted, to the extent that it has come to be seen not primarily as an alternative but as part of the establishment. Ironically, if the Forum were for some time considered an Other in relation to the stalled political positions of nation-states, the inertia of international organizations, and the shrewd economic rationality of business corporations, it is now moving into the realm of the establishment. Insofar as the structural clue to the organization lies in corporate funding and the commitment of corporate leaders to the operations of the Forum as a multistakeholder arena, it merely extrapolates the trend of increased corporate and financial involvement in politics—a trend that has grown in significance over the past few decades.[27] The strategies the Forum deploys to set it apart—exclusivity, a discretionary form of governance, and the construction of elite groupings—now signal that the organizational model of the Forum may not be conducive to solving the global problems it aims to tackle.

Modeling Future Global Governance?

Many nation-states and international institutions are facing insurmountable impediments and disincentives with respect to the regulation of such global matters as climate change, famine, terrorism, and organized crime. As an effect of this situation, it is commonly argued that contemporary global issues should be dealt with through some form of transnational governance. WEF events, projects, and diplomatic undertakings are responses to this call. Indeed, allowing political leaders to meet without the pressures of protocol and the media, deliberating off the record, can be necessary for solving the grand issues of our time, providing a remedy for global governance gaps.

After observing the Forum for several years, we believe it is honest in its interests in making the world a better place. It is not merely the voice of greedy corporations, of which it sometimes is accused.[28] The WEF is an organization in and of itself—however dependent it is on the funding of large-scale corporations—and it pursues its own interests. This is perhaps most evident in the diplomatic interests of the organization, which indicate that the Forum is on a path of its own—a path that does not always align with particular corporate interests in the global market space. Yet as a result of its attempts to stay neutral, provide an arena for multiple stakeholders, and pursue soft diplomacy, it is also an organization that remains somewhat vague even to itself. Its position on key ideological issues is sometimes wavering and ambivalent.

Moreover, as a model for global governance, the WEF comes out as debatable. A fundamental issue is its lack of attendance to the relationship between constituency and accountability. Because it has no mechanisms of representation, the Forum builds its own constituency among the people it finds brilliant and in charge. From the perspective of the world that is not invited, this can hardly qualify as democratic. Moreover, the answer to the question of how the Forum can be held accountable for what it achieves in global policy and diplomacy is wanting. The fact that the Forum is a foundation entails that formal demands on its democratic accountability are limited, in spite of being recognized by the Swiss state as an international organization. In addition, the Forum's leeway in deciding on the degree of transparency toward the larger public is related to its organizational status.

As Diane Stone decisively argues, enforcing accountability in global policymaking is difficult, given the hybrid and temporary character of the transnational networks active in this sphere.[29] The Forum provides a pivotal case in point. It becomes the daunting task of national citizens to hold participants accountable.[30] To increase the accountability of the group of elected politicians and state bureaucrats who participate in Forum activities, the principles put forth by political scientist Anne-Marie Slaughter with regard to transnational policy networks could provide a starting point.[31] The Forum could agree to be monitored by other nongovernmental organizations—by Transparency International, for instance—and pledge adherence to professional norms and standards on good governance. It may be argued that the WEF—and organizations like it—risk being used as a way for liberal states' politicians to circumvent the accountability issue at the domestic level. As our informants repeatedly stated, a much-valued aspect of its meetings is its provision of an arena that allows elected political leaders to deliberate beyond conventional political and diplomatic protocol and the prying eyes of the press. This would indicate a low interest in transparency among nation-state representatives when they are participating in WEF activities.

In line with John Ikenberry, we raise the question of how to recognize the need for granting more authority and capacity to international bodies of this sort without jeopardizing popular rule and the accountability procedures built into liberal democratic states.[32] The WEF's organizational model does not provide an answer to this fundamental question. To use wording from the field, it rather thrives on being a shy organization, determining at its own discretion if, when, and around what topics it aims for media attention and openness. The withdrawal of the elites that we have pictured throughout the book epitomizes the built-in tension between transparency and opacity. At Forum events, those who are invited mingle, debate, and perform. For better or worse, these acts will have repercussions around the world. At the same time, the map of elites is being redrawn, bypassing national maps. These are the proclaimed global elites, often involved not only in WEF events but also in diverse transnational meeting places. They represent a self-reproducing nobility, detached from local contexts—that is, until someone asks: Why does the emperor have no clothes?

In relation to accountability, the role that corporations play within the WEF construct must also be critically assessed. Admittedly, corporations are a powerful presence within the Forum, but corporate interests do not dictate what the Forum advocates, whether versions of neoliberalism or social democracy. From a democratic aspect, the troublesome part with regard to corporations has more to do with the fact that they are drawn into global public policymaking. The WEF mantra on multistakeholder deliberations not only puts the Forum in the front seat; it also opens the possibility of turning the CEOs of one thousand of the world's largest corporations into policymaking actors. In many instances, the interest in this privilege among corporate executives may be low. Funding corporations may primarily use the WEF for striking business deals. Nevertheless, the policy opening is enticing for some corporations, and the secluded WEF is an excellent arena for pursuing policy change. The feasibility of holding these corporations accountable is evidently limited. Social movement activists regularly raise their voices to make corporations accountable, and this pressure does not go unnoticed by the Forum. Still, the balance between corporate interests in participating in these events and the opportunities for the public to keep track of its activities is emphatically uneven.

Following geographers Eric Sheppard and Helga Leitner, we may consider the approach to governance taken by the WEF as yet another attempt at supplementing the deficiencies of capitalism.[33] Adhering to a trust in markets and promoting global capitalism as important ingredients in fixing the existing system, the Forum extends a neoliberal trend in the version of third way social democracy and reinforces the imaginary of capitalism rather than modifies it. The supplement—in this case, the WEF form of discretionary governance—simultaneously marks the incompleteness of globalizing capitalism and assists in reproducing it. As we have seen, this imaginary also legitimizes particular forms of expertise cultivated among a small, primarily Western elite group and promotes technological reasoning to solve complex policy problems. In this vein, we concur with anthropologist Didier Fassin that politics and forms of governing are not only about the rules of the games of governing, but also about its stakes, that is, the kind of societies and lives that are essentially desired.[34] Beyond supplementing and reinforcing a malfunctioning system, another form of governance must be possible.[35] Yet the shift in the WEF's envisioned global governance model does not involve a thorough questioning of the rules of the game. As political theorist Fredric Jameson noted, "Someone once said that it is easier to imagine the end of the world than to imagine the end of capitalism."[36] This is precisely the Forum's conundrum.

The WEF provides an answer to the fragmented global predicament by calls for more transnational cooperation. We have discussed the constructive aspects of the Forum, along with its more detrimental sides. As a model for future government, we find the Forum wanting in a fundamental democratic sense, although it may be of use for markets, policymaking, and diplomatic relations. In its vision for the years to come, Klaus Schwab sketches an expansion of the Forum.[37] It already has smaller offices in Beijing, New York, San Francisco, and Tokyo, but in order to better increase its coverage and bolster its stability, further expansion is being planned—an expansion that would entail a new phase in the history of the WEF. It would not merely increase the extent of its reach; it would also entail a reversed way of globalizing its activities. When, in the first instance the WEF became a global phenomenon, it was because the world would come to the Forum. In the new phase, the Forum globalizes by coming to the world, as it were. Like many other think tanks with expansive globalizing ambitions, the WEF will probably be found in many places in the future.

What this entails for its status and mandate remains to be seen. Since the WEF relies for its survival, agency, and authority on its ability to seduce, it cannot be certain of its longevity. It is here today but may be gone tomorrow. Yet judging by the development of the organization so far, there is no reason to believe that it will fall in the near future. To the contrary, its experimental organizational design and its successful framing of political discourse may well be used as a model for future global governance.

Perhaps it is in the interstices of the established international infrastructure of organizations that we find the resources, motivations, and capacity for social, political, and economic change. To be sure, it is here that we find the experimentation with novel forms of cultural diplomacy and with soft as well as sharp power. It is here that the particular form of discreet governance that is the signature of the WEF is crafted, refined, and deployed. What remains problematic is that these novel forms of governance are being developed under the radar, away from the sight of the general public and elected politicians, and far removed from the deliberations of citizen groups. Openings for the general public to engage are few and far between. Furthermore, as a model for future globalization and governance, it lacks essential mechanisms by which to ensure accountability—not only with regard to what the Forum decides to communicate, but also in terms of what the invitees are up to. In the interest of future global democracy, it is therefore essential to continuously reflect on and examine this model of global governance and offer viable alternatives.

Appendix

Methodological Approach

Fieldwork

Our study of the World Economic Forum (WEF) has been driven by our curiosity for new modes of global governance and politics. We posed the question, What type of governance is the WEF constructing? This in turn raised another question: How is global politics possible? The centralized yet global character of the Forum implied some methodological challenges. Following the Forum across space and over time meant working with the world at large as a field—wherever the Forum organized events and meetings and wherever we might find the participants, the field was there. As we noted in Chapter 1, we chose to understand the organization from both the inside, as it were, interviewing and observing WEF staff at its headquarters in Cologny and during its events, and externally by interacting with and posing questions to WEF funders and participants in and around events. To this end, we applied a mixed-methods approach that involved varying degrees of participant observation, different kinds of interviews, and analysis of documents.[1] We have systematically made both quantitative and qualitative use of these sources.[2]

The ethnographic material consists of transcriptions of participant and nonparticipant observations; formal and informal conversations undertaken in and around WEF meetings in Cape Town, Davos (from three consecutive years), Dubai, and Istanbul; as well as two meetings arranged by WEF event partiscipants in Stockholm and another European capitol city. Taken together, we did about eighty days of observations and around seventy interviews, of which twenty-five were recorded and transcribed interviews with Forum staff in the WEF headquarters in Cologny. Some interviews were semistructured, and others were more conversational in character. Several people have been interviewed two or three times. Typically interviews ranged from forty-five to ninety minutes. As part of our fieldwork, we also talked to and interacted with a large number of service personnel and other categories of people involved in WEF meetings and events.

With the exception of Chairman Klaus Schwab, the identities of all informants are confidential. Original names of individuals and corporations, as well as titles, nationality, and line of work, have been altered. Gender, age, and relation to the Forum have most commonly not been altered in order to provide the general picture of participants and staff. None of those who agreed to participate in recorded interviews demanded that their identities be concealed. Still, to reveal their identity would be of little importance in regard to a fair and robust analysis of the WEF. All respondents who were formally or informally interviewed were informed that we are employed at Stockholm University and that we were talking to them based on our academic interest in the WEF and our capacity as researchers. The material in its totality, including interview transcripts and the database of participant background data, has been stored electronically and safeguarded by password. Printed transcriptions have been stored in locked and fireproof cabinets. In practice, this has meant that except for the two of us, only the three research assistants involved in the project have had access to the data.

Participant Background Data

Based on presentations of participants on the WEF website of all twenty-one external Forum events between 2011 and 2013 ($N = 3{,}790$), and a sample of participants from the 2017 Annual Meeting ($n = 996$), we sought to get an understanding of the common WEF participant. Using basic statistical calculations, we have counted and charted participation in relation to background variables such as gender, age, sector, type of employer, educational level, alma mater, and in what capacity they were participating (such as guests, moderators, speakers). Because information regarding all these variables was not always attainable from the WEF website, we also had to search other open sources, such as LinkedIn and Bloomberg. With regard to the largest data set (2011–2013), we were able to do this for only a subsample, containing information of 490 randomly chosen participants.

Female participation in WEF events is increasing (Figure A.1) as a result of conscious attempts to balance the genders. In 2011, 83 percent of participants were male, whereas in 2017, the figure was 72 percent. The construction of a number of communities geared to younger people (see Chapter 5), however, seems to have had only a marginal effect in regard to mean age of participants. The mean age in the twenty-one events from 2011 to 2013 was 56.5 years, whereas the sample from the 2017 Annual Meeting in 2017 shows a mean age of 55.7 years.

Based on the information from the WEF website, we also charted average educational degree among participants. Where several educational degrees were identified, we coded only the highest degree. Educational data were coded in four levels: PhD degree or a postgraduate, master's degree or other degrees at the master's level, BA degree or another undergraduate degree, and no higher education degree. In cases where we were unable to find educational background, they were coded as unknown. The analysis from the 2017 data shows that 27 percent of participants had a PhD degree, and 42 percent had a degree at the master's level. Whereas we could not find information regarding the highest educational degree for 11 percent of the sample, only 2 percent had no educational degree. No major differences could be found in the 2011–2013 data set.

For participants who had pursued higher education (the majority of them), we also coded the information regarding which educational institution each participant had at-

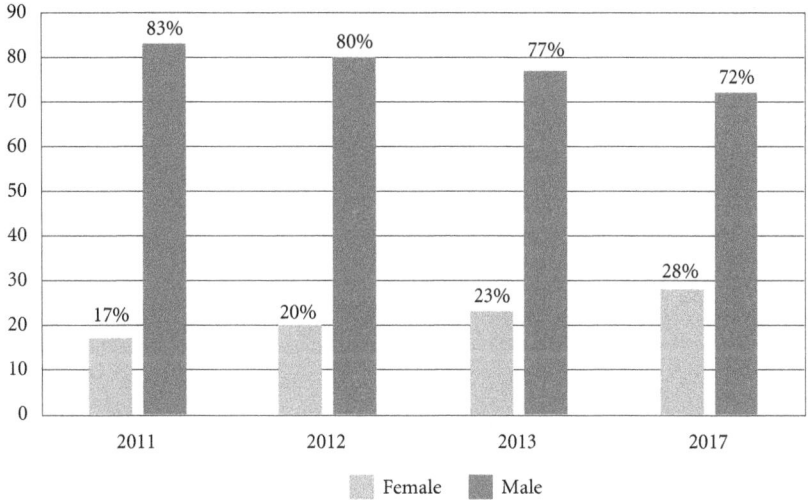

FIGURE A.1. Gender percentage in WEF meetings, 2011–2013 and 2017. Source: Garsten and Sörbom.

tended. Again, the information was found at either the WEF website or at other websites. If no information was found, we coded that as unknown/none. The alma mater ranking is based on world university rankings from 2016.[3] The ranking has been categorized in ten groups, from the highest ranking (A) to the lowest (H), plus a group for an alma mater that was not on the world university ranking list in 2016. Code I means that the educational institution could not be found and code J that it was unknown.

The subsample from meetings between 2011 and 2013 in Figure A.2 shows that almost 30 percent of the participants at some point during their education had attended one of the ten highest-ranked educational institutions in the world. A smaller ratio (18.8 percent) had received their educational degree from universities that were not on the world universities ranking list in 2016. An even smaller number (8.4 percent) of the participants had an unknown degree or could not be traced to any institution. The data set of participants in the 2017 WEF Annual Meeting in Davos included almost 25 percent participants with education from the top ten universities.

When we traced the sector to which participants were associated (that is, in which they were active or employed), we made use of the same codes that were applied by WEF itself, since participants registered in the subsample of 2011–2013 (n = 490), had been identified with regard to the sector they belonged to: (1) academia, (2) business, (3) culture, (4) government, (5) media, (6) NGO, (7), politics, (8) religion, and (9) undefined (Table A.1).

The general pattern shows that the Forum registered 36 percent of participants as associated with the business sector, indicating that the majority of participants were nonbusiness people. Among women, though, the majority of participants were registered as associated with nongovernmental organizations.

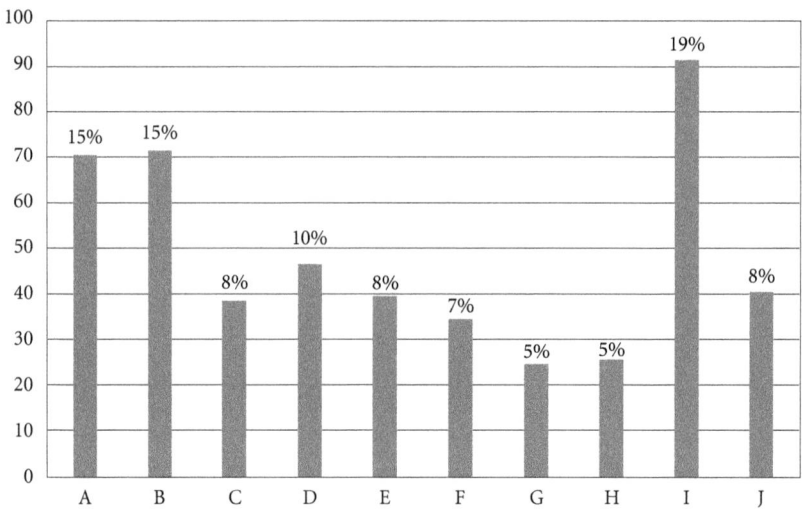

FIGURE A.2. Alma mater rankings: Subsample from 2011–2013 (in percent). Source: Garsten and Sörbom.

Sector	Gender	Number	Percentage
Academia	F	12	10
	M	54	14
Business	F	30	27
	M	171	45
Culture	F	0	0
	M	4	1
Government	F	13	12
	M	62	16
Media	F	14	13
	M	19	5
NGOs	F	33	29
	M	53	14
Politics	F	10	9
	M	12	3
Religion	F	0	0
	M	2	1
Undefined	F	0	0
	M	1	< 0.5

TABLE A.1. WEF meeting participant by sector and gender, 2011–2013. Source: Garsten and Sörbom.

An important dimension of participation is the degree to which participants are re-invited and thus are recurring participants. Being repeatedly accepted into the ranks of the Forum indicates a definite social status. For analyzing this particular aspect, we drew on the largest data set, covering all participants made public by the WEF over twenty-one events in 2011, 2012, and 2013. Since some participants may have various functions at a single event, we coded the entire set manually, checking each name for number of functions. By doing so, we could determine with some accuracy whether the participant was a recurring participant or fulfilled several functions at one event.

The examination of the data shows that the number of meetings to which the participants were invited varied among the participants in terms of gender. A larger share of the women participated twice (60 percent), whereas for men, the recurrent participation was lower (50 percent). However, as the number of invitations to meetings increased, the number of recurrent female participants decreased. Among those registered for six events, for instance, three were women and twenty-three were men.

Documents

In addition to interviews and ethnographic fieldwork, we analyzed the manifold types of written material that the Forum produces. Typically these texts have been press releases, blog posts, journal articles, op-ed articles, Facebook updates, and reports. Through use of the NVIVO software for qualitative analysis, we organized this vast source of data and identified recurring themes and concepts.[4]

In general, the Forum publishes about one hundred reports annually. Since 1999 these have been published online. We analyzed a subsample ($n = 285$) of these reports from 2000, 2005, 2010, and 2015. The reports were coded along the themes of self-per-ception (the role the Forum gives itself), political issues, and political solutions. The analysis informed the discussion in Chapters 3, 5, and 6, where we provide insights into the content of WEF reports and blogs, in search of the political sway of the Forum.

Notes

Introduction

1. World Economic Forum (2017a, 1).
2. Schwab (1988).
3. Schwab (1988, 1).
4. The identities of all informants are confidential, and all informant names are pseudonyms. The only exception is Klaus Schwab, who appears under his own name. More details about research confidentiality are provided in Chapter 1.
5. Hylland Eriksen (2007); Hannerz (1996).
6. Scholte (2005).
7. Garsten and Sörbom (2017b).
8. Interview, March 14, 2013.
9. Schwab (1971).
10. World Economic Forum (2010a, 7).
11. Code of Ethics—The Davos Manifesto.
12. Code of Ethics—The Davos Manifesto.
13. Garsten and Sörbom (2014).
14. World Economic Forum (2010), www.weforum.org/about/history.
15. Schwab (1988).
16. World Economic Forum (2010), accessed May 4, 2016, at www.weforum.org/about/history.
17. Schwab (2004).
18. At its meeting on December 17, 2014, the Federal Council recognized the WEF as an "other international body" as defined in the Host State Act (HSA, SR 192.12) and approved the agreement (accessed March 30, 2017, at https://www.admin.ch/gov/en/start/dokumentation/medienmitteilungen.msg-id-55987.html).
19. World Economic Forum (2018), accessed January 15, 2018, at https://www.weforum.org/about/world-economic-forum.
20. More regional offices are to come, as laid out in Schwab's 2020 vision (Schwab 2015).

21. World Economic Forum (2017c), accessed March 27, 2017, at www.weforum
.org/about/careers.

22. World Economic Forum (2017d), accessed March 27, 2017, at www.weforum
.org/communities/global-agenda-councils,

23. World Economic Forum (2017e), accessed March 27, 2017, at www.weforum
.org/communities/young-global-leaders.

24. The Global Leadership Fellow Programme is in this sense different, since it
is open for application. The admission decision is then made internally at the WEF.
Likewise, the Global Shapers community is open for application through the local hub,
which has some leeway in deciding on admission.

25. Chatham House Rule states that anyone who comes to the meeting is free to use
the information from the discussion, but not allowed to reveal the source.

26. See the appendix for a fuller description of these figures.

27. Djelic and Sahlin Andersson (2006); Djelic and Quack (2010); Garsten and Sörbom (2017b).

28. Sassen (1998).

29. Ruggie (2004).

30. United Nations (2015).

31. McGann (2017).

32. Smith (2007, 89). See also Arin (2013); Denham, Garnett, and Stone (1998);
McGann (2007); Medvetz (2012a, 2012b); Rich (2004); Stone (1996); Weidenbaum
(2011).

33. Barley (2010, 777).

34. See Medvetz (2012a).

35. In a similar vein, other scholars have described how think tanks may influence political and other agendas, and thus achieve power and influence. Mirowski and
Plehwe (2009) describe, with the example of the Mont Pelerin Society, how the core
ideas of neoliberalism were planted and distributed in "networks of neoliberal partisan
think-tanks." Richardson, Kakabadse, and Kakabadse (2011) outline the mechanisms
of influence at work in "the transnational power elite," with a focus on the Bilderberg
group. Researching Bible advocacy in England, Engelke (2009) maintains that the establishment of a think tank was part of what he terms "strategic secularism," a process by
which religious actors work to incorporate secular formations into religious agendas.
Medvetz (2012a), in his thorough overview of think tanks in the United States, argues
that the ambiguity of the think tank is the very key to its power and influence.

36. See, for example, Haas (1992); Stone (2005).

37. Stone (2002, 9).

38. Carroll and Carson (2003).

39. As social anthropologist Janine Wedel (2009, xi) argues, "The frameworks and
terms that we've long used to understand power and influence are not longer sufficient
to explain what is happening." These new agenda-wielding players, Wedel succinctly
contends, "actively structure, indeed create, their roles and involvements to serve their
own agendas—at the expense of the government agencies, shareholders, or the public

on whose behalf they supposedly work. These players not only flout authority, they institutionalize their subversion of it."

40. Consequently, in terms of power and authority, we stress a constructivist dimension, departing from the notion of power as suggested by Foucault, according to whom the term "designates relationships between partners" (Foucault 1982, 786). See also Lukes (2005, 12) and Luhmann (1975). We develop our understanding of power at length in Chapter 3.

41. Along the same lines, sociologists Miller and Rose (1992, 175) contend that "political power today is exercised through a profusion of shifting alliances between diverse authorities, to govern a multitude of facets of economic activity and social life."

42. Medvetz (2012a) has also taken a relational view of the role of think tanks.

43. On the concepts of "partial organization" and "partially organized fields," see Ahrne and Brunsson (2011).

44. Garsten and Sörbom (forthcoming).

45. Cf. Emerson (1962).

46. Nye (2008).

47. Nye (2004, 95).

48. Nye (2012, x).

49. Scholars in different domains have used the term *discretionary governance* to denote forms of governance that in some way go beyond the conventional in relying on informal and unofficial procedures and are not subject to established forms of democratic control or regulation. Hagendijk and Irwin (2006) discuss discretionary governance in the context of the governance of science and technology, and Heydebrand (2013) addresses the issue with regard to interactive new media.

50. See, for example, Melissen (2005).

51. See, for example, Naray (2008).

52. The notion of sociality here is meant to capture the different sets of concrete social relationships that develop around social activities (Pink, 2008, 172). Our interest in sociality thus reflects an interest in ongoing substantive social action rather than fixed or social relations defined a priori. Furthermore, sociality reflects an engagement in shared worlds of meaning and understanding, most readily emerging out of and apparent in social relations (cf. Vergunst and Vermehren 2012).

53. Interview with Paola Pakulsky (September 18, 2012).

54. Bourdieu (1987).

55. Shihadeh (2015).

56. World Economic Forum (2016e), accessed April 26, 2016, at www.weforum.org.

57. World Economic Forum (2014, 4).

58. Geertz (1972).

Chapter 1: Disentangling Discretionary Governance

1. World Economic Forum (2018), accessed January 17, 2018, at https://www.weforum.org/about/world-economic-forum.

2. Mahmoud (2014).

3. Mahmoud (2014, 17).

4. Simmel (1906).

5. Hannerz (2003).

6. On "global assemblages," see Collier and Ong (2005).

7. Marcus (1998).

8. Our ethnographic fieldwork covers four years—2011 to 2015.

9. Gusterson (1997).

10. Coleman and Collins (2007, 12).

11. Rabinow (2008).

12. Koopman (2009, 37–38).

13. Garsten and Hernes (2009).

14. The Occupy Movement is an international sociopolitical movement that works against social inequality and lack of democracy around the world. Its primary goal is to advance social and economic justice and new, more direct forms of democracy.

15. World Economic Forum (2017f), accessed January 27, 2017, at www.weforum .org/open-forum/.

16. On the production of silence and power in relation to globalist ideology, see Trouillot (2016).

17. World Economic Forum (2017g), accessed January 17, 2017, at www.global shapers.org/about-us-0.

18. Akindes (2003); Bird (2003).

19. For a more elaborate discussion of the performative role of meetings in organizations, see, for example, Garsten and Sörbom (2017a); Schwartzman (1993); Sandler and Thedvall (2017).

20. Rabinow (2003, 87).

21. Holmes and Marcus (2010, 181).

22. We interviewed approximately twenty-five staff members and about forty-five meeting participants. Some of them we met several times. As part of our fieldwork, we also talked to a large number of journalists, service personnel, and other categories of people involved in and around WEF meetings and events.

23. As a rule, we have been careful to protect the identities of our interlocutors and interviewees by using pseudonyms and not revealing more information than needed to provide relevant context. In some cases, we have intentionally altered basic facts regarding, for instance, gender, region, or occupation, in the interest of anonymity. Only in cases in which the person is widely known and a public figure, as in the case of the WEF chairman, have we kept the actual name.

24. Davidson Wassler and Bresler (1996).

25. There is now a growing literature on collaborative and team ethnography. See, for example, Clerke and Hopwood (2014); Gordon et al. (2006); Rabinow and Stavri-anakis (2014); Scales, Bailey, and Lloyd (2008); Davidson Wassler and Bresler (1996).

26. A vast number of works treat the role of documents in organizations. See, for example, Goody (1986); Hull (2012); Riles (2006); Weber (1978); Yates (1989).

27. Neumann (2012).

28. See the appendix for more information regarding, for instance, the gender, age, and educational background of participants.

29. Hull (2012).

30. See the appendix for more information regarding the analysis of texts.

31. Gupta and Ferguson (1997).

32. Faubion (2009).

33. See Rabinow (2011) for an elaborate discussion of ethically grounded anthropology and new forms of inquiry.

34. Deleuze (1997).

Chapter 2: Liquid Mandate

1. Interview with Klaus Schwab, March 2013.

2. Easton (1953).

3. Deleuze and Félix Guattari (1987, 249).

4. "Giving the World's Citizens a Voice" (2015), accessed January 11, 2017, at www.unpacampaign.org.

5. Rosenau and Czempiel (1992); Rhodes (1996); Porter (2009); Rosenau (2009).

6. See, for example, Higgot, Underhill, and Bieler (2000); Sklair (2002); Garsten and Lindh de Montoya (2004); Crane (2008); Gond, Kand, and Moon (2009); Levy and Kaplan (2009); Soule (2009).

7. Ruggie (2004).

8. Djelic and Sahlin-Andersson (2008, 7). See also Garsten and Jacobsson (2011) and Gilbert, Rasche, and Waddock (2015).

9. Garsten and Jacobsson (2011); Wilson and Swyngedouw (2014).

10. Carroll and Carson (2003).

11. Ruggie (2004).

12. Pigman (2007, 8).

13. Pigman (2007, 16).

14. World Economic Forum (2010a, 75).

15. See WEF Regulations regarding the World Economic Forum (2015a), accessed January 12, 2017, at www3.weforum.org/docs/WEF_Reglement_2015.pdf.

16. On the role of members in associations, see Ahrne (1994).

17. Interview undertaken by Adrienne together with Hans Abrahamsson in Cologny April 8, 2003.

18. See van Dijk (1997) and Fairclough (2008).

19. Adler (1997).

20. Barley (2010, 780).

21. See Jepperson and Meyer (2000) on actorhood.

22. Merton (1948).

23. Merton (1948, 193).

24. Merton (1948, 195).

25. Merton (1948, 194).

26. Interview, June 5, 2015.

27. Conversation, February 10, 2013.

28. World Economic Forum (2006, article 12).

29. The total figure of economic capital owned by the Forum foundation is not presented in Forum accounts. In the 2015–2016 annual report, the Forum notes that the foundation had increased its capital by CHF 1,240,960, a figure considerably higher than 2015 when the increase was reported as CHF 733,000 but lower than the 2014 of CHF 1,480,000 (WEF 2016a, 43).

30. World Economic Forum (2015), accessed February 13, 2017, at www.weforum .org(italics added).

31. Interview, September 21, 2012.

32. Durkheim (1995).

33. Weber (1978, 41).

34. On the dynamics of the development of transnational community formation and identity, see, for example, Anderson (1983) and Hannerz (1990).

35. Compare with Djelic and Quack (2010,12–13), who explore the formation of the transnational community in the related spheres of governance of business and economic activity.

36. Garsten and Sörbom (forthcoming).

37. Compare with Koppell (2010).

38. Interview, March 13, 2013.

39. See Strathern (2000) and Garsten and Lindh de Montoya (2008).

40. Roberts (2009, 962). See also Chua (1995).

41. Garsten and Lindh de Montoya (2008).

42. See Schweizerischen Bundesrat (2014), accessed March 27, 2017, at www.newsd .admin.ch/newsd/message/attachments/38056.pdf.

43. World Economic Forum (2016a).

44. E-mail communication with the Federal Department of Economic Affairs, Switzerland, November 3, 2016, stating that the WEF does not have to report its economic affairs to the Swiss Confederation. The confederation covers the costs for the security arrangements in Davos, coordinated by the canton of Graubünden. Only these latter costs have to be transparent. See also Arrivilaga and Schnurbein (2014) regarding the issues of transparency in Swiss foundations.

45. World Economic Forum (2016b).

46. Interview, September 8, 2011.

47. See Simmel (1964).

48. Stein (1998).

49. Simmel (1906, 466).

50. Costas and Grey (2016).

51. Compare with Knill and Lenschow (2003).

52. Morgan (1989, 242).

53. Interview, June 5, 2015.

54. Greene (2001).

Chapter 3: Setting Precedence

1. Interview, June 5, 2015.
2. Callon and Latour (1981, 279–286; italics in original).
3. Latour (1988, 191).
4. See Cooren et al. (2011) on communication as constitutive of organization.
5. On brokers and brokerage as a phenomenon, see, for example, Ingold and Varone (2012), James (2011), Lindquist (2015), Mosse and Lewis (2006), and Wolf (1956).
6. Guzzini (2004); Luhmann (1975).
7. Dahl (1957); Foucault (1979).
8. Taylor (2011).
9. Holmes (2014).
10. Seidl and Becker (2006).
11. See Coleman (1994, 70) on authority.
12. Coleman (1994, 36).
13. Weber (1997, 138).
14. In 2016, the name of this meeting and the councils it forms was renamed Annual Meeting of the Global Future Councils.
15. Hacking (2006).
16. Garsten and Sörbom (2014).
17. Cf. Cooren et al. (2006).
18. Interview, September 19, 2012.
19. Interview, September 19, 2012.
20. Lakoff (1993).
21. Lukes (2005).
22. Interview, June 4, 2015.
23. World Economic Forum (2013a); "The Green Growth Alliance," PowerPoint material from Annual Meeting in Davos, 2013.
24. Interview, June 4, 2015.
25. Dahl (1957, 202–203).
26. Rose and Miller (1992).
27. Luhmann (1995).
28. On the Forum and informal diplomacy, see Pigman (2005). See also Stone (1999) on informal diplomacy.
29. Gilboa (2005).
30. Jones (2015).
31. Graz (2003).
32. On deep lobbying, see also Clemons (2003) and Garsten (2013).
33. See Coleman (1994,66).
34. Coleman (1994, 70).
35. Lukes (2005).
36. Garsten and Sörbom (2014).

Chapter 4: The Status Machinery

1. World Economic Forum (2013c), accessed January 31, 2017, at www.weforum. org/events/world-economic-forum-annual-meeting-2013.

2. Interview, June 5, 2015.

3. Deleuze (2004).

4. World Economic Forum (2012). Interestingly, the expression "community of communities" echoes the expression of the global justice movement—"movement of movements"—aimed at capturing the mosaic of movements currently challenging neoliberal globalization. See, for example, Mertes (2003).

5. Interview, September 21, 2012.

6. World Economic Forum (2016e), accessed February 8, 2017, at www.weforum .org/press/2016/01/world-economic-forum-announces-new-board-of-trustees-3447 f94a-fd22-406d-bfbc-ec2fefd833b6/.

7. World Economic Forum (2013d), accessed September 27, 2013, at www.weforum .org/community/forum-young-global-leaders.

8. Scarry (2014, 4).

9. Cf. Tolmach Lakoff (2000, 21).

10. Djelic and Quack (2010, 13).

11 Stone (2008, 24).

12. Stone (2008, 30).

13. Cf. Barley (2010); Bond, Glouharova, and Harrigan (2010); Hillman, Keim, and Schuler (2004).

14. Ahrne and Brunsson (2011).

15. Ahrne and Brunsson (2011) and Garsten and Sörbom (forthcoming).

16. See Ahrne and Brunsson (2011) on elements of organization.

17. See Bourdieu (1987) on the minute details of social distinction and pretension.

18. Goffman (1959).

19. Goode (1978).

20. Cf. Podolny (1993).

21. Sheridan (1994).

22. Benedict (1946).

23. Greene (2001, 403).

24. Hilde Schwab—Crystal Awards, accessed January 31, 2017, at www.youtube .com/watch?v=AqBxgaLtZ24.

25. Moeran (2001).

26. Sahlins (1963).

27. Garton Ash (2005), accessed January 15, 2017, at https://www.theguardian.com /world/2005/feb/03/globalisation.comment.

28. "Leaders without Followers" (2013), accessed September 21, 2013, at www.econ omist.com/blogs/newsbook/2013/01/world-economic-forum-davos.

29. Gustini (2011), accessed February 8, 2017, at www.theatlantic.com/business/ archive/2011/01/the-untold-story-of-davos-mistresses/339081/.

30. The Global Agenda Council on Women's Empowerment was one such initia-

tive, working to raise awareness and share best practices on gender issues. The *Global Gender Gap Report*, issued annually by the Forum since 2006, shows the magnitude of gender disparities between women and men across the four key areas of health, education, economy, and politics and tracks their progress over time. The 2016 report covers 144 countries.

31. In recent years, the Forum has worked on rectifying the imbalance, with some results. For a more detailed picture of gender balance at WEF events, see the appendix.

32. Granovetter (1973).

33. Interview, September 21, 2012.

34. Interview, September 21, 2012.

35. Interview, September 20, 2012.

36. Interview, August 22, 2011.

37. As Carroll and Sapinsky (2015) noted, the transnational corporate policy network continues to be carried by an elite inner circle of well-connected persons and organizations, centered in Europe and North America but weighted increasingly toward Europe. This would be consistent with our findings.

38. In 2017, 28 percent of the female participants and 27 percent of male participants had a PhD degree, while 43 percent of the female participants and 42 percent of the male participants had a master's degree as their highest degree indicated.

39. The data set consisted of 3,790 participants registered in WEF meetings over the period 2011 to 2013. See the appendix for more information on the data set.

40. Sklair (2001, 5).

41. Weber (1978, 932).

Chapter 5: Mobilizing for the Future

1. Walton (2008, 155).

2. Anderson (1983).

3. Hannerz (2016, 170).

4. E-mail conversation, 2012.

5. Global Shapers movie (2016), accessed May 16, 2016, at www.weforum.org.

6. See Global Shapers Community (2016), accessed June 6, 2016, at www.global shapers.org/search?search_api_views_fulltext=london.

7. World Economic Forum (2014, 4).

8. World Economic Forum (2014, 3).

9. See World Economic Forum (2016d), accessed May 25, 2016, at www.weforum .org/communities/young-global-leaders.

10. Schwab (2014, 4).

11. Schwab (2014, 4).

12. Schwab (2014, 4).

13. Millar (2013, 1).

14. See World Economic Forum (2016f), accessed May 13, 2016, at www.weforum .org/communities/global-leadership-fellows.

15. Millar (2012, 44).

16. Khurana and Baldwin (2013, 5).

17. See World Economic Forum (2016g), accessed May 15, 2016, at www.weforum.org/communities/global-leadership-fellows.

18. Khurana and Baldwin (2013, 1).

19. Millar (2012, 43).

20. Khurana and Baldwin (2013, 7).

21. Khurana and Baldwin (2013, 5).

22. Ramya Krishnaswamy, information movie on GLF (May 11, 2016).

23. Ehrnooth and Siurala (1991, 10).

24. Watson (2009, 14).

25. Hall (1904). See also Bohlin (2004).

26. Watson (2009).

27. World Economic Forum (2011).

28. See Bessant (2004) for a discussion on the need to bring in young people to legitimize politics.

29. Alexandria Global Shapers, Facebook, accessed June 19, 2016.

30. On "age set" as a concept, see, for example, Foner and Kertzer (1978) and Evans-Pritchard (1940).

31. See Ahrne and Brunsson (2011) on the concept of "partial organizing."

32. Bourdieu (1978).

33. In this case "industries and communities" refer to funders and other members of WEF-constructed communities.

34. Interview, September 9, 2012.

35. Hannerz (2015).

36. See Andersson (2006, 280).

37. Hannerz.

38. Inayatullah (1998).

39. Interview, September 9, 2012.

40. World Economic Forum (2015b, 2017b).

41. Interview, September 9, 2012.

42. Interview, September 9, 2012.

43. Interview, September 9, 2012.

44. World Economic Forum (2015b, 8).

45. Inayatullah (1998).

46. World Economic Forum (2013b).

47. World Economic Forum (2015b, 6).

48. World Economic Forum (2015b, 16).

49. World Economic Forum (2015b).

50. World Economic Forum (2011).

51. Schwab (2015, 1).

52. Koselleck (2004).

53. Law (2011).

54. Hinchliffe (2014, 30).

55. Law (2011).

56. Gusterson (2008).

Chapter 6: Political Sway

1. Klein (2016), accessed February 7, 2017, at www.theguardian.com/commentis free/2016/nov/09/rise-of-the-davos-class-sealed-americas-fate?CMP=share_btn_link.

2. Cirilli (2017).

3. Harvey (2005).

4. Carroll and Carson (2006, 59).

5. See Rupert (2005, 223) and Fougner (2008, 321).

6. Harvey (2005, 2).

7. A presentation of the material underlying this section was provided in Chapter 1.

8. World Economic Forum (2010c).

9. World Economic Forum (2009).

10. World Economic Forum (2010b).

11. Barnett (2005, 5).

12. Friesen (2010).

13. Schwab and Smadja (1996).

14. Schumpeter (1942).

15. Schwab and Smadja (1996)

16. This turn is recognizable in other organizations too. Sheppard and Leitner, for instance, argue that in regard to policies on aid and development, two remakings of global capitalist governance could be identified after the 1997 Asian financial crisis: a "post-Washington consensus" whose relationship to neoliberalism was complex, and a "new development economics," advocating Keynesian principles (2009, 185). Particularly after the 2008 global finance crisis, they argue, these remakings can be conceptualized as supplements reinforcing an imaginary of capitalism as the solution to, rather than progenitor of, uneven development.

17. Schwab (2012).

18. Compare with the analysis of economic historian Jenny Andersson (2009). Andersson shows that the two key dilemmas of the third way are how to critique capitalism and reform it and how to capitalize on the intervention of capitalist structures in relation to their social effects. Social democracy, she argues, is an ideological "ism" or an agent; its goal is to "intervene in the relationship between the economic and the social, mediating it and arbitrating it, indeed constructing economy and society as fields of action, existence and intervention" (13). This handling of market and politics comes close to the WEF strategy.

19. Giddens (1998, 99).

20. These changes in the views of markets and states, on behalf of both the WEF and social democracy, can be seen as parallel and partially symbiotic with alterations of neoliberalism stances. Partly as a response to economic and political changes, neoliberalism in its general interpretations has gone from a phase in the 1970s of "aggressive neoliberalism," through a phase during the 1980s and 1990s of "euphoric neoliberalism,

to a third stage of "disciplinary neoliberalism," during which social democratic regimes have consolidated the neoliberal framework by strengthening corporatist forms of socioeconomic cooperation (Bieling 2006).

21. See Berman (2006) for an analysis of how European social democracy has treated the relation between policy and markets.

22. Bieling (2006).

23. Bieling (2006, 217–218).

24. WEF (2016c, v).

25. Elias (2013). See also Fisher (2012).

26. Peck and Tickle (2002, 390).

27. See Harvey (2005, 36, 62–63).

28. Schwab (2015).

29. Schwab (2010).

30. Schwab (2008).

31. Schwab (2009).

32. Schwab (2015).

33. Cf. Rose (2000). In the same vein, Jessop argues that the politics born out of neoliberal concerns "tends to promote 'community' (or a plurality of self-organizing communities) as a flanking, compensatory mechanism for the inadequacies of the market mechanism" (Jessop, 2006, 4).

34. Schwab (1971).

35. Schwab (2010).

36. Burkitt and Ashton (1996).

37. Burkitt and Ashton (1996, 10).

38. Cf. Dryzek (1993).

39. Lakoff (1996).

40. Mouffe (2005).

41. Mouffe (1993, 6).

42. Mouffe (2005).

43. Mouffe (2005).

Conclusion: A New Narrative for Future Globalization?

1. Schwab (2017).

2. Schwab (2017).

3. Schwab (2017).

4. Schwab (2017), accessed March 25, 2017, at www.weforum.org/agenda/2017/03/klaus-schwab-new-narrative-for-globalization.

5. Nye (2011).

6. Nye (2011, 82).

7. Greene (2001, 3).

8. Greene (2001, 194).

9. See also Carroll and Carson (2003).

10. Coleman (1974).

11. Luhmann (1995).

12. Clegg (1989).

13. Cf. Powell (1990) on the lightness of networks.

14. See Ahrne and Brunsson (2010) regarding partial organization.

15. Garsten and Sörbom (forthcoming).

16. On euphemism and politics, see, for example, van Dijk (1997).

17. See Meyer and Jepperson (2000) on actorhood.

18 Stone (2007).

19. Lakoff (1996).

20. Brown (2015).

21. Polanyi (1944).

22. Fukuyama (1992).

23. Cf. Beneria (1999); Munck(2006); Burgoon (2009); Osterhammel (2013).

24 See Mishra (2017) on the globalization of rage and the age of anger.

25. Wright Mills ([1956], 2000, 290).

26. Meyer, Drori, and Hwang (2006).

27. Garsten and Sörbom (2017).

28. Even if that was the case—that the Forum is an instrument for its funding corporations—these funders are probably examples of liberal ones. Consider the organizations that would never even attempt to take part in the lofty arena of the WEF, let alone be invited by the Forum. Unless one argues that corporations are by definition greedy, it may be that the one thousand corporations that choose to put money into the Forum are those one would turn to if one is interested in using corporations for improving the state of the world.

29. Stone (2008, 28).

30. Cf. Slaughter (1997).

31. Slaughter (2004).

32. Eikenberry (2009).

33. Sheppard and Leitner (2009).

34. Fassin (2009).

35. We are here paraphrasing Fassin (2009), who uses the expression "another politics of life must be possible" to emphasize the importance of meaning and values in politics. The expression also speaks to the well-known social justice movement expression "another world is possible," which is also the slogan of the World Social Forum.

36. Jameson (2003, 76).

37. Schwab (2015).

Appendix: Methodological Approach

1. Cf. Cresswell (2013).

2. The quantitative analyses were conducted by our assistants, Måns Ljungstedt, MA, who collected and coded the data for the quantitative and the qualitative analyses, and Júlía Birnudóttir Sigurðardóttir, MA, who calculated the statistics.

3. "World University Rankings 2015–2016," *Times Higher Education* (2016),

accessed January 15, 2017, at www.timeshighereducation.com/world-university-rank ings/2016/world-ranking#!/page/0/length/25/sort_by/scores_overall/sort_order/asc/ cols/stats.

    4. Cf. Bringer, Johnston and Brackenridge (2006).

References

Adler, Jonathan. 1997. "Lying, Deceiving or Falsely Implicating." *Journal of Philosophy* 94:435–452.

Ahrne, Göran. 1994. *Social Organizations: Interaction inside, outside and between Organizations.* London: Sage.

Ahrne, Göran, and Nils Brunsson. 2011. "Organization outside Organizations: The Significance of Partial Organization." *Organization* 18:83–104.

Akindes, Fay Yokomizo. 2003. "Methodology as Lived Experience: Rhizomatic Ethnography in Hawai'i." In *Global Media Studies: Ethnographic Perspectives*, edited by Patrick D. Murphy and Marwan Kraidy, 147–165. London: Routledge.

Andersen, H. C. 1837. *The Emperor's New Clothes (Kejserens nye Klæder].* Copenhagen: C. A. Reitzel.

Anderson, Benedict. 1983. *Imagined Communities: Reflections on the Origin and the Spread of Nationalism.* London: Verso.

Andersson, Jenny. 2006. "Choosing Futures: Alva Myrdal and the Construction of Swedish Future Studies, 1967–1972." *International Review of Social History* 51:277–295.

Arin, Kubilay Yado. 2013. *Think Tanks: The Brain Trusts of US Foreign Policy.* Berlin: Springer

Arrivilaga, Lucas, R., and Georg von Schnurbein. 2014. "The Swiss Legal Framework on Foundations and Its Principles on Transparency." *International Journal on Non-for-Profit Law* 16:30–58.

Barley, Stephen. 2010. "Building an Institutional Field to Corral a Government: A Case to Set an Agenda for Organization Studies." *Organization Studies* 31:777–805.

Benedict, Ruth. 1946. *The Chrysanthemum and the Sword.* Boston: Mariner Books.

Beneria, Lourdes. 1999. "Globalization, Gender and the Davos Man." *Feminist Economics* 5:61–83.

Berman, Sheri. 2006. *The Primacy of Politics: Social Democracy and the Making of Europe's Twentieth Century.* Cambridge: Cambridge University Press.

Bessant, Judith. 2004. "Mixed Messages: Youth Participation and Democratic Practice." *Australian Journal of Political Science* 39:387–404.

Bieling, Hans-Jürgen. 2006. "Neoliberalism and Communitarianism: Social Conditions, Discourses and Politics." In *Neoliberal Hegemony: A Global Critique*, edited by Dieter Plehwe, Bernard Walpen, and Gisela Neunhoffer, 207–222. London: Routledge.

Bird, S. Elizabeth. 2003. *The Audience in Everyday Life: Living in a Media World*. New York: Routledge.

Bohlin, Göran. 2004. "Themed Section Introduction: Research on Youth and Youth Cultures." *Young* 12:237–243.

Bond, M., S. Glouharova, and N. Harrigan. 2010. "The Political Mobilization of Corporate Directors: Socio-Economic Correlates of Affiliation to European Pressure Groups." *British Journal of Sociology* 61:306–335.

Bourdieu, Pierre. 1987. *Distinction: A Social Critique of the Judgment of Taste*. Translated by Richard Nice. Cambridge, MA: Harvard University Press.

———. 1996. *Sur la television*. Paris: Raison d'agir.

Bringer, J. D., L. H. Johnston, and C. H. Brackenridge. 2006. "Using Computer-Assisted Qualitative Data Analysis Software to Develop a Grounded Theory Project." *Field Methods* 18:245–266.

Brown, Wendy. 2015. *Undoing the Demos: Neoliberalisms' Stealth Revolution*. Cambridge, MA: MIT Press.

Burgoon, Brian. 2009. "Globalization and Backlash: Polayni's Revenge?" *Review of International Political Economy* 16:145–177.

Burkitt, Brian, and Frances Ashton. 1996. "The Birth of Stakeholder Society." *Critical Social Policy* 16:3–16.

Callon, Michel, and Bruno Latour. 1981. "Unscrewing the Big Leviathans: How Do Actors Macrostructure Reality?" In *Advances in Social Theory and Methodology: Toward an Integration of Macro and Micro Sociologies*, edited by Karin Knorr Cetina and Aaron Cicourel, 277–303. London: Routledge.

Carroll, William, K., and Colin Carson. 2003. "Forging a New Hegemony? The Role of Transnational Policy Groups in the Network and Discourses of Global Corporate Governance." *Journal of World-Systems Research* 9:67–102.

Carroll, William K., and Jean Philippe Sapinsky. 2010. "The Global Corporate Elite and the Transnational Policy Planning Network, 1996–2006: A Structural Analysis." *International Sociology* 25:501–538.

Chua, Wai Fong. 1995. "Experts, Networks and Inscriptions in the Fabrication of Accounting Images: A Story of the Representation of Three Public Hospitals." *Accounting, Organizations and Society* 20:111–145.

Cirilli, Kevin. 2017. "Trump Team Shunning Davos Meeting of World's Economic Elites." *Bloomberg Politics*, January 14. Accessed March 27, 2017, at www.bloomberg.com/news/articles/2017-01-13/trump-team-shunning-davos-gathering-of-world-s-economic-elite.

Clegg, Stuart. 1989. "Radical Revisions: Power, Discipline and Organizations." *Organization Studies* 10:97–115.

Clemons, Steven C. 2003. "The Corruption of Think Tanks." *JPRI Critique* 10:97–115.

Clerke, Teena, and Nick Hopwood. 2014. "Ethnography as Collective Research Endeavour." In *Doing Ethnography in Teams: A Case Study of Asymmetries in Collaborative Research,* edited by Teena Clerke and Nick Hopwood, 5–18. London: Springer.

Coleman, James. (1974) 1994. *Power and the Structure of Society.* New York: Norton.

Coleman, Simon, and Peter Collins. 2007. "Introduction: 'Being . . . Where?' Performing Fields on Shifting Grounds." In *Locating the Field: Space, Place and Context in Anthropology,* edited by Simon Coleman and Peter Collins, 1–23. London: Bloomsbury.

Collier, Stephen J., and Aihwa Ong, eds. 2005. *Global Assemblages: Technology, Politics, and Ethics as Anthropological Problems.* Malden, MA: Blackwell.

Cooren, François, Timothy Kuhn, Joep P. Cornelissen, and Timothy Clark. 2011. "Communication, Organizing and Organization: An Overview and Introduction to the Special Issue." *Organization Studies* 32:1149–1170.

Costas, Jana, and Christopher Grey. 2016. *Secrecy at Work: The Hidden Architecture of Organizational Life.* Stanford: Stanford University Press.

Crane, Andrew, ed. 2008. *The Oxford Handbook of Corporate Social Responsibility.* New York: Oxford University Press.

Cresswell, John W. 2013. *Research Design: Qualitative, Quantitative and Mixed Methods.* London: Sage.

Dahl, Robert A. 1957. "The Concept of Power." *Systems Research and Behavioral Science* 2:201–215.

Davidson Wassler, Judith, and Liora Bresler. 1996. "Working in the Interpretive Zone: Conceptualizing Collaboration in Qualitative Research Teams." *Educational Researcher* 25, no. 5: 5–15.

Deleuze, Gilles. 1997. "Desire and Pleasure." In *Foucault and His Interlocutors,* edited by Arnold Ira Davidson, 185–186. Chicago: University of Chicago Press.

———. 2004. *Desert Islands and Other Texts, 1953–1974.* Los Angeles: Semiotext(e).

Deleuze, Gilles, and Felix Guattari. 1987. *A Thousand Plateaus: Capitalism and Schizophrenia.* London: Continuum.

Denham, Andrew, Mark Garnett, and Diane Stone, eds. 1998. *Think Tanks across Nations: A Comparative Approach.* Manchester: Manchester University Press.

Djelic, Marie-Laure, and Kerstin Sahlin Andersson. 2006. *Transnational Governance: Institutional Dynamics of Regulation.* Cambridge: Cambridge University Press.

Djelic, Marie-Laure, and Sigrid Quack. 2010. *Transnational Communities: Shaping Global Economic Governance.* Cambridge: Cambridge University Press.

Durkheim, Emile. (1915) 1995. *The Elementary Forms of Religious Life.* New York: Free Press.

Easton, David. 1953. *The Political System: An Inquiry into the State of Political Science.* New York: Knopf.

Ehrnooth, J., and Lars Siurala, eds. 1991. *Construction of Youth.* Helsinki: VAPK Publishing, Finnish Youth Research Society.

Eikenberry, John G. 2009. "Liberal Internationalism 3.0: America and the Dilemma of the New World Order." *Perspectives on Politics* 7:71–87.

Elias, Juanita. 2013. "Davos Woman to Rescue of Global Capitalism: Postfeminist Politics and Competitiveness Promotion at the World Economic Forum." *International Political Sociology* 7:152–169.

Emerson, Richard M. 1962. "Power Dependence Relations." *American Sociological Review* 27:31–41.

Engelke, Matthew. 2009. "Strategic Secularism: Bible Advocacy in England." *Social Analysis* 53:39–54.

Evans-Pritchard, Edward E. 1940. *The Nuer: A Description of the Modes of Livelihood and Political Institutions of a Nilotic People*. Oxford: Clarendon Press.

Fairclough, Norman. (1992) 2008. *Discourse and Social Change*. Cambridge: Polity Press. 2008.

Fassin, Didier. 2009. "Another Politics of Life Is Possible." *Theory, Culture and Society* 26:44–60.

Faubion, James D. 2009. "The Ethics of Fieldwork as an Ethics of Connectivity, or The Good (Anthropologist (Isn't What She Used to Be)." In *Fieldwork Is Not What It Used to Be: Learning Anthropology's Method in a Time of Transition*, edited by James D. Faubion and George E. Marcus, 145-166. Ithaca, NY: Cornell University Press.

Fisher, Melissa S. 2012. *Wall Street Women*. Durham: Duke University Press.

Foner, Anne, and David Kertzer. 1978. "Transitions over the Life Course: Lessons from Age-Set Societies." *American Journal of Sociology* 83:1081–1104.

Foucault, Michel. 1979. *Discipline and Punish: The Birth of the Prison*. New York: Vintage Books.

Fougner, Tore. 2008. "Neoliberal Governance of States: The Role of Competitiveness Indexing and Country Benchmarking." *Millennium Journal of International Studies* 37:303–326.

Friesen, Elisabeth. 1982. "The Subject and Power." *Critical Inquiry* 8:777–795.

———. 2010. "Boomerang Politics and International Finance: Transnational Civil Society Activism and the Contestation over Debt Cancellation." Paper prepared for the Canadian Political Association Conference, Concordia University, Montreal.

Fukuyama, Francis. 1997. *The End of History and the Last Man*. New York: Avon Books.

Garsten, Christina. 2013. "All about Ties: Think Tanks and the Economy of Connections." In *Organizational Anthropology: Doing Ethnography in and among Complex Organizations*, edited by Christina Garsten and Anette Nyqvist, 139–154. London: Pluto.

Garsten, Christina, and Tor Hernes, eds. 2009. *Ethical Dilemmas in Management*. Abingdon: Routledge.

Garsten, Christina, and Kerstin Jacobsson. 2011. "Post-Political Regulation: Soft Power and Post-Political Visions in Global Governance." *Critical Sociology* 39:421–437.

Garsten, Christina, and Monica Lindh de Montoya, eds. 2004. *Market Matters: Exploring Cultural Processes in the Global Market Place*. Basingstoke: Palgrave MacMillan.

———, eds. 2008. *Transparency in a New Global Order: Unveiling Organizational Visions*. Cheltenham: Elgar.

Garsten, Christina, and Adrienne Sörbom. 2014. "Values Aligned: The Organization of Conflicting Values within the World Economic Forum." In *Configuring Value Conflicts in Markets*, edited by Susanna Alexius and Kristina Tamm Hallström, 159–177. Cheltenham: Edward Elgar.

———. 2017a. "Small Places, Big Stakes Meetings as Moments of Ethnographic Momentum." In *Meeting Ethnography: Meetings as Key Technologies of Contemporary Governance, Development, and Resistance*, edited by Jen Sandler Jen and Renita Thedvall, 126–144. London: Routledge.

———, eds. 2017b. *Power, Policy and Profit: Corporate Engagement in Politics and Governance*. Cheltenham: Edward Elgar.

———. Forthcoming. "A Global Network: World Economic Forum and the Partial Organizing of Global Agendas." In *Organizing outside Organizations*, edited by Göran Ahrne and Nils Brunsson. Oxford: Oxford University Press.

Garton Ash, Timothy. 2005. "Davos Man's Death Wish." *Guardian*, February 3. https://www.theguardian.com/world/2005/feb/03/globalisation.comment.

Geertz, Clifford. 1972. "Religion as a Cultural System." In *Reader in Comparative Religion: An Anthropological Approach*, 3rd ed., edited by William A. Lessa and Evon Z. Vogt, 167–178. New York: Harper.

Giddens, Anthony. 1998. *The Third Way: The Renewal of Social Democracy*. Malden, MA: Polity Press.

Gilbert, Dirk U., Andreas Rasche, and Sandra Waddock. 2015. "Accountability in a Global Economy: The Emergence of International Accountability Standards." *Business Ethics* 21:23–44.

Gilboa, Eytan. 2005. "Media-Broker Diplomacy: When Journalists Become Mediators." *Critical Studies in Media Communication* 22:99–120.

Global Shapers Community. 2016. *Young Global Shapers*. Cologny: World Economic Forum. www.globalshapers.org/search?search_api_views_fulltext=london.

Goffman, Erving. 1959. *The Presentation of Self in Everyday Life*. New York: Anchor Books.

Gond, Jean-Pascal, Nahee Kang, and Jeremy Moon. 2009. "The Government of Self-Regulation: On the Comparative Dynamics of Corporate Social Responsibility." *Economy and Society* 40:640–671.

Goode, William J. 1978. *The Celebration of Heroes: Prestige as a Social Control System*. Berkeley: University of California Press.

Goody J. 1986. *The Logic of Writing and the Organization of Society*. Cambridge: Cambridge University Press.

Gordon, Tuula, Pirkko Hynninen, Elina Lahelma, Tuija Metso, Tarja Palmu, and Tarja Tolonen. 2006. "Collective Ethnography, Joint Experiences and Individual Pathways." *Nordisk Pedagogik* 26:3–15.

Granovetter, Mark S. 1973. "The Strength of Weak Ties." *American Journal of Sociology* 78:1360–1380.

Graz, Jean-Christophe. 2003. "How Powerful Are Transnational Elite Clubs? The So-cial Myth of the World Economic Forum." *New Political Economy* 8:321–340.

Greene, Robert. 2001. *The Art of Seduction*. New York: Penguin Books.

Gupta, Akhil, and James Ferguson. 1997. "'The Field' as Site: Method and Location in Anthropology." In *Anthropological Locations: Boundaries and Grounds of a Field Science*, edited by Akhil Gupta and James Ferguson, 101–146. Berkeley: University of California Press.

Gusterson, Hugh. 1997. "Studying Up Revisited." *Political and Legal Anthropology Review* 20:114–119.

———. 2008. "Nuclear Futures: Anticipatory Knowledge, Expert Judgment, and the Lack That Cannot Be Filled." *Science and Public Policy* 35:551–556.

Gustini, Ray. 2011. "The Untold Story of Davos Mistresses." *Atlantic*, January 27.

Guzzini, Stefano. 2004. "The Concept of Power: A Constructivist Analysis." *Millennium: Journal of International Studies* 33:495–521.

Haas, Peter, M. 1992. "Introduction: Epistemic Communities and International Policy Coordination." *International Organization* 46:1–35.

Hacking, Ian. 2006. "Kind of People: Moving Targets." *Proceedings of the British Academy* 151:285–318.

Hagendijk, Rob, and Allan Irwin. 2006. "Public Deliberation and Governance: Engaging with Science and Technology in Contemporary Europe." *Minerva* 44:167–184.

Hall, Stuart, G. 1904. *Adolescence: Its Psychology and Its Relations to Physiology, Anthropology, Sociology, Sex, Crime, Religion, and Education*. New York: Appleton.

Hannerz, Ulf. 1990. "Cosmopolitans and Locals in World Culture." *Theory, Culture and Society* 7:237–251.

———. 1996. *Transnational Connections: Culture, People, Places*. London: Routledge.

———. 2003. "Being There . . . and There . . . and There! Rerhizomatic Reflections on Multi-Site Ethnography." *Ethnography* 4:201–216.

———. 2016. *Writing Future Worlds: An Anthropologist Explores Global Scenarios*. Basingstoke: Palgrave Macmillan.

Harvey, David. 2005. *A Brief History of Neoliberalism*. Oxford: Oxford University Press.

Higgot, Richard, Geoffrey Underhill, and Anders Bieler, eds. 2000. *Non-State Actors and Authority in the Global System*. Abingdon: Routledge.

Hillman, Amy, J., Gerald, D. Keim, and Douglas Schuler. 2004. "Corporate Political Activity: A Review and Research Agenda." *Journal of Management* 30:837–857.

Hinchliffe, Steve. 2014. "More Than One World, More Than One Health: Re-Configuring Interspecies Health." *Social Science and Medicine* 129:28–35.

Holmes, Douglas R. 2014. *Economy of Words: Communicative Imperatives in Central Banks*. Chicago: University of Chicago Press.

Holmes, Douglas R., and George E. Marcus. 2010. "Prelude to a Re-functioned Ethnography." In *Ethnographic Practice in the Present*, edited by Marit Melhuus, Jon P. Mitchell, and Helena Wulff, 176–184. Oxford: Berghahn Books.

Hull, Mathew, S. 2012. *Government of Paper: The Materiality of Bureaucracy in Urban Pakistan*. Berkeley: University of California Press.

Hylland Eriksen, Thomas. 2007. *Globalization: The Key Concepts*. Oxford: Berg.

Inayatullah, Sohail. 1998. "Causal Layered Analysis: Poststructuralism as Method." *Futures* 30:815–829.

Ingold, Karin, and Frédérik Varone. 2012. "Treating Policy Brokers Seriously: Evidence from the Climate Policy." *Journal of Public Administration Research* 22:319–346.

James, Deborah. 2011. "The Return of the Broker: Consensus, Hierarchy and Choice in South African Land Reform." *Journal of the Royal Anthropological Institute* 17:318–338.

Jameson, Fredric. 2003. "Future City." *New Left Review* 21:65–79.

Jessop, Bob. 2006. "The Third-Way: Neoliberalism with a Human Face." In *New Labour und die Modernisierung Gros Britanniens*, edited by Sebastian Berg and Andre Kaiser. Augsberg: Wissener Verlag.

Jones, Peter. 2015. *Track Two Diplomacy in Theory and Practice*. Stanford: Stanford University Press.

Khurana, Rakesh, and Eric Baldwin. 2013. "The World Economic Forum's Global Leadership Fellowship Program." Harvard Business School case study 9-413-118.

Klein, Naomi. 2016. "It Was the Democrats' Embrace of Neoliberalism That Won It for Trump." *Guardian*, November 9. www.theguardian.com/commentisfree/2016/nov/09/rise-of-the-davos-class-sealed-americas-fate?CMP=share_btn_link.

Knill, Christoph, and Andrea Lenschow. 2003. "Modes of Regulation in the Governance of the European Union: Towards a Comprehensive Evaluation." European Integration Online Papers 7. Accessed October 17, 2014, at www.eiop.or.at/eiop/texte/2003-001a.htm.

Koopman, Colin. 2009. *Pragmatism as Transition: Historicity and Hope in James, Dewey, and Rorty*. New York: Columbia University Press.

Koppell, Jonathan, G. S. 2010. *World Rule, Accountability, Legitimacy, and the Design of Global Governance*. Chicago: University of Chicago Press.

Koselleck, Reinhart. 2004. *Futures Past: On the Semantics of Historical Time*. New York: Columbia University Press.

Lakoff, George. 1993. "The Contemporary Theory of Metaphor." In *Metaphor and Thought*, 2nd ed., edited by Andrew Ortony, 202–251. Cambridge: Cambridge University Press.

———. (1996) 2002. *Moral Politics: How Liberals and Conservatives Think*. Chicago: University of Chicago Press.

Latour, Bruno. 2007. *Reassembling the Social*. Oxford: Oxford University Press.

Law, John. 2011. "What's Wrong with a One-World?" *Heterogenities.net*.

"Leaders without Followers: Readers' Comments. Swiss Banker in Reply to Simon Fischer." 2013. *Economist*. Accessed September 21, 2013, at ww.economist.com/blogs/newsbook/2013/01/world-economic-forum-davos.

Levy, David L., and Rami Kaplan. 2009. "Corporate Social Responsibility and Theories of Global Governance: Strategic Contestation in Global Issue Arenas." In *The Oxford Handbook of Corporate Social Responsibility*, edited by Andrew Crane,

Abigail McWilliams, Dirk Matten, Jeremy Moon, and Donald S. Siegel, 432–451. Oxford: Oxford University Press.

Lindquist, Johan. 2015. "The Anthropology of Brokers and Brokerage." In *International Encyclopedia of Social and Behavioral Science*, 2nd ed., edited by James Wright, 870–874. Amsterdam: Elsevier.

Luhmann, Niklas. 1975. *Macht*. Stuttgart: Ferdinand Enke Verlag.

———. 1995. *Social Systems*. Stanford: Stanford University Press.

Lukes, Steve. 2005. *Power: A Radical View*, 2nd ed. London: Palgrave Macmillan.

Mahmoud, Lilith. 2014. *The Brotherhood of Freemason Sisters: Gender, Secrecy, and Fraternity in Italian Masonic Lodges*. Chicago: University of Chicago Press.

Marcus, George E. 1998. *Ethnography through Thick and Thin*. Princeton, NJ: Princeton University Press.

McGann, James G. 2007. *Think Tanks and Policy Advice in the United States: Academics Advisors and Advocates*. Oxon: Routledge.

———. 2017. "2016 Global Go To Think Tank Index Report." *TTCSP Global GO To Think Tank Index Reports* 12. Accessed January 18, 2018, at https://repository.upenn.edu/think_tanks/12/.

Medvetz, Tom. 2012a. *Think Tanks in America*. Chicago: Chicago University Press.

———. 2012b. "Murky Power: 'Think Tanks' as Boundary Organizations." In *Rethinking Forms of Power in Organizations, Institutions, and Markets*, edited by David Courpasson, Damon Golsorkhi, and Jeffrey J. Sallaz, 113–134. Bradford, UK: Emerald Group.

Melissen, Jan, ed. 2005. *Wielding Soft Power: The New Public Diplomacy*. The Hague: Netherlands Institute of International Relations Clingendael.

Mertes, Tom, ed. 2003. *Movement of Movements: Is Another World Really Possible?* London: Verso.

Meyer, John, Gili S. Drori, and Hokyo Hwang. 2006. "World Society and the Proliferation of Formal Organization." In *Globalization and Organization: World Society and Organizational Change*, edited by Gili S. Drori, John M. Meyer, and Hokyo Hwang, 25–49. Oxford: Oxford University Press.

Meyer, John, and Ronald Jepperson. 2000. "The 'Actors' of Modern Society: The Cultural Construction of Social Agency." *Sociological Theory* 18:100–120.

Millar, Roderick. 2012. "Leaders for the Future: Nurturing Generation Y." *Developing Leaders, Executive Education in Practice* 6:42–50.

———. 2013. "Getting Personal: The World Economic Forum and the Power of Coaching." *Developing Leaders: Executive Education in Practice* 10:42–48.

———. 2014. "Global Leaders for Tomorrow." *Developing Leaders* 6:44–50.

Miller, Peter, and Nicholas Rose. 1992. "Political Power Beyond the State: Problematics of Government." *British Journal of Sociology* 43:173–205.

Mirowski, Philip, and Dieter Plehwe. 2009. *The Road from Mont Pélerin*. Cambridge, MA: Harvard University Press.

Mishra, Pankaj. 2017. *The Age of Anger: A History of the Present*. New York: Farrar, Straus and Giroux.

Moeran, Brian. 2001. *Celebrities, Culture and a Name Economy.* Copenhagen: Copenhagen Business School, Department of Intercultural Communication and Management.

Morgan, Gareth. 1989. *Creative Organization Theory.* Newbury Park, CA: Sage.

Mosse, David, and David Lewis. 2006. "Theoretical Approaches to Brokerage and Translation in Development." In *Development Brokers and Translators: The Ethnography of Aid and Agencies,* edited by David Mosse and David Lewis, 1–27. Bloomfield, CT: Kumarian Press.

Mouffe, Chantal. 1993. *The Return of the Political.* London: Verso.

———. 2005. *On the Political.* London: Routledge.

Munck, Ronaldo. 2006. "Globalization and Contestation: A Polanyian Problematic." *Globalizations* 3:175–186.

Naray, Olivier. 2008. "Commercial Diplomacy: A Conceptual Overview." Paper presented at Seventh World Conference of TPOs, The Hague, Netherlands.

Neumann, Iver B. 2012. *At Home with the Diplomats: Inside a European Foreign Ministry.* Ithaca, NY: Cornell University Press.

Nye, Joseph. 2004. *Soft Power: The Means to Success in World Politics.* New York: Public Affairs Press.

———. 2008. "Public Diplomacy and Soft Power." *Annals of the American Academy of Political Science* 616:94–109.

———. 2011. *The Future of Power.* New York: Public Affairs Press.

———. 2012. *Soft Power: The Means to Success in World Politics.* New York: Public Affairs Press.

Osterhammel, Jürgen. 2013. "Nationalism and Globalization." In *The Oxford Handbook of the History of Nationalism,* edited by John Breuilly, 694–712. Oxford: Oxford University Press.

Peck, Jamie, and Adam Tickle. 2002. "Neoliberalizing Space." *Antipode* 34:380–404.

Pigman, Geoffrey, A. 2005. "Making Room at the Negotiating Table: The Growth of Diplomacy between Nation-State Governments and Non-State Elites." *Diplomacy and Statecraft* 16:385–401.

———. 2007. *The World Economic Forum: A Multi-Stakeholder Approach to Global Governance.* London: Routledge.

Pink, Sarah. 2008. "An Urban Tour: The Sensory Sociality of Ethnographic Place-Making." *Ethnography* 9:175–196.

Podolny, Joel M. 1993. "A Status-Based Model of Market Competition." *American Journal of Sociology* 98, no. 4: 829–872.

Polanyi, Karl. (1944) 2001. *The Great Transformation: The Political and Economic Origins of our Time.* Boston: Beacon Press.

Porter, Tony. 2009. "Global Governance as Configurations of State/Non-State Activity." In *Palgrave Advances in Global Governance,* edited by Jim Whitman, 87–104. London: Palgrave Macmillan.

Powell, Walter, W. 1990. "Neither Market, Nor Hierarchy: Network Forms of Organization." *Research in Organizational Behavior* 12:295–336.

Rabinow, Paul. 2003. *Anthropos Today: Reflections on Modern Equipment*. Princeton, NJ: Princeton University Press.

———. 2008. *Marking Time: On the Anthropology of the Contemporary*. Princeton, NJ: Princeton University Press.

———. 2011. *The Accompaniment: Assembling the Contemporary*. Chicago: University of Chicago Press.

Rabinow, Paul, and Anthony Stavrianakis. 2014. *Designs of the Contemporary: Anthropology Tests*. Chicago: University of Chicago Press.

Rhodes, Roderick, A. W. 1996. "The New Governance: Governing without Government." *Political Studies* 44:652–667.

Rich, Andrew. 2004. *Think Tanks, Public Policy and the Politics of Expertise*. Cambridge: Cambridge University Press.

Richardson, Ian, Andrew Kakabadse, and Nada Kakabadse. 2011. *Bilderberg People: Elite, Power and Consensus in World Affairs*. New York: Routledge.

Riles, Annelise, ed. 2006. *Documents: Artifacts of Modern Knowledge*. Ann Arbor: University of Michigan Press.

Roberts, John. 2009. "No One Is Perfect: The Limits of Transparency and an Ethic for 'Intelligent' Accountability." *Accounting, Organizations and Society* 34:957–970.

Rose, Nikolas. 2000. "Community, Citizenship and the Third Way." *American Behavioral Scientist* 43:1395–1411.

Rose, Nikolas, and Peter Miller. 1992. "Power beyond the State: Problematics of Government." *British Journal of Sociology* 43:173–205.

Rosenau, James N. 2009. "Global Governance or Global Governances?" In *Palgrave Advances in Global Governance*, edited by Jim Whitman, 1–8. London: Palgrave Macmillan.

Rosenau, James, N., and Ernst-Otto Czempiel. 1992. *Governance without Government: Order and Change in World Politics*. Cambridge: Cambridge University Press.

Ruggie, Gerard, J. 2004. "Reconstituting the Global Public Domain: Issues, Actors and Practices." *European Journal of International Relations* 10:499–531.

Rupert, Mark. 2005. "Class Powers and the Politics of Global Governance." In *Power in Global Governance*, edited by Michael Barnett and Raymond Duvall, 205–228. Cambridge, MA: Cambridge University Press.

Sahlins, Marshall. 1963. "Poor Man, Rich Man, Big Man, Chief: Political Types in Melanesia and Polynesia." *Comparative Studies in Society and History* 5:285–303.

Sandler, Jen, and Renita Thedvall, eds. 2017. *Meeting Ethnography; Meetings as Key Technologies of Contemporary Governance, Development, and Resistance*. London: Routledge.

Sassen, Saskia. 1998. *Globalization and Its Discontents: Essays on the New Mobility of People and Money*. New York: New Press.

Scales, Kezia, Simon Bailey, and Joanne Lloyd. 2008. "Separately and Together: Reflections on Conducting a Collaborative Team Ethnography in Dementia Care." *Enquire* 4:22–44.

Scarry, Eileen. 2014. *Thermonuclear Monarchy: Choosing between Democracy and Doom*. New York: Norton.

Scholte, Jan A. 2005. *Globalization: A Critical Introduction*. Basingstoke: Palgrave Macmillan.

Schumpeter, Joseph, A. 1942. *Capitalism, Socialism and Democracy*. New York: Harper.

Schwab, Klaus. 1971. *Moderne Unternehmensführung im Maschinenbau*. Frankfurt: Maschinenbau-Verlag GmbH.

——. 1988, "Dialogue for Action among the World's 33333." *World Link* 1:1.

——. 2004. "Welcome to the Annual Meeting 21.01.2004." News release, World Economic Forum, January 13.

——. 2008. "Brave New World." August 10. Accessed December 27, 2015, at www.forbes.com.

——. 2009. "Managing Global Inter-Dependence." Address at the University of Latvia, Riga, September 28. www.lu.lv/eng/news/t/467/.

——. 2010. "A Breakdown in Our Values." *Guardian*, January 6.

——. 2012. "The End of Capitalism—So What's Next?" *Huffington Post*, April 13.

——. 2014. "Foreword." In *The Forum of Young Global Leaders: A Generation Change*, edited by World Economic Forum. Cologny: World Economic Forum.

——. 2015. *Visions 2020*. Cologny: World Economic Forum.

——. 2017. "We Need a New Narrative for Globalization." World Economic Forum, March. www.weforum.org/agenda/2017/03/klaus-schwab-new-narrative-for-globalization.

Schwab, Klaus, and Claude Smadja. 1996. "Start Taking the Backlash against Globalization Seriously." *New York Times*, February 1.

Schwartzman, Helen B. 1993. *Ethnography in Organizations*. Newbury Park, CA: Sage.

Schweizerischen Bundesrat. 2014. "Abkommen zwischen dem Schweizerischen Bundesrat und der Stiftung World Economic Forum zur Festlegung des Status der Stiftung World Economic Forum in der Schweiz." Accessed March 27, 2017, at www.newsd.admin.ch/newsd/message/attachments/38056.pdf.

Seidl, David, and Kai Helge Becker. 2006. "Organization as Distinction Generating and Processing Systems: Niklas Luhmann's Contribution to Organization Studies." *Organization* 13:9–35.

Sheppard, Eric, and Helga Leitner. 2009. "Quo Vadis Neoliberalism? The Remaking of Global Capitalist Governance after the Washington Consensus?" *Geoforum* 41:185–194.

Sheridan, Alan. 1994. "Translator's Note." In Jacques Lacan, *The Four Fundamental Concepts of Psycho-analysis*. London: Norton.

Shihadeh, Amir. 2015. "Davos Best Practices and Tips." Accessed January 26, 2017, at www.globalshapers.org/es/node/27592.

Simmel, Georg. 1906. "The Sociology of Secrecy and of Secret Societies." *American Journal of Sociology* 11:441–498.

———. 1964. "The Secret Society." In *The Sociology of Georg Simmel*, edited by K. H. Wolf. Glencoe, IL: Free Press.

Sklair, Leslie. 2001. *The Transnational Capitalist Class*. Oxford: Blackwell.

———. 2002. "The Transnational Capitalist Global Class and Global Politics: Deconstructing the Corporate-State Connection." *International Political Science Review* 23:159–174.

Slaughter, Anne-Marie. 1997. "The Real New World Order." *Foreign Affairs* 76:183–197.

———. 2004. *A New World Order*. Princeton, NJ: Princeton University Press.

Smith, James, A. 1991. *The Idea Brokers: Think Tanks and the Rise of the New Policy Elite*, New York: Free Press.

Smith, Mark, A. 2007. *The Right Talk: How Conservatives Transformed the Great Society into the Economic Society*. Princeton: Princeton University Press.

Soule, Sarah, A. 2009. *Contention and Corporate Social Responsibility*. Cambridge: Cambridge University Press.

Stein, Howard, F. 1998. "Organizational Euphemism and the Cultural Mystification of Evil." *Administrative Theory and Praxis* 3:346–357.

Stone, Diane. 1996. *Capturing the Political Imagination: Think Tanks and the Policy Process*. London: Frank Cass.

———. 1999. "Private Authority, Scholarly Legitimacy and Political Credibility: Think Tanks and Informal Diplomacy." In *Non State Actors and Authority in Global Order*, edited by Richard Higgott, Geoffrey Underhill, and Anders Bieler, 211–225. London: Routledge.

———. 2004. "Knowledge Networks and Global Policy." In *Global Knowledge Networks and International Development: Bridges across Boundaries*, edited by Diane Stone and Simon Maxwell, 89–105. London: Routledge.

———. 2007. "Transfer Agents and Global Networks in the 'Transnationalization' of Policy." *Journal of European Public Policy* 11:545–566.

———. 2008. "Global Public Policy: Transnational Policy Communities and Their Networks." *Policy Studies Journal* 36:19–38.

———. 2012. "Governance Via Knowledge: Actors: Institutions and Networks." In *OUP Handbook of Governance*, edited by David Levi-Faur, 339–353. Oxford: Oxford University Press.

Strathern, Marilyn. 2000. "The Tyranny of Transparency." *British Educational Research Journal* 26, no. 3: 309–321.

Taylor, James, R. 2011. "Organizations as an (Imbricated) Configuring of Transactions." *Organization Studies* 32:1273–1294.

Times Higher Education. "World University Rankings 2016." www.timeshighereduca tion.com/world-university-rankings/2016/world-ranking#!/page/0/length/25/sort _by/scores_overall/sort_order/asc/cols/stats.

Tolmach Lakoff, Robin. 2000. *The Language War*. Berkeley: University of California Press.

Trouillot, Michel-Rolph. 2016. *Global Transformations: Anthropology and the Modern World*. Basingstoke: Palgrave Macmillan.

United Nations. 2015. *The United Nations Regional Commissions and the 2030 Agenda for Sustainable Development: Moving to Deliver on a Transformative and Ambitious Agenda.* September. New York: United Nations.

United Nations Parliamentary Assembly. 2015. "Campaign for a United Nations Parliamentary Assembly. Giving the World's Citizens a Voice." www.unpacampaign.org.

Van Dijk, A. Teun. 1997. *Discourse as Structure and Process of Discourse Studies: A Multidisciplinary Introduction.* London: Sage.

Vergunst, Jo, and Anna Vermehren. 2012. "The Art of Slow Sociality: Movement, Aesthetics and Shared Understanding." *Cambridge Anthropology* 30:127–142.

Walton, John, S. 2008. "Scanning beyond the Horizon: Exploring the Ontological and Epistemological Basis for Scenario Planning." *Advances in Developing Human Resources* 10:147–165.

Wasser, Judith D., and Liora Bresler. 1996. "Working in the Interpretive Zone: Conceptualizing Collaboration in Qualitative Research Teams." *Educational Researcher* 25:5–15.

Watson, Cate. 2009. "Futures Narratives, Possible Worlds, Big Stories: Causal Layered Analysis and the Problems of Youth." *Sociological Research Online* 14.

Weber, Max. 1978. *Economy and Society.* Berkeley: University of California Press.

———. (1922) 1997. "Class, Status and Party." In *Classical Sociological Theory: A Reader,* edited by Ian McIntosh. New York: New York University Press.

Wedel, Janine. 2009. *Shadow Elite.* New York: Basic Books.

Weidenbaum, Murray. 2011. *The Competition of Ideas: The World of Washington Think Tanks,* 2nd ed. New Brunswick, NJ: Transaction.

Wilson, Japhy, and Eric Swyngedouw, eds. 2014. *The Post-Political and Its Discontents: Spaces of Depoliticisation, Spectres of Radical Politics.* Edinburgh: Edinburgh University Press.

Wolf, Eric. 1956. "Aspects of Group Relations in a Complex Society: Mexico." *American Anthropologist* 58:1065–1078.

Wolff, Kurt H. 1964. *The Sociology of Georg Simmel.* New York: Free Press of Glencoe.

World Economic Forum. 2006. *Foundation Statutes.* Cologny: World Economic Forum. www3.weforum.org/docs/WEF_Forum_Statutes_2015.pdf.

———. 2009. *Task Force on Low Carbon Prosperity: Recommendations.* Cologny: World Economic Forum.

———. 2010a. *A Partner in Shaping History: The First 40 Years, 1971–2010.* Cologny: World Economic Forum

———. 2010b. *Global Enabling Trade Report.* Cologny: World Economic Forum. www3.weforum.org/docs/WEF_GlobalEnablingTrade_Report_2010.pdf.

———. 2010c. *Annual Meeting of the New Champions, 2010, Driving Growth through Sustainability.* Cologny: World Economic Forum. www.weforum.org/reports/annual-meeting-new-champions-2010-driving-growth-through-sustainability.

———. 2011. *Forum of Young Global Leaders.* Cologny: World Economic Forum.

———. 2012. *World Economic Forum.* Cologny: World Economic Forum. www3.weforum.org/docs/WEF_InstitutionalBrochure.pdf.

———. 2013a. *Strategic Infrastructure in Africa: A Business Approach to Project Acceleration.* www3.weforum.org/docs/AF13/WEF_AF13_African_Strategic_Infrastructure.pdf.

———. 2013b. *Annual Report 2012–2013.* Cologny: World Economic Forum. www.weforum.org/reports/annual-report-2012-2013.

———. 2013c. *World Economic Forum Annual Meeting 2013, Watch the Highlights.* Cologny: World Economic Forum. www.weforum.org/events/world-economic-forum-annual-meeting-2013.

———. 2013d. *The Forum of Young Global Leaders.* Cologny: World Economic Forum. www.weforum.org/community/forum-young-global-leaders

———. 2014. *Network of Global Agenda Councils 2012–2014: Midterms Report.* Cologny: World Economic Forum. www3.weforum.org/docs/GAC/2013/WEF_GAC_MidtermReports_2012-14.pdf.

———. 2015a. *Regulations regarding the World Economic Forum.* Cologny: World Economic Forum. www3.weforum.org/docs/WEF_Reglement_2015.pdf.

———. 2015b. *Global Risks Report 2015.* Cologny: World Economic Forum. www3.weforum.org/docs/WEF_Global_Risks_2015_Report15.pdf.

———. 2015c. *The Global Context.* Cologny: World Economic Forum. http://www3.weforum.org/docs/WEF_AM15_Report.pdf

———. 2016a. *Annual Report of 2015–2016.* Cologny: World Economic Forum. www3.weforum.org/docs/WEF_Annual_Report_2015-2016.pdf.

———. 2016b. *Code of Conduct.* Cologny: World Economic Forum.www3.weforum.org/docs/WEF_Code_of_Conduct_2016.pdf.

———. 2016c. *The Global Gender Gap Report.* Cologny: World Economic Forum. www.reports.weforum.org/global-gender-gap-report-2016.

———. 2016d. *Young Global Leaders.* Cologny: World Economic Forum. Accessed May 25, 2016, at www.weforum.org/communities/young-global-leaders.

———. 2016e. "World Economic Forum Announces New Board of Trustees." Cologny: World Economic Forum. Accessed January 17, 2018, at https://www.weforum.org/press/2016/08/world-economic-forum-announces-new-board-of-trustees-2016/.

———. 2016f. *The Forum of Young Global Leaders.* Cologny: World Economic Forum. Accessed May 25, 2016, at www.weforum.org/communities/young-global-leader.

———. 2016g. *Global Leadership Fellows.* Cologny: World Economic Forum. Accessed May 15, 2016, at www.weforum.org/communities/global-leadership-fellows.

———. 2017a. *The 47th Annual Meeting to Call for New Model of Leadership Championing Collaboration, Growth, Reformed Capitalism and Preparedness for the Fourth Industrial Revolution.* Cologny: World Economic Forum. Accessed January 27, 2017, at www.weforum.org/press/2017/01/47th-annual-meeting-to-call-for-new-model-of-leadership-championing-collaboration-growth-reformed-capitalism-and-preparedness-for-the-fourth-industrial-revolution/.

———. 2017b. *Global Risk Report.* Cologny: World Economic Forum. www.weforum.org/reports/the-global-risks-report-2017.

———. 2017c. *Careers*. Cologny: World Economic Forum. Accessed January 27, 2017, at www.weforum.org/about/careers,

———. 2017d. *Global Agenda Action Councils*. Cologny: World Economic Forum. Accessed January 27, 2017, at www.weforum.org/communities/global-agenda-councils.

———. 2017e. *Young Global Leaders*. Cologny: World Economic Forum. www.weforum.org/communities/young-global-leaders.

———. 2017f. *Open Forum*. Cologny: World Economic Forum. Accessed January 27, 2017, at www.weforum.org/open-forum.

———. 2017g. *Building a Movement*. Cologny: World Economic Forum. Accessed January 27, 2017, at www.globalshapers.org/about-us-0.

———. 2018. *Our Mission*. Cologny: World Economic Forum. Accessed January 27, 2017, at www.weforum.org/about/world-economic-forum.

Wright Mills, Charles. (1956) 2000. *The Power Elite*. Oxford: Oxford University Press.

Yates, JoAnne. 1989. *Control through Communication: The Rise of System in American Management*. Baltimore, MD: Johns Hopkins University Press.

Index

Lightning Source UK Ltd.
Milton Keynes UK
UKHW01f0244010618
323565UK00001B/15/P

9 781503 606043